HUMAN BODY!

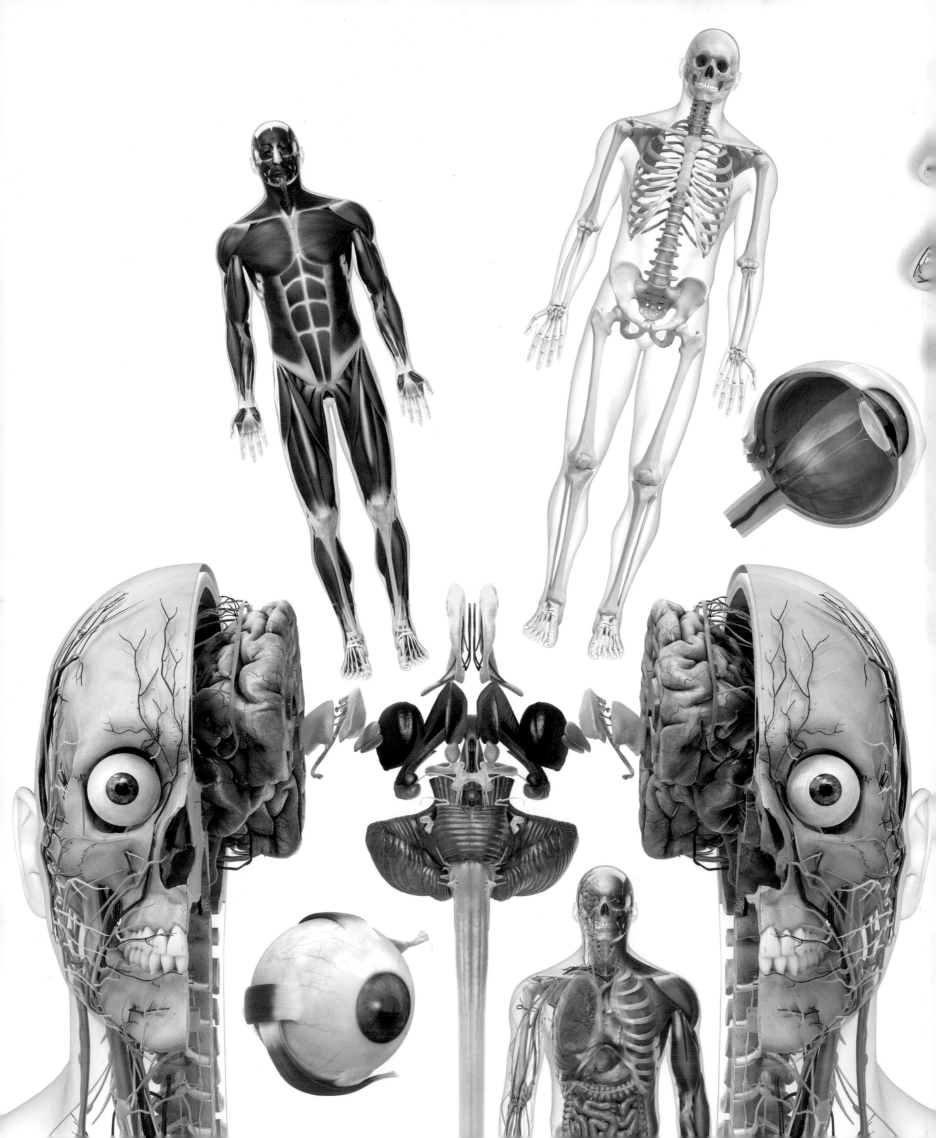

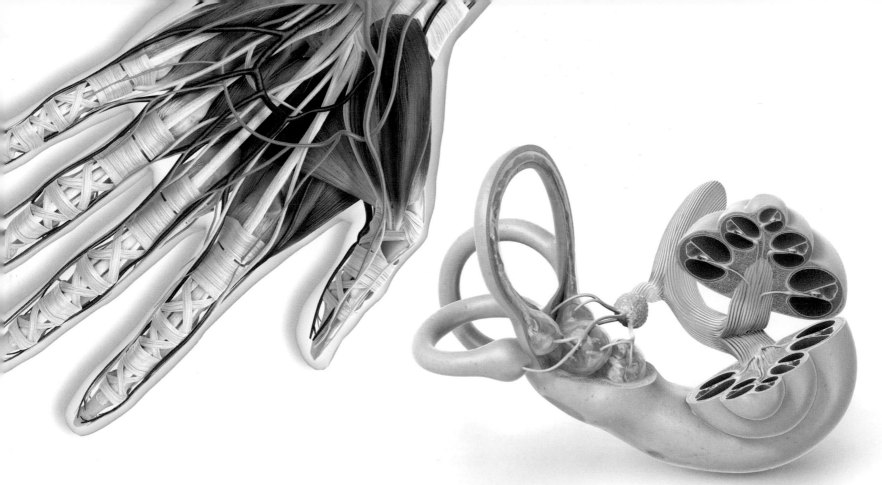

DK SMITHSONIAN ✹
HUMAN BODY!

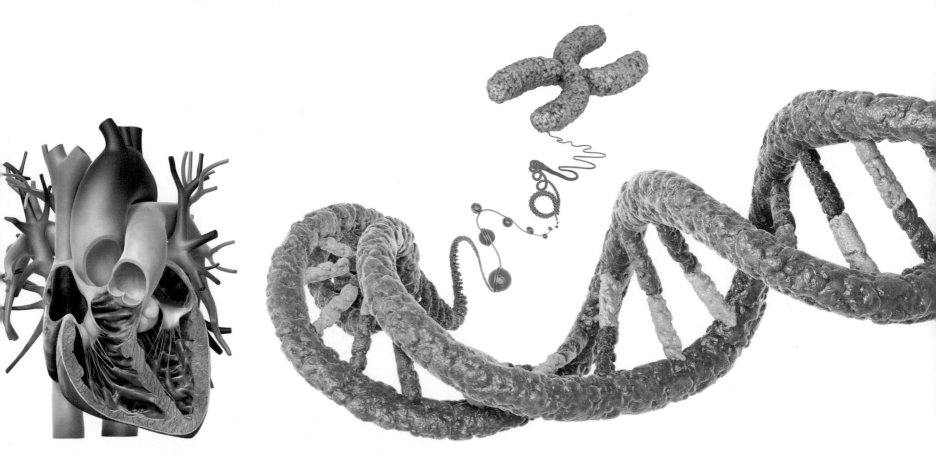

Senior Art Editor Smiljka Surla
Senior Editor Rona Skene
US Editors Megan Douglass, Margaret Parrish
Medical Consultant Dr Kristina Routh
Contributors Anna Claybourne, John Farndon,
John Friend, Nicola Temple
Illustrator Arran Lewis
Additional Illustrations Michael Parkin,
Maltings Partnership
Editors Tim Harris, Andrea Mills
Designer Simon Murrell
DK Picture Library Romaine Werblow
Picture Researcher Deepak Negi
Managing Editor Lisa Gillespie
Managing Art Editor Owen Peyton Jones
Producer, Pre-Production Catherine Williams
Senior Producer Anna Vallarino
Jacket designers Suhita Dharamjit, Surabhi Wadhwa
Jackets design development manager Sophia MTT
Senior DTP designer Harish Aggarwal
Jackets editorial coordinator Priyanka Sharma
Jackets editor Claire Gell
Publisher Andrew Macintyre
Art Director Karen Self
Associate Publishing Director Liz Wheeler
Design Director Phil Ormerod
Publishing Director Jonathan Metcalf

First American Edition, 2017
Published in the United States by DK Publishing
345 Hudson Street, New York, New York 10014
Copyright © 2017 Dorling Kindersley Limited
DK, a Division of Penguin Random House LLC
17 18 19 20 21 10 9 8 7 6 5 4 3 2
003–299419–August/2017

DK books are available at special discounts when purchased in bulk
for sales promotions, premiums, fund-raising, or educational use.
For details, contact: DK Publishing Special Markets,
345 Hudson Street, New York, New York 10014
SpecialSales@dk.com
Printed and bound in China

A world of ideas:
see all there is to know
www.dk.com

THE SMITHSONIAN
Established in 1846, the Smithsonian—the world's largest
museum and research complex—includes 19 museums and galleries
and the National Zoological Park. The total number of artifacts, works of art,
and specimens in the Smithsonian's collection is estimated at 154 million.
The Smithsonian is a renowned research center, dedicated to public education,
national service, and scholarship in the arts, sciences, and history.

CONTENTS

BODY BASICS

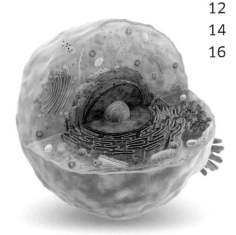

BODY SYSTEMS

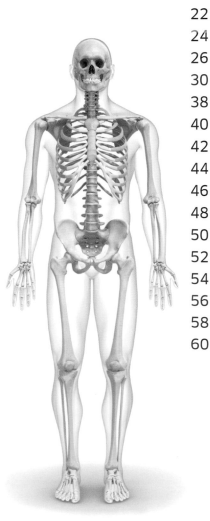

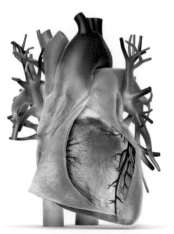

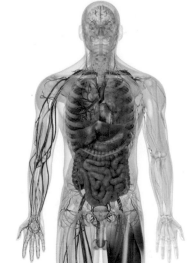

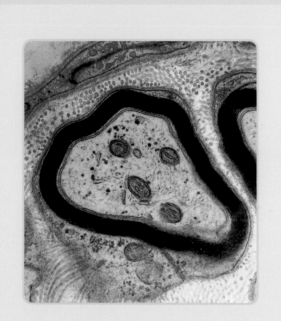
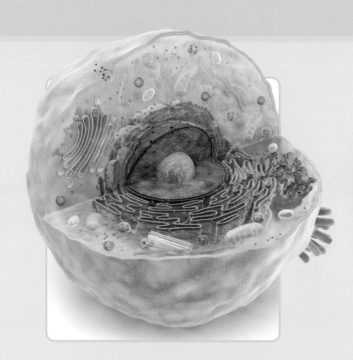

BODY BASICS

The smallest structure found in living things is the cell, and trillions of them make up each human body. These building blocks of life each have a specific job. They are constantly dividing to produce new cells that allow the body to grow and repair itself.

MAKING A HUMAN

Everything in the body is made up of atoms, the tiniest building blocks of matter. Atoms combine to form molecules. Millions of molecules form every cell in the body. There are more than 200 types of cell, with similar cells working in teams called tissues. The body's many organs and systems are made up of different tissues.

Atoms and molecules

The smallest parts in the body are atoms. These tiny building blocks form the elements in the body, such as carbon. Atoms from different elements can also join together in groups called molecules—for example, water is a molecule, made from a combination of hydrogen and oxygen atoms.

Cell

Molecules build up to create body cells. There are about 75 trillion cells in the average human, with different types of cells carrying out a variety of body functions, from transporting oxygen to sensing light and color in the eye.

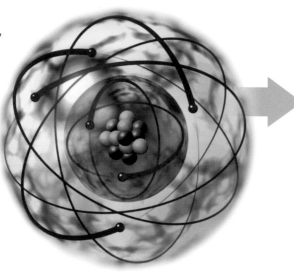

ATOM

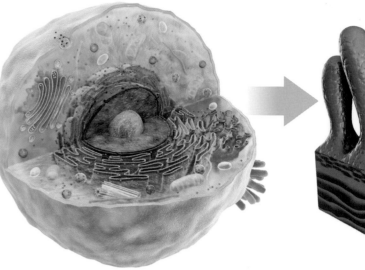

CELL

WHAT MAKES A BODY?

The human body is made from the same components as every other living thing. It is the way that they are put together that makes our bodies uniquely human. The basic materials are simple chemicals such as water, carbon, and oxygen, but they join to create more complex compounds. Trillions of microscopic cells become the building blocks of life, grouping together to form skin, bone, blood, and organs, until the body becomes complete.

TYPES OF TISSUE

Tissues are groups of connected cells. Many tissues are made entirely from one type of cell. The four main types of tissue in the human body are connective, epithelial, muscular, and nervous.

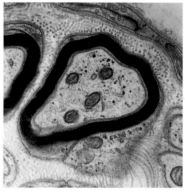

THE HARDEST **TISSUE IN THE** HUMAN BODY **IS TOOTH ENAMEL.**

Nerve tissue

Large groups of nerve cells create nervous tissue. This forms the brain, spinal cord, and masses of nerves that work together in the nervous system, the body's high-speed communications network.

BODY BASICS

More than 93 percent of the human body consists of three chemical elements—oxygen (65%), carbon (18.5%), and hydrogen (10%). Nitrogen (3%), calcium (1.5%), and phosphorus (1%) are also present in significant amounts. At least 54 chemical elements feature in total, but most of these are tiny traces.

A 10-YEAR-OLD'S BODY CONTAINS **66 GRAMS OF POTASSIUM,** THE SAME AMOUNT AS IN **156 BANANAS.**

Others 6.5%

Hydrogen 10%
The most common element in the universe, hydrogen has the tiniest atoms, and is mostly bonded with carbon or oxygen in the body.

Other elements = less than 1.0%

Iron 0.006%

Sodium 0.2%

Potassium 0.4%

Phosphorus 0.4%

Calcium 1.5%

Nitrogen 3.2%

ENLARGEMENT

Oxygen 65%
About two-thirds of the body is oxygen. Most of the oxygen is bonded with hydrogen to form H_2O—the chemical formula for water.

Carbon 18.5%
Nearly one-fifth of the body is carbon, the same element that coal, diamond, and the lead of pencils are made from.

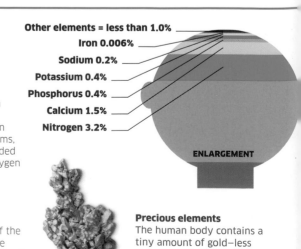

Precious elements
The human body contains a tiny amount of gold—less than the weight of a grain of sand. Most of the body's gold is in the blood.

Tissue
Cells performing the same function are grouped together to form body tissues, such as skin, fat, or heart muscle. Blood is also a tissue, in liquid form.

Organ
Different kinds of tissue combine to make larger structures called organs. Each organ works like a machine, performing its own role. An example of an organ is the stomach, which plays a part in the process of digesting food.

Body system
Organs are at the center of 12 internal body systems. Each system has a specific job to keep the body in working order. The stomach is one of the main organs of the digestive system.

Complete human
When this complex combination of integrated systems, organs, and tissues works together, the human body is complete. Each individual component plays its part in maintaining a fully functioning body.

STOMACH TISSUE

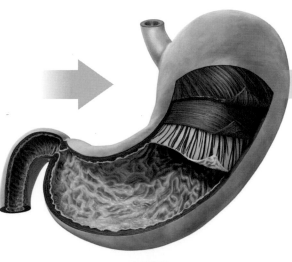

STOMACH

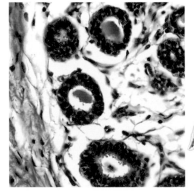

DIGESTIVE SYSTEM

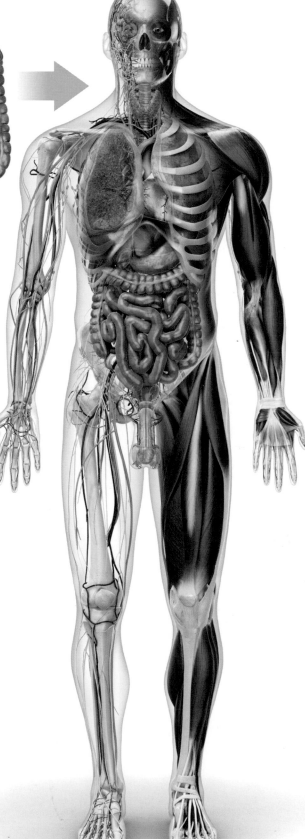

HUMAN BODY

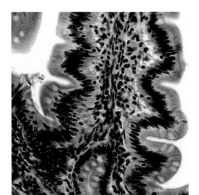

Epithelial tissue
Made up of three main shapes of cell, epithelial tissue lines and covers surfaces inside and outside the body. It forms skin and the linings of body cavities such as the gut and lungs.

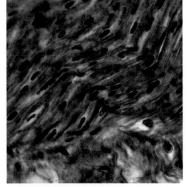

Muscle tissue
Built from long, thin cells, muscle tissue can relax and contract to allow muscles to move bones. It also helps sustain blood pressure and carry food through the digestive system.

Connective tissue
This dense tissue is the body's "glue," filling the space between other tissues and organs, and binding them together. Examples include adipose tissue (fat), bone, and blood.

CARBON COMPOUNDS

The human body is made from chemicals containing the element carbon. Called organic compounds, they often contain hydrogen and oxygen, too. Although these organic compounds are based on only a few elements, they produce more than 10 million different compounds. Four main types of carbon compound exist inside the human body.

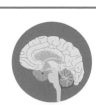

Proteins
Proteins are vital body molecules. Organs such as the brain are made of protein, as well as muscles, connective tissues, hormones that send chemical messages, and antibodies that fight infection.

Fats
Fats are made from carbon and hydrogen atoms. They form the outer barrier of cells. The layer of fat beneath the skin stores energy and helps the body to keep out the cold.

Nucleic acids
The molecules DNA and RNA carry all the instructions for making the proteins that our bodies are made of. They also carry code that controls how cells work and reproduce.

Carbohydrates
Carbohydrates are made from carbon, oxygen, and hydrogen and are the body's main source of energy. Carbohydrates circulate in the blood as sugars or are stored in the liver and muscles.

Types of cell

Each type of cell has a shape and size related to its own vital task in the body.

Red blood cells
are doughnut shaped, and this lets them pick up and carry oxygen easily.

Nerve cells
are long, thin, and carry electrical signals over long distances.

Muscle cells
can contract (shorten) and relax to produce movement.

Epidermal cells
in the skin fit tightly together to form a protective layer.

Fat cells
are filled with droplets of liquid fat as an energy store.

Cone cells
in the eye detect light, enabling us to see.

Cell life spans

Different types of body cell have different life spans. Some, such as skin cells, are worn away. Other cells wear out and self-destruct. They are replaced with more of their kind by special cells called stem cells.

Less than 1 day
White blood cells fighting infection

30 days
Skin cells

12–18 months
Liver cells

15 years
Muscle cells

A whole lifetime
Some nerve cells in the brain

Inside a cell

The body is made of trillions of cells, each too small to see without a microscope. These cells aren't all the same. There are about 200 different types, each with its own size, shape, and contents. Each type of cell has a particular task.

Just as the body has organs, such as the heart, the cell has organelles, such as mitochondria. These parts work together to make the cell a living unit. In addition, tiny rods, including microtubules, move organelles and form a kind of "skeleton" that supports and shapes the cell.

Golgi apparatus
The Golgi apparatus processes and packages proteins made on ribosomes, ready for use inside or outside the cell.

Vesicle
This bag takes proteins from the Golgi apparatus and carries them to where they are needed.

Cell membrane
This flexible membrane surrounds the cell and controls what enters and exits. It consists of a double layer of lipid (fat) molecules containing proteins that have different jobs to do.

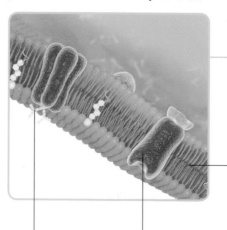

Lipid layer
A double layer of lipid (fat) molecules forms the main part of the membrane.

Protein
This protein channel transports substances into and out of the cell.

Glycoprotein
This "tag" identifies the cell to other cells.

1 million years—the time it would take to count all the **body's cells** at a rate of one per second.

Red blood cells make up about **70%** of the total number of cells in the body.

11

Vacuole
This bag contains water and food taken into the cell.

Microtubules
These structures help to shape the cell and move organelles.

Cell structure

No cell is exactly like the one shown here, but this example shows the features that are found in many body cells. Each busy, living cell consists of an outer membrane, cytoplasm, and different types of organelles. Most cells have a control center called the nucleus.

The longest cells in the body
are the neurons
that stretch almost 3 ft (1 m) from the spinal cord to the feet.

Cytoplasm
A jelly-like fluid in which organelles float, the cytoplasm contains proteins and other substances.

Lysosome
This membrane bag contains enzymes that break down unwanted substances and recycle worn-out organelles.

Nucleus
The nucleus is the cell's control centre, containing genetic material called DNA.

Ribosome
This tiny structure makes the many proteins that build and run the cell.

Rough endoplasmic reticulum
This network of tubes and flattened bags makes and transports proteins and other substances.

Microvilli
These structures increase the area of a cell's surface so it is better at taking in substances—but not all cells have them.

Inner membrane
This folded membrane provides a large surface for making ATP.

ATP synthase
This is where the energy-carrier ATP is made.

Mitochondria
These sausage-shaped organelles are the cell's power stations. They release the energy from glucose and other foods that cells use to drive their many activities.

Centrioles
These two bunches of microtubules play a key part in cell division.

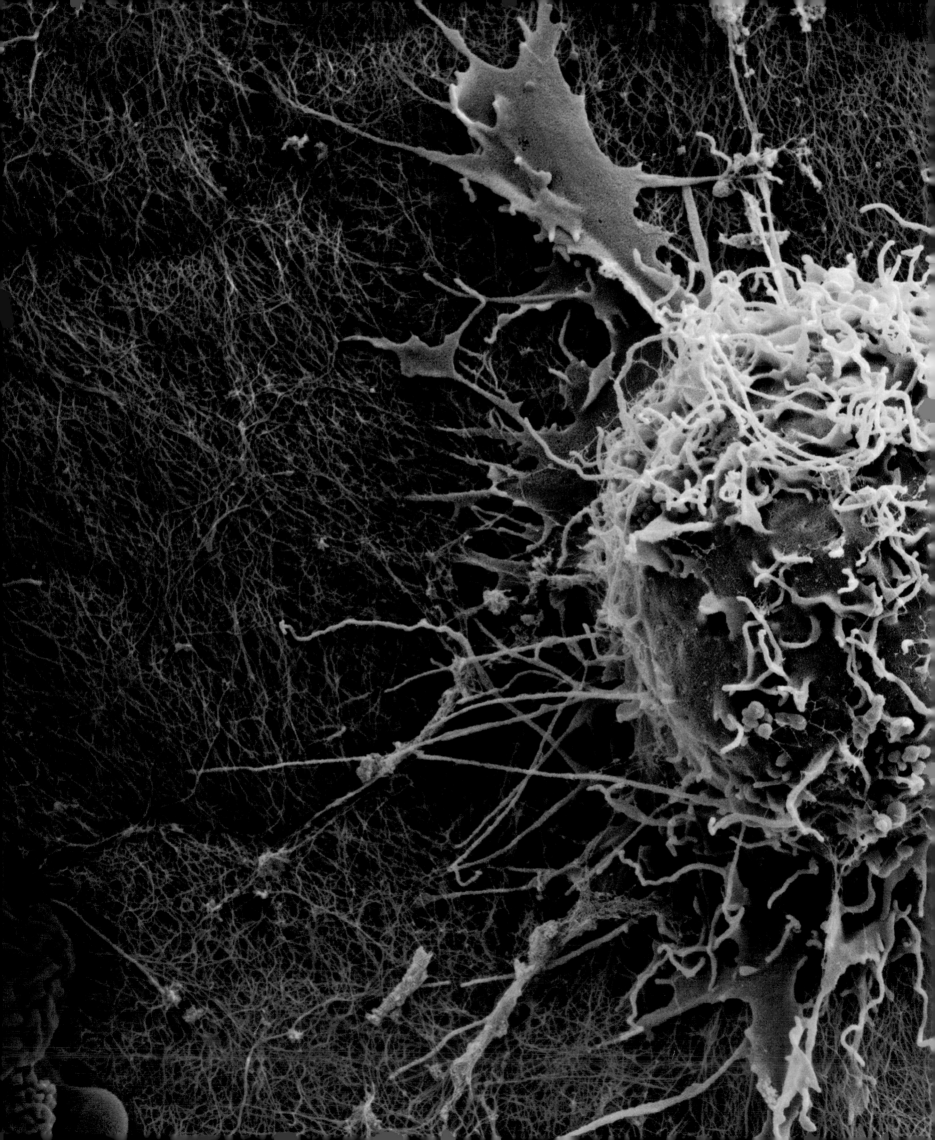

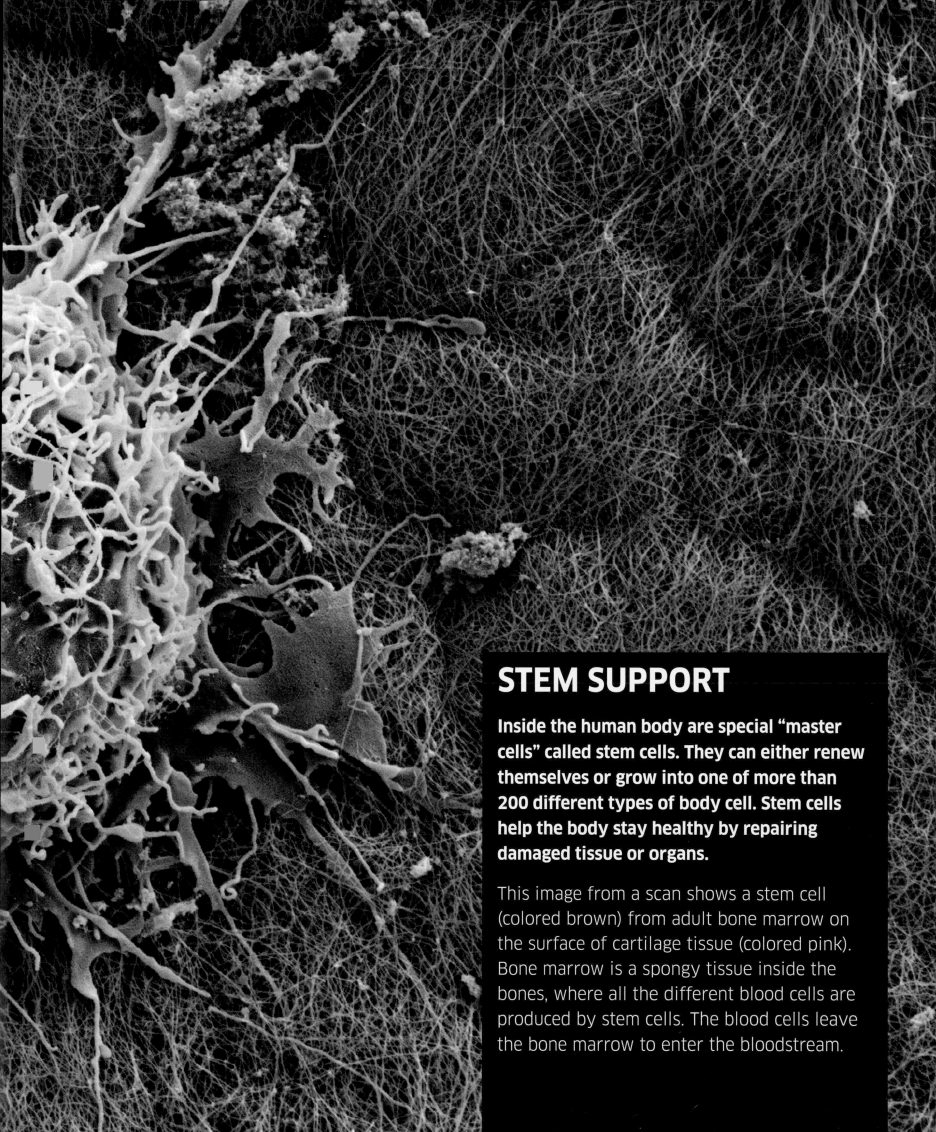

STEM SUPPORT

Inside the human body are special "master cells" called stem cells. They can either renew themselves or grow into one of more than 200 different types of body cell. Stem cells help the body stay healthy by repairing damaged tissue or organs.

This image from a scan shows a stem cell (colored brown) from adult bone marrow on the surface of cartilage tissue (colored pink). Bone marrow is a spongy tissue inside the bones, where all the different blood cells are produced by stem cells. The blood cells leave the bone marrow to enter the bloodstream.

DNA—instructions for life

The nucleus of every human cell carries a set of unique codes for making new cells to build and maintain the body. These instructions are called genes, and they are made of a substance called DNA.

Inside the cell nucleus, there are 46 tiny structures called chromosomes. These are made of tightly coiled strands of DNA, which contain all the information the cell needs to make a new, identical version of itself. Every time a cell divides so the body can grow or repair itself, a DNA strand "unzips" down the middle. Each unzipped half then rebuilds itself into a new DNA strand, identical to the original and carrying all the same codes.

The sequence of DNA bases is different for everyone—except **identical twins**, whose DNA is exactly the same.

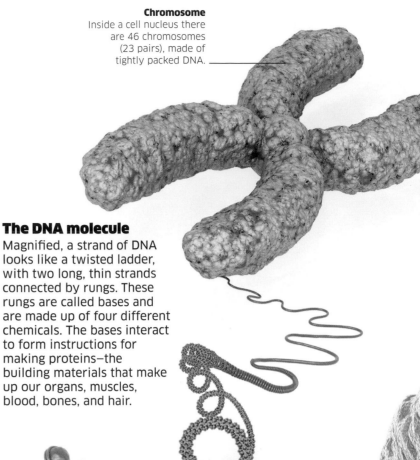

Chromosome
Inside a cell nucleus there are 46 chromosomes (23 pairs), made of tightly packed DNA.

The DNA molecule

Magnified, a strand of DNA looks like a twisted ladder, with two long, thin strands connected by rungs. These rungs are called bases and are made up of four different chemicals. The bases interact to form instructions for making proteins—the building materials that make up our organs, muscles, blood, bones, and hair.

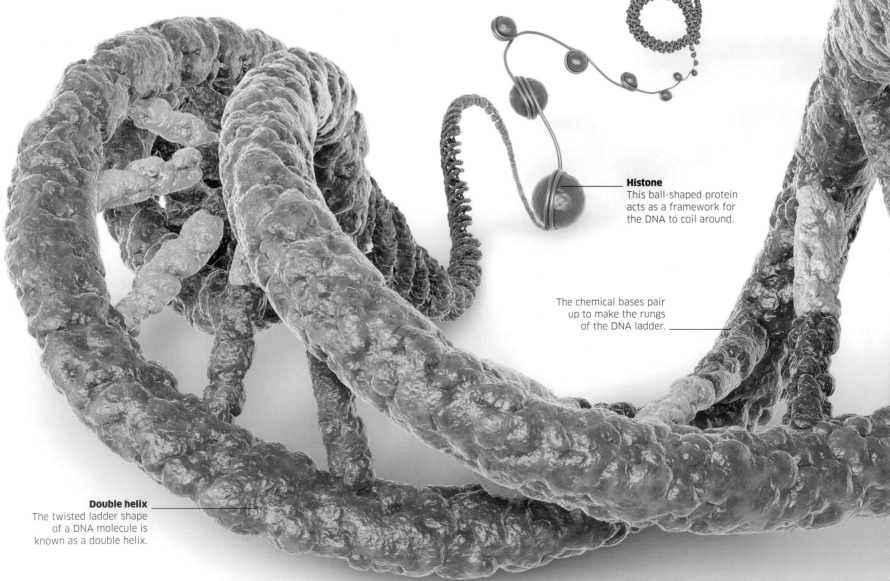

Histone
This ball-shaped protein acts as a framework for the DNA to coil around.

The chemical bases pair up to make the rungs of the DNA ladder.

Double helix
The twisted ladder shape of a DNA molecule is known as a double helix.

A human has around **20,000 different genes**—more than a chicken, but fewer than a mouse.

Humans and chimpanzees share **almost 99% of the same DNA.**

The order of the base pairs creates different codes to form different proteins.

If the DNA strands in just one cell were laid out in a line, it would be about 6½ ft (2 m) long.

KEY TO BASES

Adenine
Thymine
Cytosine
Guanine

Adenine always links to thymine

Guanine always joins with cytosine

Pairing up
DNA bases are made of four chemicals—adenine, cytosine, guanine, and thymine. The bases link together in pairs. The specific order of the base pairs along the ladder gives the instructions for making different proteins.

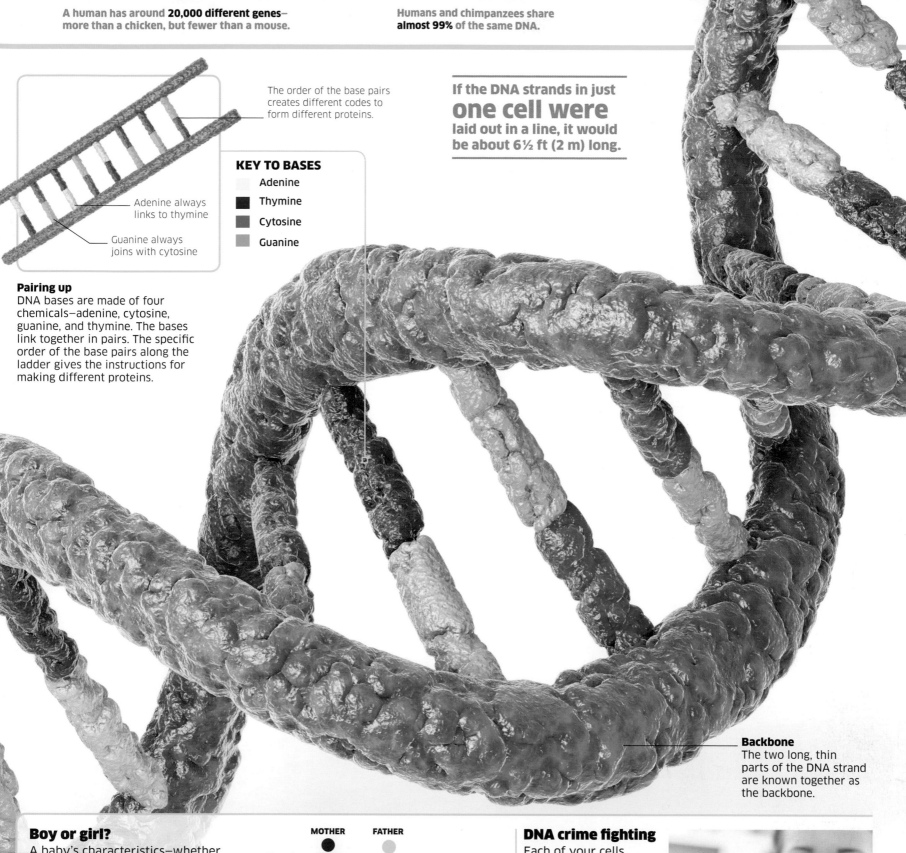

Backbone
The two long, thin parts of the DNA strand are known together as the backbone.

Boy or girl?
A baby's characteristics—whether it will be tall or short, have curly or straight hair, or brown or blue eyes—are set by the DNA it inherits from its parents. Two special chromosomes, called X and Y, determine whether a baby will be male or female.

Genetic mix
An embryo is created when a sperm cell fertilizes a female egg. All eggs contain an X chromosome, but a sperm can carry either an X or a Y chromosome. So it is the sperm that determines the baby's sex.

MOTHER

FATHER

Females have two X chromosomes.

Males have one X and one Y chromosome.

XY

A sex cell (egg) carries an X chromosome.

Y

X

Sex cells (sperm) can carry either an X or a Y chromosome.

XY

XX

BOY (XY)

GIRL (XX)

A baby receives an X chromosome from its mother and an X or Y chromosome from its father.

DNA crime fighting
Each of your cells contains a copy of your genome—all the DNA that you inherited from your parents. Just like a fingerprint, everyone (except an identical twin) has a slightly different, unique genome. This means that a criminal who leaves hair, skin, blood, or saliva at a crime scene can be identified by their DNA.

Matching DNA
A DNA fingerprint from a sample is recorded as a series of rungs, similar to a supermarket bar code. Crime investigators use software to search databases of offenders' DNA to look for a match.

STAGES OF LIFE

Throughout life, the human body is constantly changing as it experiences different stages of development. From a single cell, the body goes through a process of cell division and multiplication as it grows and develops. By adulthood the body is fully grown, and cells no longer divide for growth. Instead, they divide to replace worn out or damaged cells.

HOW CELLS MULTIPLY

We each start out as a single cell. To develop different organs and tissues for the body to grow, our cells must multiply. As adults, cells need to be replaced when damaged or when they complete their life cycle.

Mitosis

The body produces new cells by a process called mitosis. This is when a cell's DNA, which carries all the instructions to build and run a new cell, duplicates itself. The cell then splits to form two identical cells. This is how cells grow—by making exact copies of themselves.

1 CHECKING
The parent cell gets ready for mitosis. It checks its DNA for damage and makes any necessary repairs.

6 OFFSPRING
Two daughter cells are formed. Each one contains a nucleus with an exact copy of the DNA from the parent cell.

5 SPLITTING
A membrane forms around each group of chromosomes. The cell membrane starts to pull apart to form two cells.

THE CHANGING BODY

From babyhood to old age, the body changes as it grows and ages. At the age of around 20-30, humans have reached maximum height and are physically at their strongest. After that, the body very gradually decreases in power with age. However, the brain actually continues to improve over several more years. As it gains more experience, it gets better at analyzing situations and making decisions.

ONLY A FEW **BODY CELLS LAST** A LIFETIME—THEY **INCLUDE NEURONS IN** THE BRAIN AND **HEART MUSCLE CELLS.**

Standing tall
A surge in hormones produces a big growth spurt.

Making a man

Here are the stages of life for a human male, from a baby to an elderly man. Size and height are the most obvious changes, but there are many other changes on the way to adulthood and old age.

Permanent teeth
Baby teeth are replaced by adult teeth by the age of about 11.

Starting small
Learning to stand and walk is a gradual process for growing babies.

1 BABY
Babies have a large head and short arms and legs. By around 18 months, they have gained enough strength and muscle control to stand and start to walk.

2 TODDLER
At about age 2, the arms and legs grow so the head no longer looks as large. The brain develops rapidly, and children learn to talk and use their hands with more precision.

3 CHILD
From the ages of 5-10, children continue to grow and learn complex physical skills, such as riding a bike and swimming.

4 TEENAGER
During puberty, hormones trigger major changes: height increases, the body takes on more adult features, and emotional swings are common.

2 PREPARATION
The chromosomes duplicate themselves, then the originals join together with their copies.

3 LINING UP
Each doubled chromosome attaches to special fibers, which help them to line up in the center of the cell.

4 SEPARATION
The chromosomes break apart at the point where they were attached. Each half is pulled to the opposite end of the cell.

HEALTHY CELL

CELL SHRINKS AND BREAKS APART

FRAGMENTS EATEN BY CLEANER CELL

OUT WITH THE OLD
When cells reach the end of their natural life span, they undergo a process of shrinking and breaking down into small fragments. These pieces are then eaten up by special cleaner cells called phagocytes.

In with the new
The natural breakdown of cells and the cleanup operation by phagocytes leaves room for new cells to replace them.

USE IT OR LOSE IT
The speed of aging varies widely between people. Although genetics plays its part, evidence suggests that keeping both mind and body active can help to slow down the aging process and may help you live longer.

Staying active
Briton Fauja Singh holds many senior running records, including marathons. In 2013, he ran in the Mumbai Marathon at the age of 102.

5 YOUNG ADULT
The body reaches its adult height, and bones stop growing. People are physically capable of reproducing—having children.

6 ADULT
Humans are physically strongest between 20 and 35 years of age. Muscle development is complete and body systems continue to function well.

7 MIDDLE-AGED ADULT
Between the ages of 50 and 70, the skin becomes less stretchy and wrinkles appear. Muscles weaken. Vision and hearing begin to deteriorate.

8 ELDERLY ADULT
A person gets shorter as they age because their spine shortens. Their muscles also get weaker, and together with stiff joints this can make movement slower.

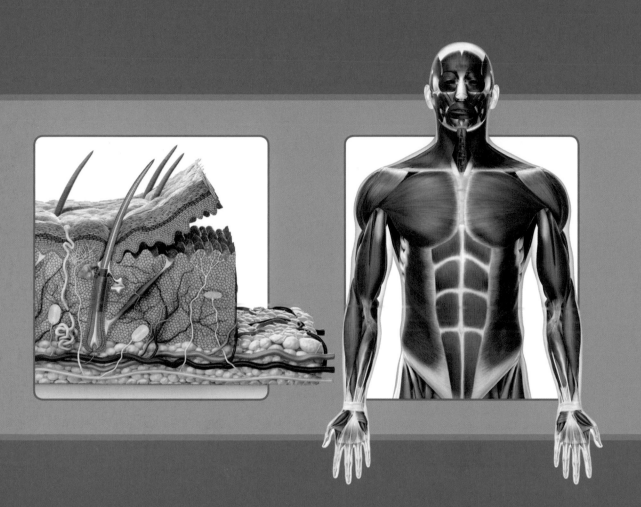
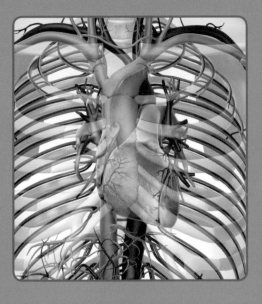

BODY SYSTEMS

The human body works like a machine, running multiple systems at once to keep it operating at optimum levels. Each body system has its own unique function, but also depends on all the other systems to perform at its best.

All systems go

Humans could not survive without all 12 of the body systems—groups of body parts that carry out different tasks. The systems communicate continually by passing instructions to each other, so the body works as one.

The 12 systems are the skin, hair, and nails; muscular; skeletal (bones); nervous (brain and nerves); cardiovascular (heart and blood); lymphatic (drainage); immune (defense); respiratory (lungs and breathing); digestive (processing food); urinary (kidneys and bladder); reproductive (sex); and endocrine (hormones) systems.

Working together

Body systems are interdependent, which means they rely on each other to function. Some organs belong to more than one system—the pancreas plays a role in digestion but also releases hormones, so it belongs to both the digestive and endocrine systems.

Every single part of the human body is connected to the central **nervous system.**

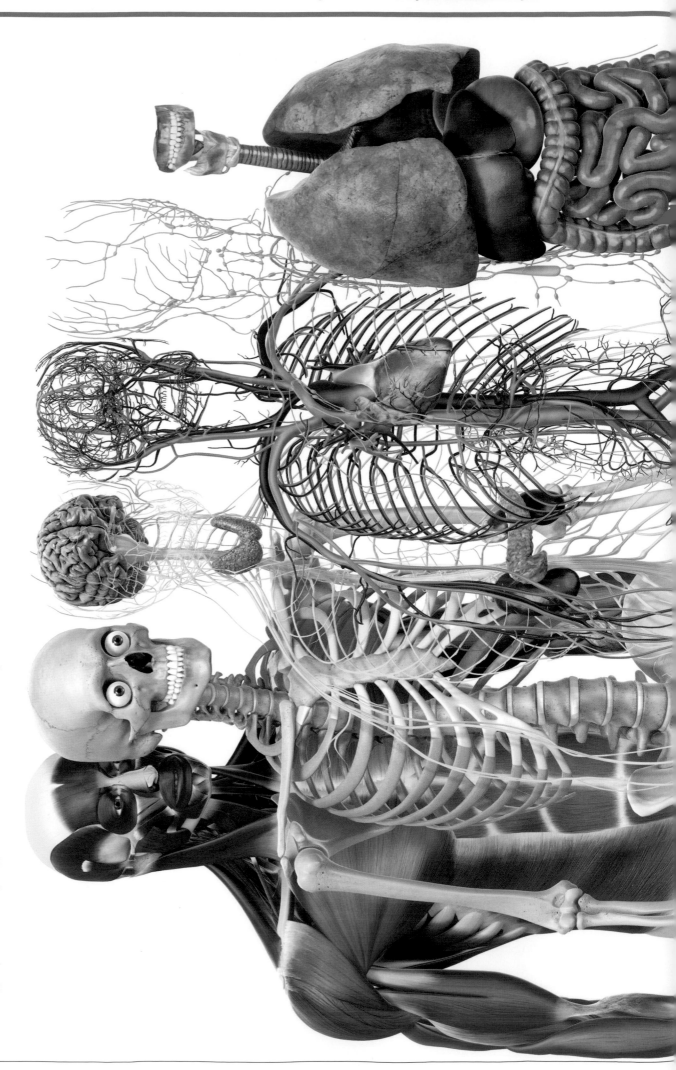

Muscles **push food through your system** so efficiently that food would reach your stomach even if you ate standing on your head.

Your body makes **two million new red blood cells** every second, to replace the same number that die.

21

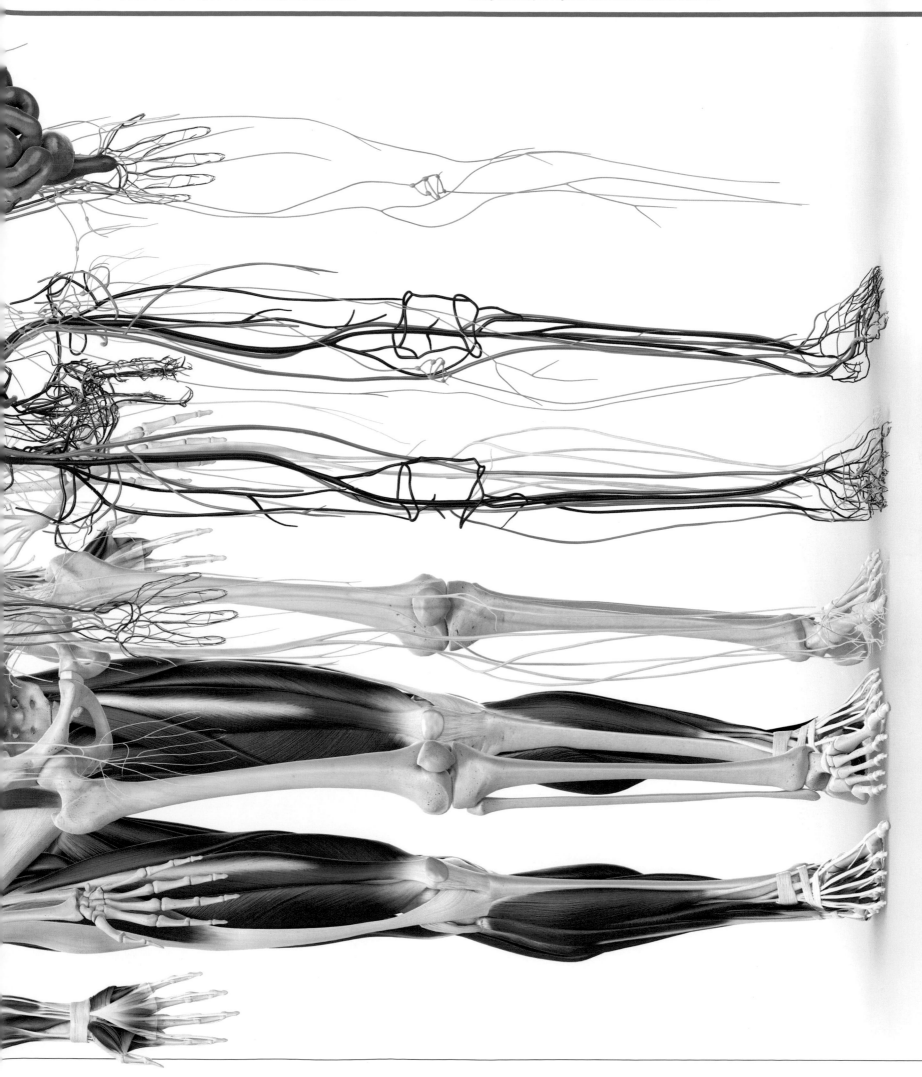

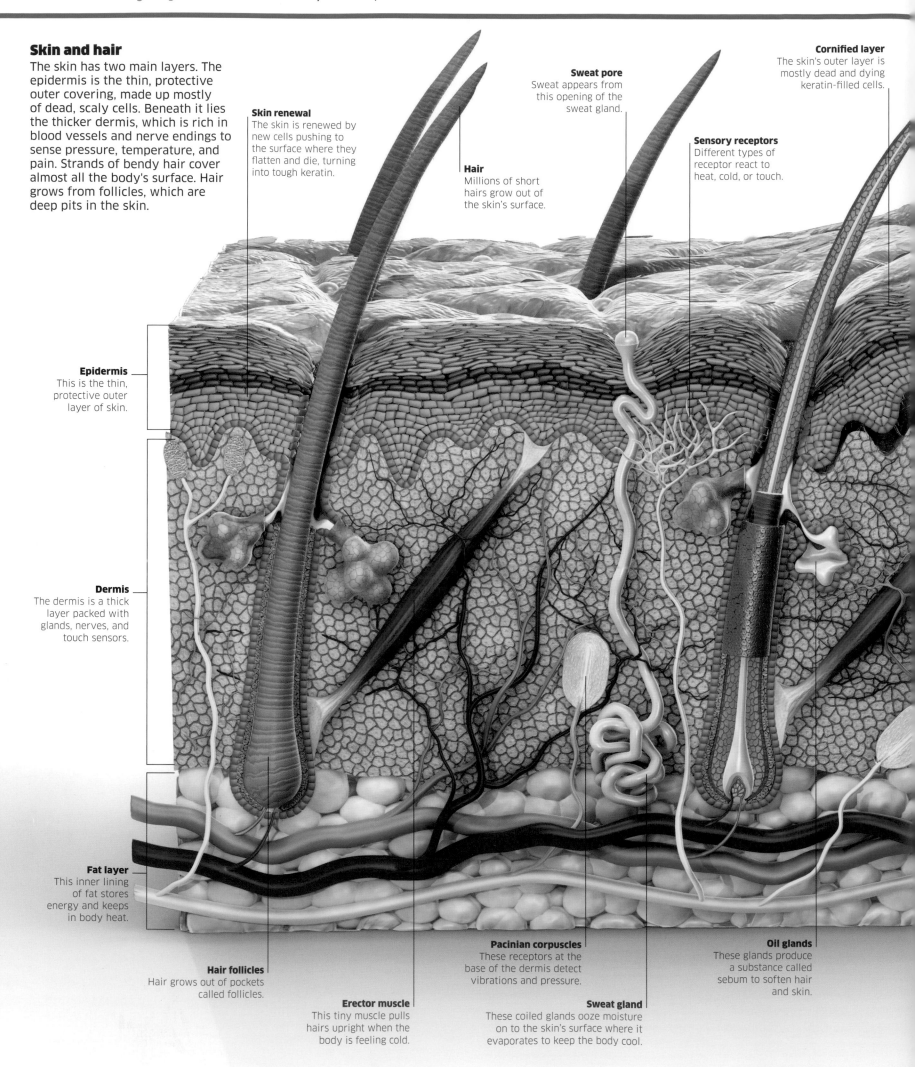

Skin and hair

The skin has two main layers. The epidermis is the thin, protective outer covering, made up mostly of dead, scaly cells. Beneath it lies the thicker dermis, which is rich in blood vessels and nerve endings to sense pressure, temperature, and pain. Strands of bendy hair cover almost all the body's surface. Hair grows from follicles, which are deep pits in the skin.

Skin renewal
The skin is renewed by new cells pushing to the surface where they flatten and die, turning into tough keratin.

Sweat pore
Sweat appears from this opening of the sweat gland.

Cornified layer
The skin's outer layer is mostly dead and dying keratin-filled cells.

Hair
Millions of short hairs grow out of the skin's surface.

Sensory receptors
Different types of receptor react to heat, cold, or touch.

Epidermis
This is the thin, protective outer layer of skin.

Dermis
The dermis is a thick layer packed with glands, nerves, and touch sensors.

Fat layer
This inner lining of fat stores energy and keeps in body heat.

Hair follicles
Hair grows out of pockets called follicles.

Erector muscle
This tiny muscle pulls hairs upright when the body is feeling cold.

Pacinian corpuscles
These receptors at the base of the dermis detect vibrations and pressure.

Sweat gland
These coiled glands ooze moisture on to the skin's surface where it evaporates to keep the body cool.

Oil glands
These glands produce a substance called sebum to soften hair and skin.

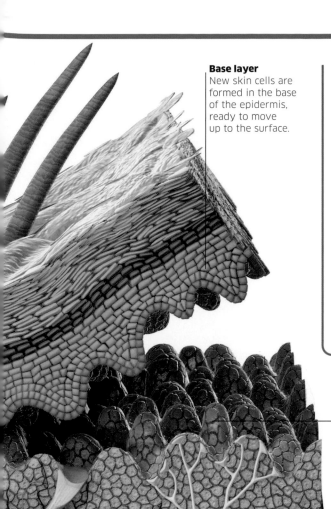

Base layer
New skin cells are formed in the base of the epidermis, ready to move up to the surface.

Protective shield

Skin protects the body, while being flexible enough to let you move around easily. The hair on your head keeps you warm and gives the scalp an extra layer of defense. Fine hairs on the rest of your body make you more sensitive to touch.

Nail structure

Nails are hard plates of dead cells that protect the ends of your fingers and toes. They also help you to grip and pick things up. New cells grow in the root of the nail, and as these cells move forward, they harden and die. It takes about six months for cells to move from the base of a nail to the tip.

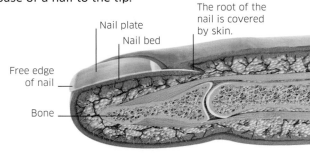

Nail plate

The root of the nail is covered by skin.

Nail bed

Free edge of nail

Bone

CROSS-SECTION OF A FINGER

Finger layer
Fingerlike bulges hold the epidermis in place—and create the ridges that make fingerprints.

Skin, hair, and nails

There is one system that extends over the entire surface of your body. Known as the integumentary system, it consists of the skin, hair, and nails, which together cover and protect the other body systems against the outside world.

The skin is the largest organ of the body, wrapping it in a waterproof and germproof barrier. It is also essential in helping you to touch and feel things around you, to control the body's temperature, and to filter out harmful rays from the sun. Hair and nails provide extra protection for some parts of the body. They grow from the skin and are made from dead cells of a tough substance called keratin.

Artery
This supplies oxygen and nutrients to the skin.

Nerves
These networks carry signals between touch receptors and the brain.

16% of your total body mass is **made up of skin.**

BODY COVER

The human body is almost entirely covered in a layer of skin and hair for protection and warmth. Together, the skin and hair form the body's largest sensory organ, with an advanced array of sensors that give the brain detailed data about the body's surroundings. The body has different skin and hair types, depending on where they are and their role.

HAIRY OR SMOOTH

The main skin types are hairy or hairless (also called glabrous skin). Most of the body is covered in hairy skin, even though the hair is sometimes too fine for us to see it easily.

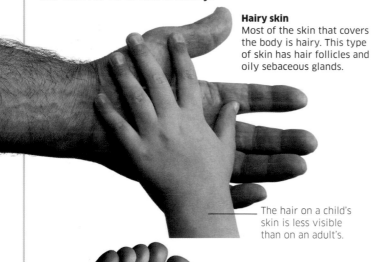

Hairy skin
Most of the skin that covers the body is hairy. This type of skin has hair follicles and oily sebaceous glands.

The hair on a child's skin is less visible than on an adult's.

Glabrous skin
Without any hair follicles, glabrous skin is much smoother than hairy skin. It provides padding for the lips, palms of the hands, and soles of the feet.

Glabrous skin has no hair.

THE BODY'S THINNEST SKIN IS ON THE EYELIDS, AND THE THICKEST IS ON THE SOLES OF THE FEET.

BODY TEMPERATURE

When it's too hot or cold, skin and hair play important roles in keeping the temperature at a safe and comfortable level. A thermostat in the brain's hypothalamus monitors signals from the body's sensors. It then sends signals for the body to act to cool itself down or stay warm.

Sweating
Sweat cools the skin as it evaporates.

SUN SHIELD

One of the skin's many functions is to make vitamin D by harnessing the sun's rays. However, ultraviolet light from the sun can damage the skin, so the body produces a substance called melanin to protect it. Melanin is what makes skin look darker or lighter.

Skin color

Human skin has adapted to suit the conditions on Earth. Near the equator, the Sun's rays are most intense. The body produces lots of melanin for maximum protection, so skin is darker. Far from the equator, less melanin is needed, so skin is lighter.

Dark skin
Lots of melanin is produced by cells called melanocytes.

Pale skin
The skin produces smaller amounts of melanin pigment.

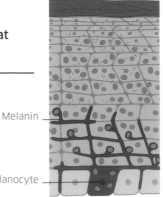
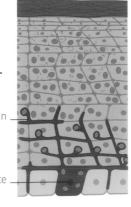
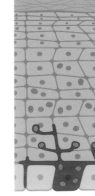

Melanin

Melanocyte

Keeping cool
If the temperature rises above 100.4°F (38°C), sweat glands produce watery sweat to cool the skin. Blood vessels at the skin's surface widen, so heat can escape easily. Hair relaxes, so heat is released into the air.

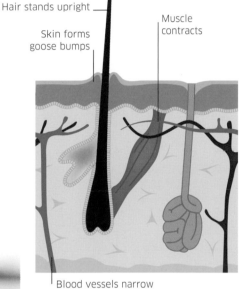

Hair is flattened

Muscle relaxes

Blood vessels are wide

Sweat gland releases droplets of sweat

Hair stands upright

Skin forms goose bumps

Muscle contracts

Blood vessels narrow

Keeping warm
When the temperature drops, skin goes into heat-retention mode. Blood vessels become narrower to prevent heat loss from the warm body. Muscles contract to make the skin's hairs stand upright to trap warm air. These muscles pull on the skin above, making lumps known as goose bumps.

HAIR
Unlike most warm-blooded land animals, humans have no fur to keep them warm— most of the hair that covers our bodies is very fine. Bare skin is good for keeping the body cool, but in colder climates, humans need to wear clothes to maintain their body temperature.

Hair growth
Each hair grows out of a deep, narrow shaft called a follicle. At the base of the hair, living cells divide and push the hair upward. Hair does not grow constantly. Instead it grows in spurts and has periods of rest in between.

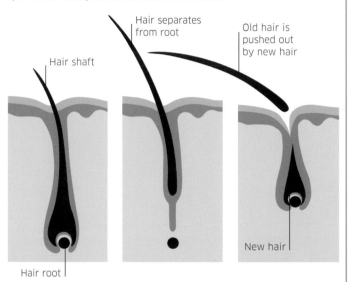

Hair separates from root

Old hair is pushed out by new hair

Hair shaft

New hair

Hair root

1 ACTIVE FOLLICLE
The active follicle creates new cells inside the hair root. As these die, they are pushed out to form the shaft, which gets longer and longer.

2 RESTING STAGE
The follicle becomes narrower, and the hair stops growing. The hair gets pulled away from the root, losing its blood supply.

3 NEW GROWTH
The follicle begins a new cycle. As people age, their hair becomes thinner because fewer follicles reactivate and grow new hairs.

Hair styles
The type of hair you have depends on the shape and size of the follicle it grows from. Small follicles produce fine hair, while bigger follicles produce thick hair. Hair on the head can be straight, wavy, or curly. About 100 head hairs are lost every day, and these are replaced by new growth.

STRAIGHT HAIR

Round follicle

WAVY HAIR

Oval follicle

CURLY OR COILED HAIR

Flat follicle

Hair types
There are two main types of hair on the human body—vellus and terminal. Vellus hairs are the fine, soft hairs that are usually found covering the skin of children and women. Terminal hairs are thicker, and are found on the head, in the armpits and pubic area, and on other parts of the body, especially in men.

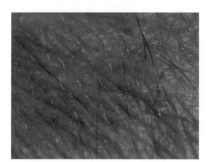

Vellus hair
Fine, short vellus hairs are pale-colored or translucent and grow over most areas of the body.

Terminal hair
Thicker hair on top of the head provides warmth and gives cover from the sun.

Freckles
Some people have a gene for freckles. These small dots show where many melanocyte cells have grouped together. They can become more visible when exposed to sunlight.

Freckled face
Freckles are most common on the face, but they appear on arms and shoulders, too.

Skeletal system

The skeleton shapes and supports the body, allows it to move, and protects internal organs. It is constructed from 206 bones that, far from being dry and dusty, are moist, living organs. Together, those bones create a framework that is strong but light.

Without a skeleton, the body would collapse in a heap. Yet it is not a rigid structure. Flexible joints between bones allow the body to move when those bones are pulled by muscles. The skeleton has other roles. It protects delicate organs such as the brain and heart. Its bones also make blood cells and store calcium, a mineral that is essential for healthy teeth.

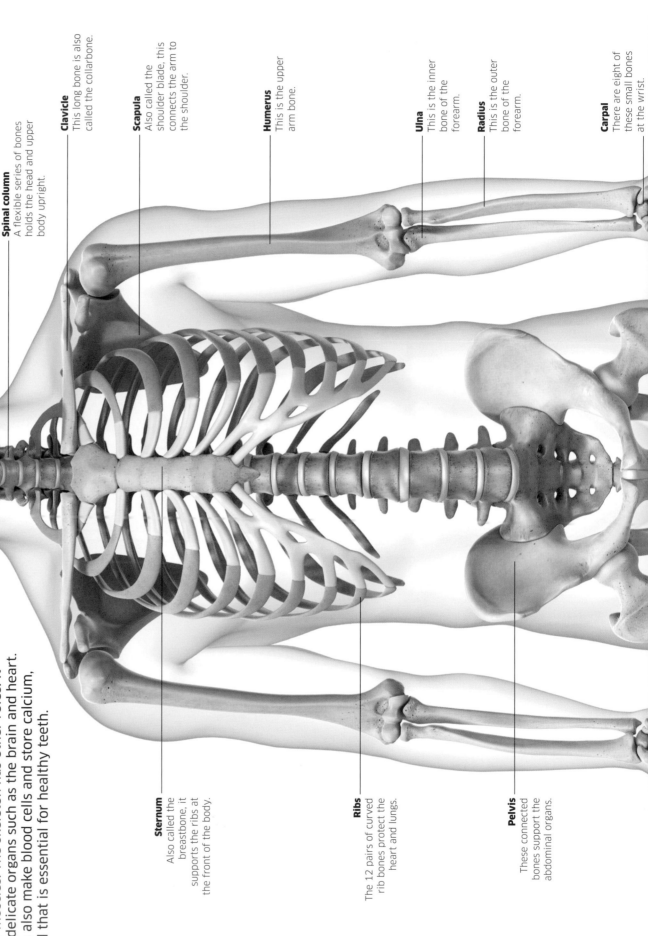

Skeleton front view
This is the front view of an adult male skeleton. The female skeleton is usually smaller and lighter than a male's, with a wider pelvis, which makes childbirth easier.

Cranium
This contains and protects the brain, eyes, ears, and nose.

Lower jawbone (mandible)
The only part of the skull that can move is the mandible.

Spinal column
A flexible series of bones holds the head and upper body upright.

Clavicle
This long bone is also called the collarbone.

Scapula
Also called the shoulder blade, this connects the arm to the shoulder.

Humerus
This is the upper arm bone.

Ulna
This is the inner bone of the forearm.

Radius
This is the outer bone of the forearm.

Carpal
There are eight of these small bones at the wrist.

Sternum
Also called the breastbone, it supports the ribs at the front of the body.

Ribs
The 12 pairs of curved rib bones protect the heart and lungs.

Pelvis
These connected bones support the abdominal organs.

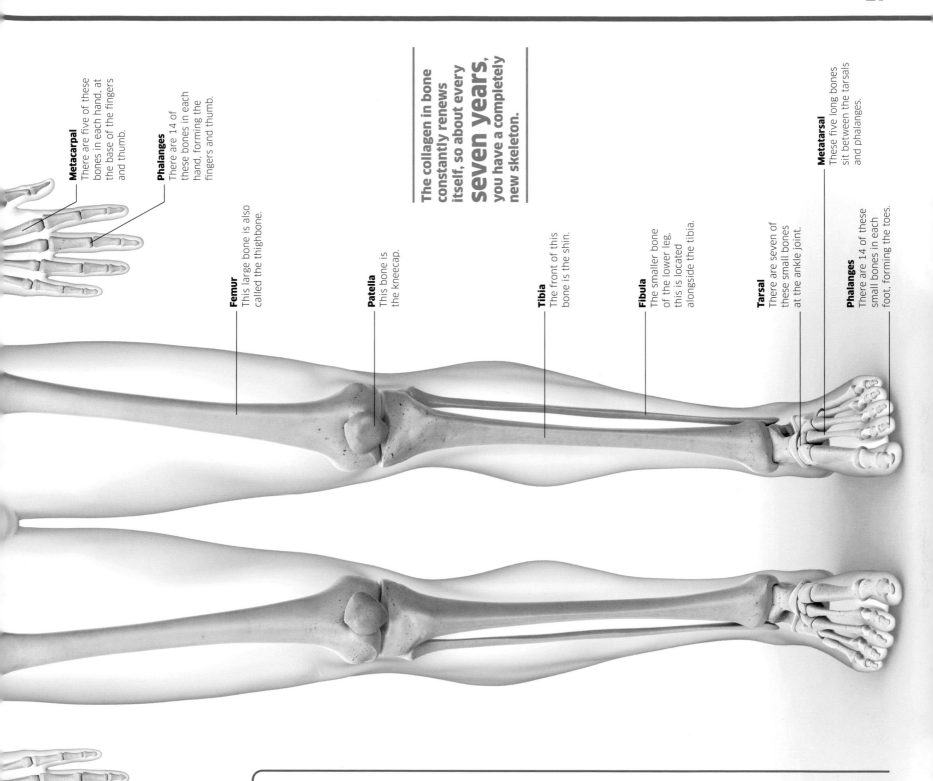

Metacarpal
There are five of these bones in each hand, at the base of the fingers and thumb.

Phalanges
There are 14 of these bones in each hand, forming the fingers and thumb.

Femur
This large bone is also called the thighbone.

Patella
This bone is the kneecap.

Tibia
The front of this bone is the shin.

Fibula
The smaller bone of the lower leg, this is located alongside the tibia.

Tarsal
There are seven of these small bones at the ankle joint.

Metatarsal
These five long bones sit between the tarsals and phalanges.

Phalanges
There are 14 of these small bones in each foot, forming the toes.

The collagen in bone constantly renews itself, so about every **seven years,** you have a completely new skeleton.

Two skeletons in one

The skeleton can be divided into two parts. The axial skeleton (red) forms a central core that supports the upper body and protects important organs. The appendicular skeleton (blue) consists of the arm and leg bones, and the bony girdles that connect them to the axial skeleton.

Axial skeleton
This is made up of the 80 bones of the skull, vertebral column, ribs, and breastbone.

Appendicular skeleton
This consists of the 126 bones of the upper and lower limbs, and the shoulder and hip girdles.

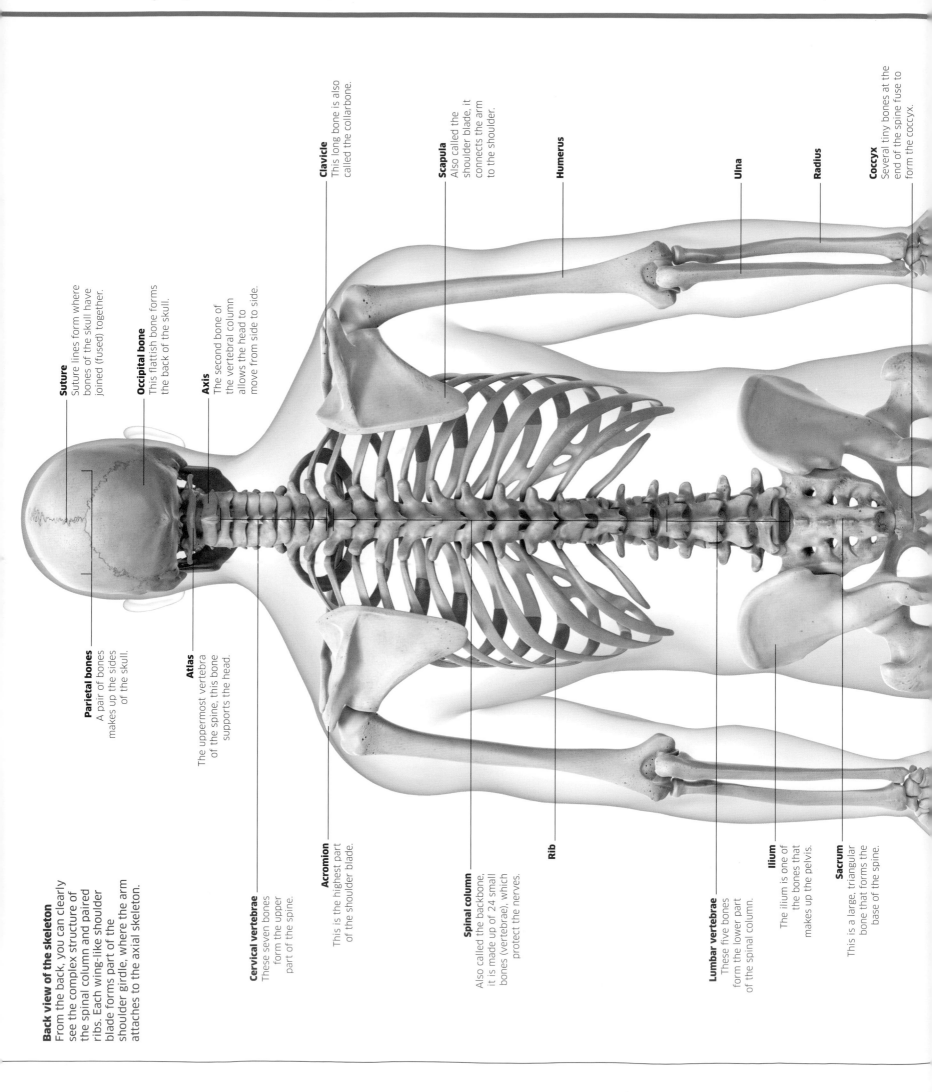

Back view of the skeleton
From the back, you can clearly see the complex structure of the spinal column and paired ribs. Each wing-like shoulder blade forms part of the shoulder girdle, where the arm attaches to the axial skeleton.

Suture
Suture lines form where bones of the skull have joined (fused) together.

Occipital bone
This flattish bone forms the back of the skull.

Axis
The second bone of the vertebral column allows the head to move from side to side.

Clavicle
This long bone is also called the collarbone.

Scapula
Also called the shoulder blade, it connects the arm to the shoulder.

Humerus

Ulna

Radius

Coccyx
Several tiny bones at the end of the spine fuse to form the coccyx.

Parietal bones
A pair of bones makes up the sides of the skull.

Atlas
The uppermost vertebra of the spine, this bone supports the head.

Cervical vertebrae
These seven bones form the upper part of the spine.

Acromion
This is the highest part of the shoulder blade.

Spinal column
Also called the backbone, it is made up of 24 small bones (vertebrae), which protect the nerves.

Rib

Lumbar vertebrae
These five bones form the lower part of the spinal column.

Ilium
The ilium is one of the bones that makes up the pelvis.

Sacrum
This is a large, triangular bone that forms the base of the spine.

Femur
The femur, or thigh bone, is the longest bone in the body.

Femoral condyles
These rounded, knobbly ends of the femur form part of the knee joint.

Babies are born with **about 300 bones,** but adults have just 206. Some bones fuse together as we grow.

Tibia

Fibula

Heel bone
The largest bone in the foot, this is also called the calcaneus.

Types of bone

Bones have different shapes and sizes, depending on their functions. There are five kinds of bone in the human skeleton.

FEMUR
(thigh bone)

Long bones
These bones are longer than they are wide and are found in the arms, hands, legs, and feet. They support the body's weight and allow it to move.

Short bones
Roughly cube-shaped bones in the wrist and ankle allow some movement and provide stability to the joints.

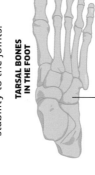

TARSAL BONES IN THE FOOT

Tarsal

Flat bones
Shield-like flat bones protect organs such as the heart and brain.

SCAPULA
(shoulder blade)

Irregular bones
These bones have complex shapes to perform specific roles. For example, the vertebrae allow the back to bend and rotate, and protect the spinal cord.

VERTEBRA

Sesamoid bones
These small, roundish bones protect tendons and joints from wear and tear. The patella protects the knee joint. It sits inside the tendon that attaches the thigh muscle to the tibia.

PATELLA
(kneecap)

Muscular system

Every single movement your body makes is produced by the muscular system. Muscles are layers of hardworking tissue that shape the body, keep it upright, and move it around.

Muscle tissue is made of long cells called fibers, which use energy to contract, or shorten, pulling different parts of the body into position. Movements are controlled by nerve signals from the brain. Sometimes you move your muscles consciously, such as when you sit down, or turn to look at something. But other muscle movements, such as your heartbeat, or when you blink your eyes, happen without you thinking about them.

Deep muscles, front view

This front view of the skeleton shows the body's deepest layer of skeletal muscles. Skeletal muscles in the back and neck work to keep the body upright, while those in the arms and legs are used for walking, running, and all kinds of other physical activities.

An adult's body weight is made up of about 40% muscle.

FRONT VIEW OF DEEP MUSCLES

Sternothyroid
This straplike muscle at the front of the neck pulls the larynx down.

Brachialis
The brachialis helps to bend the elbow.

Posterior rectus sheath
This tissue is formed by the tendons of the abdominal muscle.

Flexor digitorum profundus
This muscle helps to bend the fingers.

Gluteus medius
This muscle moves the thigh outward.

Pectoralis minor
This muscle helps to stabilize the shoulder blade when the arm moves.

Intercostal muscles
These muscles between the ribs help with breathing by raising the ribs up and out.

Transversus abdominis
This muscle helps to stabilize the pelvis and lower back when moving.

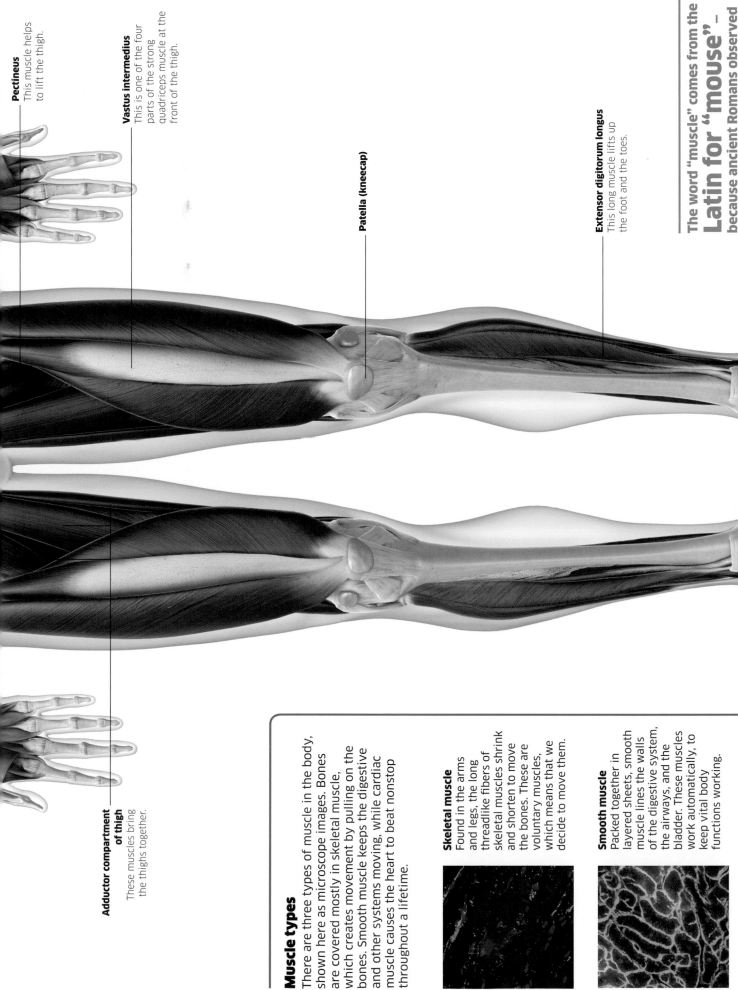

Pectineus
This muscle helps to lift the thigh.

Vastus intermedius
This is one of the four parts of the strong quadriceps muscle at the front of the thigh.

Patella (kneecap)

Extensor digitorum longus
This long muscle lifts up the foot and the toes.

The word "muscle" comes from the **Latin for "mouse"** – because ancient Romans observed that **muscles moving** under the skin looked like mice running around.

Adductor compartment of thigh
These muscles bring the thighs together.

Muscle types

There are three types of muscle in the body, shown here as microscope images. Bones are covered mostly in skeletal muscle, which creates movement by pulling on the bones. Smooth muscle keeps the digestive and other systems moving, while cardiac muscle causes the heart to beat nonstop throughout a lifetime.

Skeletal muscle
Found in the arms and legs, the long threadlike fibers of skeletal muscles shrink and shorten to move the bones. These are voluntary muscles, which means that we decide to move them.

Smooth muscle
Packed together in layered sheets, smooth muscle lines the walls of the digestive system, the airways, and the bladder. These muscles work automatically, to keep vital body functions working.

Cardiac muscle
The walls of the heart are formed by cardiac muscle. This must contract continually to keep the heart beating. Cardiac muscle never gets tired, unlike other types of muscle.

If all the body's muscles pulled in the same direction at once, they could create a force strong enough to **lift a small truck.**

Deep muscles, back view
This rear view of the deep muscles shows skeletal muscles from the head to the feet. They hold the head and back upright, keep the shoulders steady, pull the arms back, straighten the thighs, bend the knees, and point the toes down.

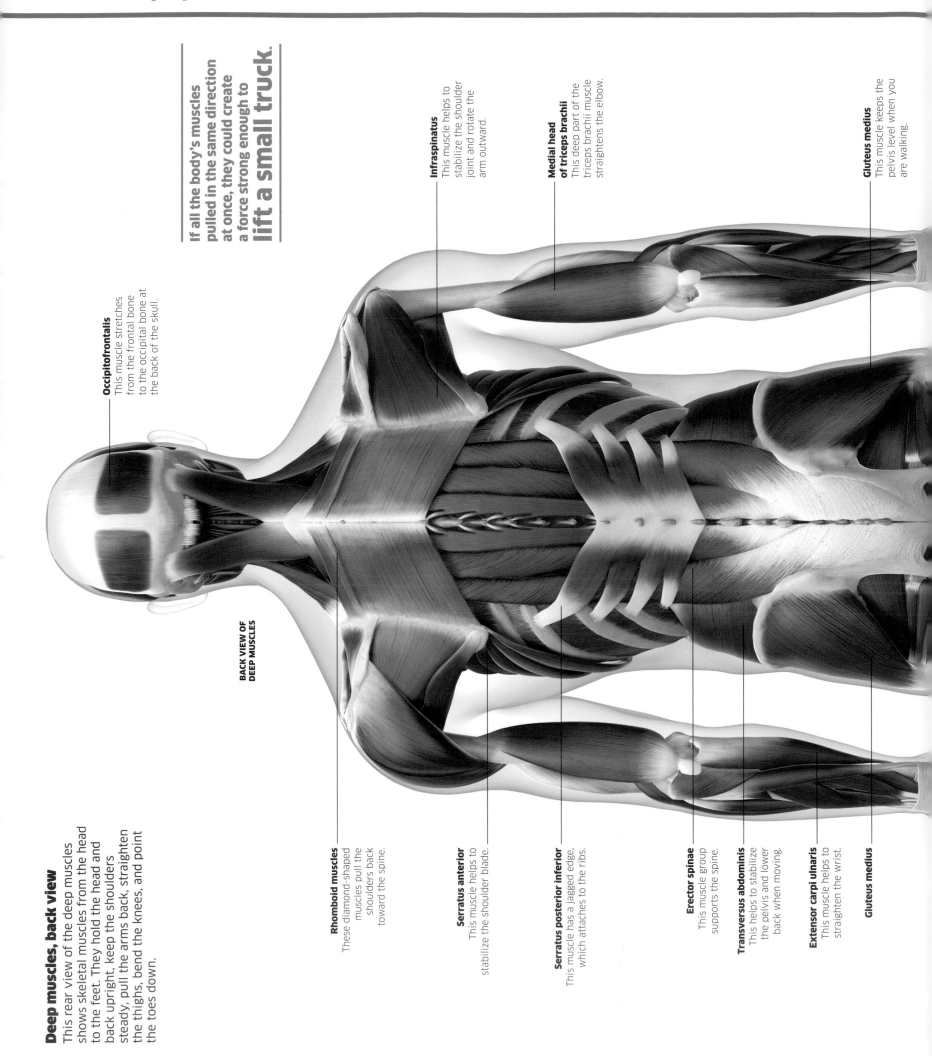

BACK VIEW OF DEEP MUSCLES

Occipitofrontalis
This muscle stretches from the frontal bone to the occipital bone at the back of the skull.

Infraspinatus
This muscle helps to stabilize the shoulder joint and rotate the arm outward.

Medial head of triceps brachii
This deep part of the triceps brachii muscle straightens the elbow.

Gluteus medius
This muscle keeps the pelvis level when you are walking.

Rhomboid muscles
These diamond-shaped muscles pull the shoulders back toward the spine.

Serratus anterior
This muscle helps to stabilize the shoulder blade.

Serratus posterior inferior
This muscle has a jagged edge, which attaches to the ribs.

Erector spinae
This muscle group supports the spine.

Transversus abdominis
This helps to stabilize the pelvis and lower back when moving.

Extensor carpi ulnaris
This muscle helps to straighten the wrist.

Gluteus medius

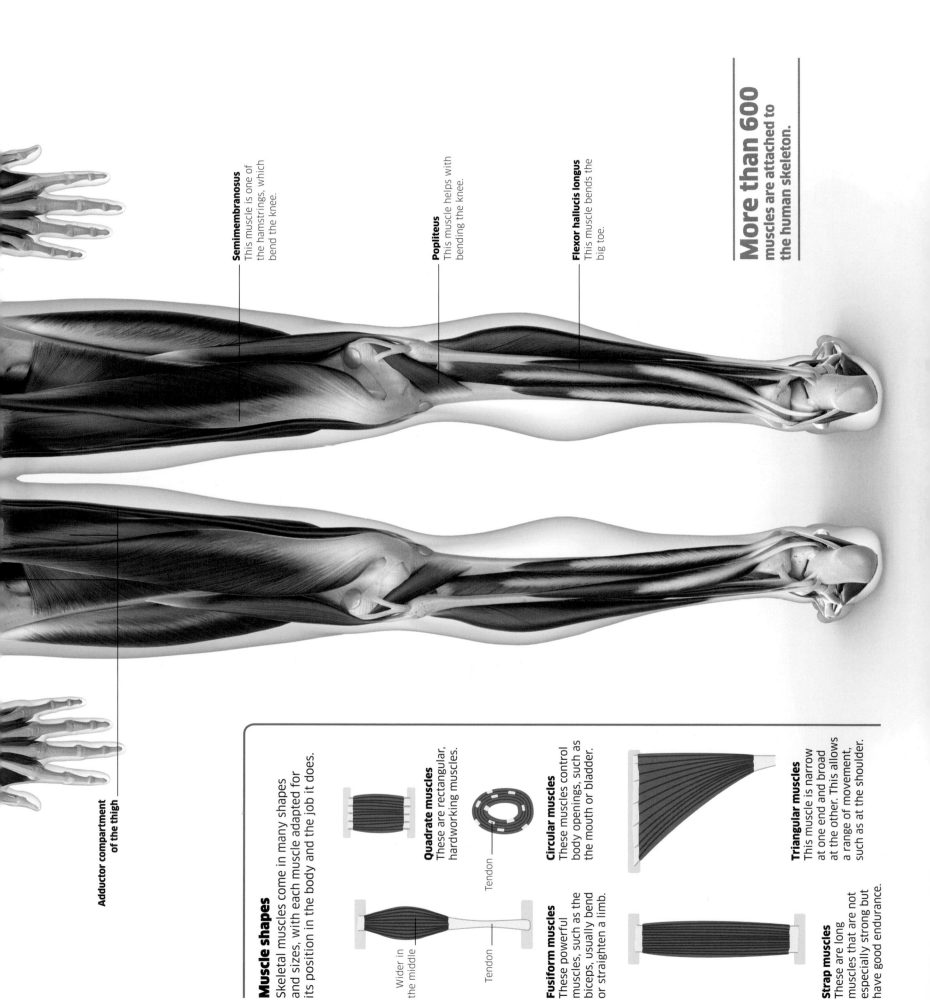

Semimembranosus
This muscle is one of the hamstrings, which bend the knee.

Popliteus
This muscle helps with bending the knee.

Flexor hallucis longus
This muscle bends the big toe.

More than 600
muscles are attached to the human skeleton.

Adductor compartment of the thigh

Muscle shapes

Skeletal muscles come in many shapes and sizes, with each muscle adapted for its position in the body and the job it does.

Quadrate muscles
These are rectangular, hardworking muscles.

Circular muscles
These muscles control body openings, such as the mouth or bladder.

Tendon

Triangular muscles
This muscle is narrow at one end and broad at the other. This allows a range of movement, such as at the shoulder.

Fusiform muscles
These powerful muscles, such as the biceps, usually bend or straighten a limb.

Wider in the middle

Tendon

Strap muscles
These are long muscles that are not especially strong but have good endurance.

Superficial muscles, front view

Superficial muscles are just beneath the skin. Those at the front of the body create different facial expressions, move the head forward and sideways, bend the arms and move them forward, bend the body forward and sideways, bend the legs, straighten the knees, and lift the feet.

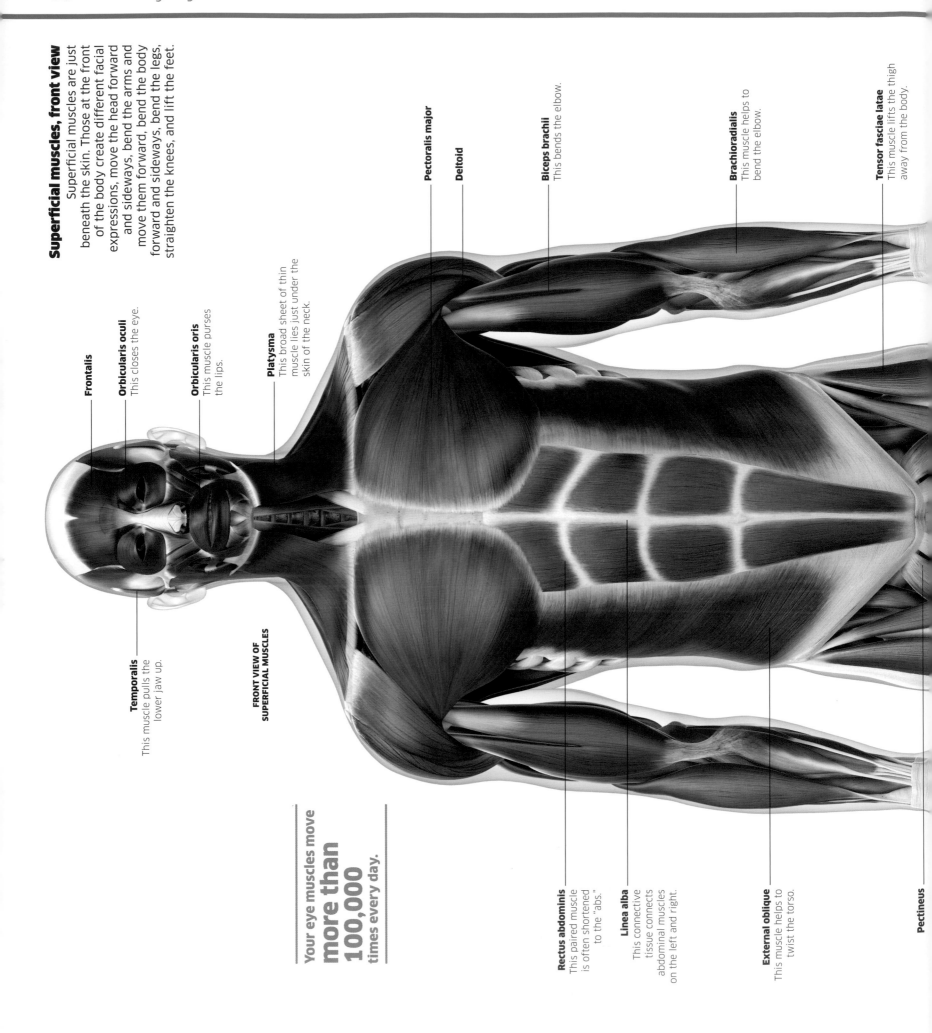

Temporalis
This muscle pulls the lower jaw up.

Frontalis

Orbicularis oculi
This closes the eye.

Orbicularis oris
This muscle purses the lips.

Platysma
This broad sheet of thin muscle lies just under the skin of the neck.

FRONT VIEW OF SUPERFICIAL MUSCLES

Pectoralis major

Deltoid

Biceps brachii
This bends the elbow.

Brachioradialis
This muscle helps to bend the elbow.

Tensor fasciae latae
This muscle lifts the thigh away from the body.

Your eye muscles move **more than 100,000** times every day.

Rectus abdominis
This paired muscle is often shortened to the "abs."

Linea alba
This connective tissue connects abdominal muscles on the left and right.

External oblique
This muscle helps to twist the torso.

Pectineus

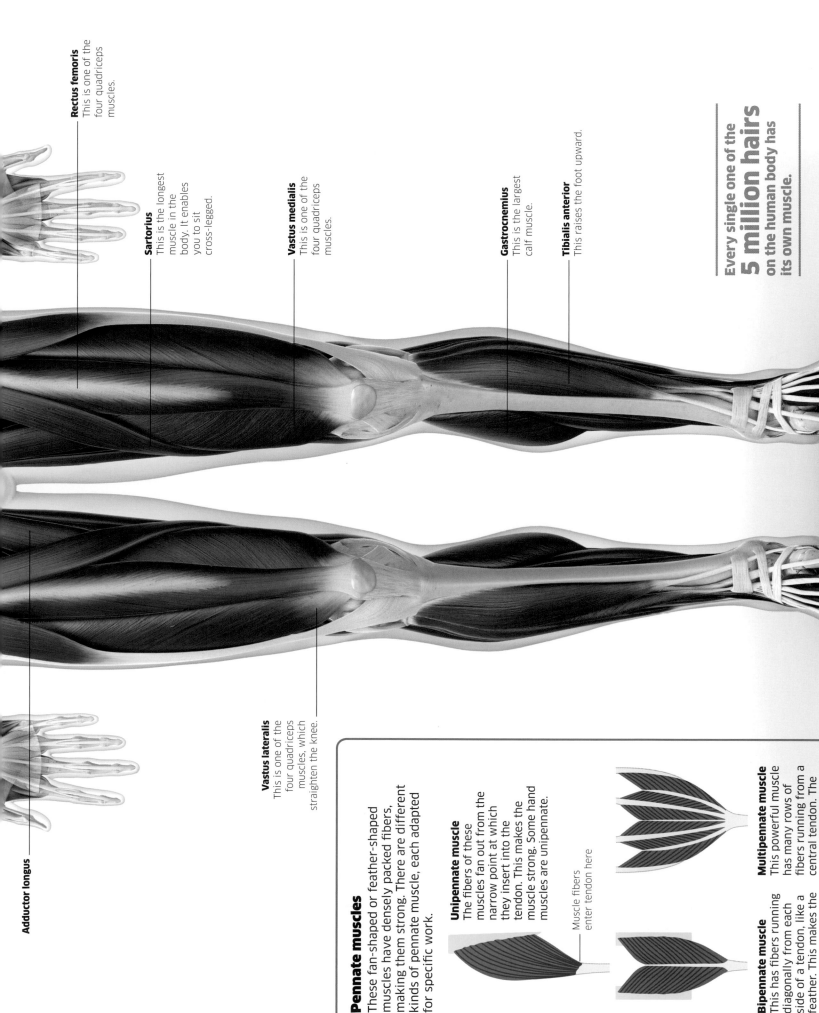

Rectus femoris
This is one of the four quadriceps muscles.

Sartorius
This is the longest muscle in the body. It enables you to sit cross-legged.

Vastus medialis
This is one of the four quadriceps muscles.

Gastrocnemius
This is the largest calf muscle.

Tibialis anterior
This raises the foot upward.

Adductor longus

Vastus lateralis
This is one of the four quadriceps muscles, which straighten the knee.

Every single one of the **5 million hairs** on the human body has its own muscle.

Pennate muscles

These fan-shaped or feather-shaped muscles have densely packed fibers, making them strong. There are different kinds of pennate muscle, each adapted for specific work.

Bipennate muscle
This has fibers running diagonally from each side of a tendon, like a feather. This makes the muscle even stronger, but less mobile. The rectus femoris muscle at the front of the thigh is bipennate.

Unipennate muscle
The fibers of these muscles fan out from the narrow point at which they insert into the tendon. This makes the muscle strong. Some hand muscles are unipennate.

Muscle fibers enter tendon here

Multipennate muscle
This powerful muscle has many rows of fibers running from a central tendon. The deltoid (shoulder) muscle is multipennate.

Superficial muscles, back view

At first glance, muscle names may appear difficult to read, but they have all been given a unique Latin name to describe them. This name can be understood around the world. The chosen name relates to specific characteristics of the muscle, such as its size, shape, location, and what it does.

BACK VIEW OF SUPERFICIAL MUSCLES

There are three times as many **skeletal muscles** as there are bones in the human body.

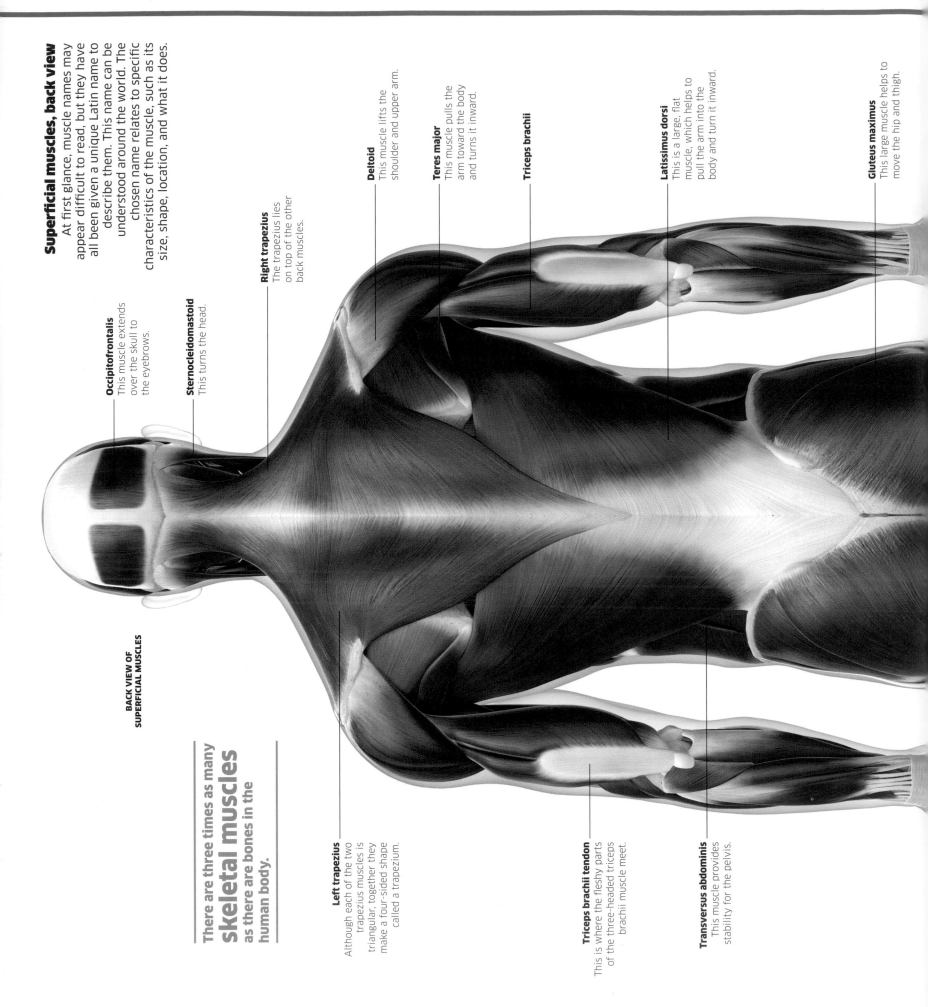

Occipitofrontalis
This muscle extends over the skull to the eyebrows.

Sternocleidomastoid
This turns the head.

Right trapezius
The trapezius lies on top of the other back muscles.

Deltoid
This muscle lifts the shoulder and upper arm.

Teres major
This muscle pulls the arm toward the body and turns it inward.

Triceps brachii

Latissimus dorsi
This is a large, flat muscle, which helps to pull the arm into the body and turn it inward.

Gluteus maximus
This large muscle helps to move the hip and thigh.

Left trapezius
Although each of the two trapezius muscles is triangular, together they make a four-sided shape called a trapezium.

Triceps brachii tendon
This is where the fleshy parts of the three-headed triceps brachii muscle meet.

Transversus abdominis
This muscle provides stability for the pelvis.

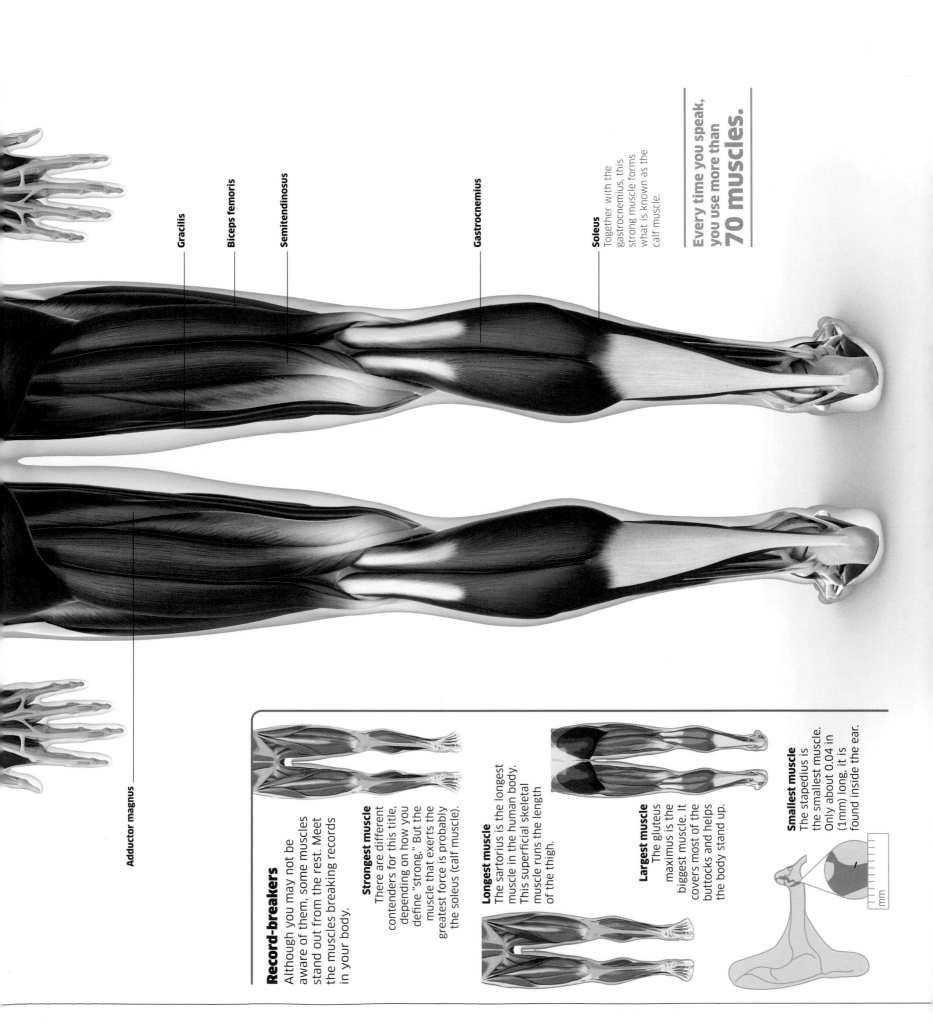

Gracilis

Biceps femoris

Semitendinosus

Gastrocnemius

Soleus
Together with the gastrocnemius, this strong muscle forms what is known as the calf muscle.

Every time you speak, you use more than **70 muscles.**

Adductor magnus

Record-breakers

Although you may not be aware of them, some muscles stand out from the rest. Meet the muscles breaking records in your body.

Strongest muscle
There are different contenders for this title, depending on how you define "strong." But the muscle that exerts the greatest force is probably the soleus (calf muscle).

Longest muscle
The sartorius is the longest muscle in the human body. This superficial skeletal muscle runs the length of the thigh.

Largest muscle
The gluteus maximus is the biggest muscle. It covers most of the buttocks and helps the body stand up.

Smallest muscle
The stapedius is the smallest muscle. Only about 0.04 in (1mm) long, it is found inside the ear.

mm

Nervous system

This is the body's communication and control network. The brain sends and receives messages along the spinal cord and billions of interconnecting nerve cells wired up to every part of the body.

The nervous system works like high-speed internet, sending electrical signals at great speed through nerve cells called neurons. Sensory nerves send signals to the brain from sense receptors all over your body. At the same time, going in the opposite direction, motor nerves send signals from the brain, telling the muscles to move.

Bundle of nerves

The brain and the spinal cord—the mass of nerves running down the backbone—make up the central nervous system (CNS). This coordinates most of the body's activities, from blinking and breathing to seeing and standing. Nerves branch out to the rest of the body via the peripheral nervous system (PNS).

Brain
The control center of the nervous system, this is home to more than 100 billion neurons.

Cranial nerves
Twelve pairs of cranial nerves relay signals between the brain and the head, face, and neck.

Spinal cord
The body's primary communications highway, this carries all nerve signals between the body and brain.

Musculocutaneous nerve
This nerve supplies muscles in the upper arm and gives feeling in the forearm.

Axillary nerve
The axillary nerve supplies muscles and sensation in the shoulder.

Phrenic nerve
Messages to and from the diaphragm are carried by this nerve.

Ulnar nerve
Supplying muscles in the forearm and hand, this nerve gives the "funny bone" tingle if you hit your elbow.

Sciatic nerve
The thickest and longest nerve in the body, this links the spinal cord to muscles in the legs and feet.

Brachial plexus
This collection of nerves supplies the muscles and skin of the arm and hand.

Intercostal nerve
The intercostal nerve supplies the muscles and skin of the thorax (chest).

Median nerve
Most of the muscles in the forearm and hand, and some skin of the hand, is supplied by this nerve.

Radial nerve
This nerve supplies muscles in the back of the arm and the skin of the lower arm.

Lumbar plexus
A "plexus" is a branching network. The lumbar plexus supplies the skin and muscle of the lower back.

Femoral nerve
This supplies sensation and muscles in the thigh and inner leg.

Sacral plexus
The skin and muscle of the pelvis and leg are supplied by this web of nerves.

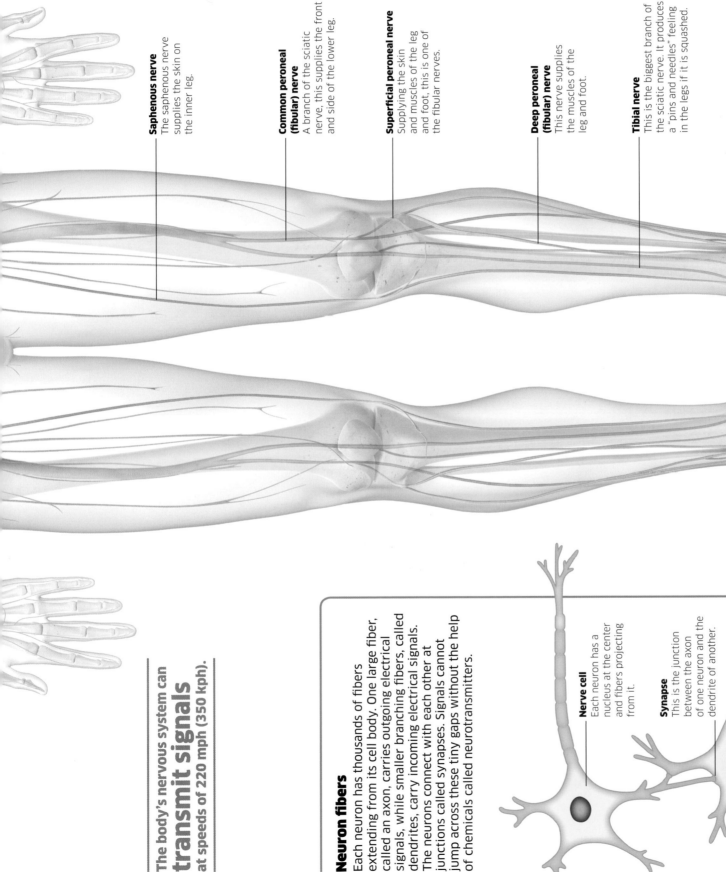

Saphenous nerve
The saphenous nerve supplies the skin on the inner leg.

Common peroneal (fibular) nerve
A branch of the sciatic nerve, this supplies the front and side of the lower leg.

Superficial peroneal nerve
Supplying the skin and muscles of the leg and foot, this is one of the fibular nerves.

Deep peroneal (fibular) nerve
This nerve supplies the muscles of the leg and foot.

Tibial nerve
This is the biggest branch of the sciatic nerve. It produces a "pins and needles" feeling in the legs if it is squashed.

Plantar nerve
The plantar nerve is responsible for the tickling sensation when the soles of the feet are touched.

The body's nervous system can **transmit signals** at speeds of 220 mph (350 kph).

Neuron fibers

Each neuron has thousands of fibers extending from its cell body. One large fiber, called an axon, carries outgoing electrical signals, while smaller branching fibers, called dendrites, carry incoming electrical signals. The neurons connect with each other at junctions called synapses. Signals cannot jump across these tiny gaps without the help of chemicals called neurotransmitters.

Nerve cell
Each neuron has a nucleus at the center and fibers projecting from it.

Synapse
This is the junction between the axon of one neuron and the dendrite of another.

Axon
An axon is a large fiber that transmits an electrical signal to the next neuron.

Dendrite
These smaller fibers receive signals from nearby neurons.

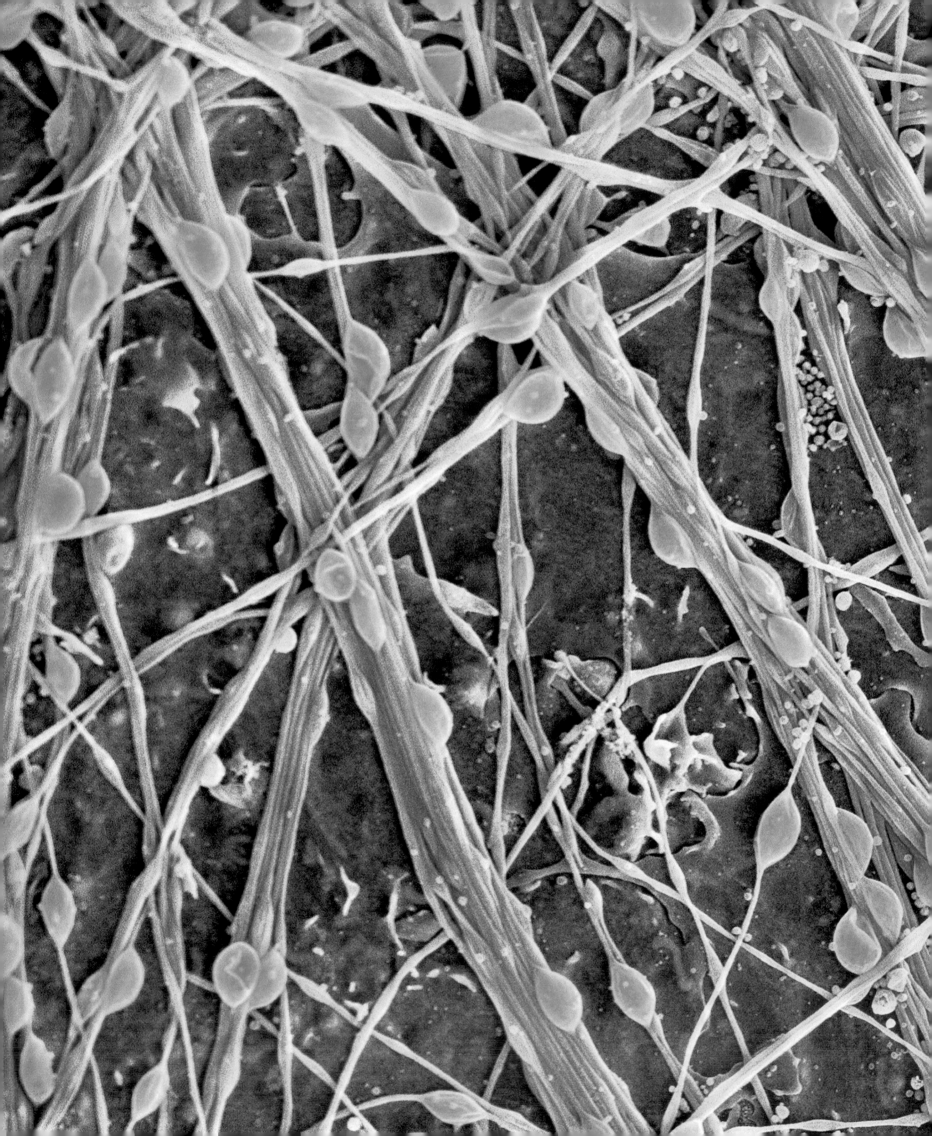

NEURON NETWORK

This image shows the network of nerve cells called neurons. Every nerve is made up of neurons, and there are billions of them. If all the body's neurons were put end to end they would stretch 37 miles (60 km).

Electrical signals pass from one neuron (colored green) to another by moving down their long extensions, which are called axons (colored blue). Signals cross a tiny space to the receiving parts of the next neuron, which are called dendrites (also blue). Messages travel at high speeds, going all the way from the brain to the feet in 0.01 seconds.

Endocrine system

In addition to sending high-speed signals along the nervous system, the body also uses chemicals called hormones to carry messages to specific parts. These hormones are produced and released into the bloodstream by the tissues and glands of the endocrine system.

There are about 50 different kinds of hormone, made by a dozen or so major glands as well as some organs. As it travels around the body, each hormone targets a particular cell or tissue to alter how it works. Hormones control growth, hunger, sleep, reproduction, and many other functions of the body.

Stroking a pet dog or cat releases the hormone oxytocin, which lowers blood pressure and reduces feelings of anxiety.

Pineal gland
This gland makes melatonin, which affects sleep.

Hypothalamus
This part of the brain links the nervous and endocrine systems.

Pituitary gland
Hormones that control other glands are produced here.

Hormone factory
The main hormone-producing glands are in the brain, neck, abdomen, and groin. Other organs, such as the stomach, liver, and heart, release hormones, too. Hormones are released only when the gland receives the correct trigger—a change in blood, a nerve signal, or an instruction from another hormone.

Thyroid gland
This gland releases thyroxine, which controls the body's metabolic rate—the speed at which cells use up the oxygen that fuels them.

Thymus
The thymus secretes hormones to boost the production of disease-fighting white blood cells. It is only active during childhood and early teenage years and shrinks to be almost invisible in adults.

Parathyroid glands
These four small glands regulate levels of calcium, which is vital for healthy teeth and bones.

Heart
The heart releases hormones that control blood pressure.

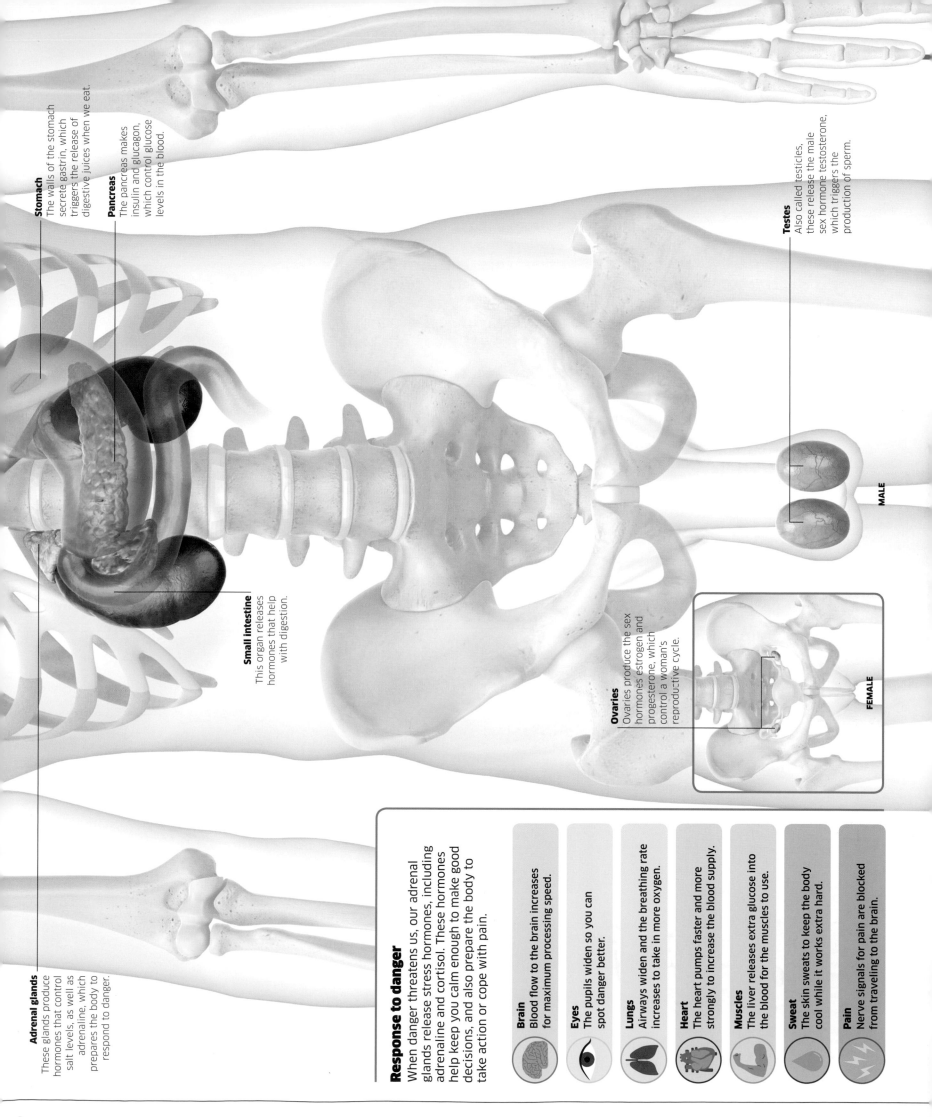

Stomach
The walls of the stomach secrete gastrin, which triggers the release of digestive juices when we eat.

Pancreas
The pancreas makes insulin and glucagon, which control glucose levels in the blood.

Testes
Also called testicles, these release the male sex hormone testosterone, which triggers the production of sperm.

MALE

Adrenal glands
These glands produce hormones that control salt levels, as well as adrenaline, which prepares the body to respond to danger.

Small intestine
This organ releases hormones that help with digestion.

Ovaries
Ovaries produce the sex hormones estrogen and progesterone, which control a woman's reproductive cycle.

FEMALE

Response to danger

When danger threatens us, our adrenal glands release stress hormones, including adrenaline and cortisol. These hormones help keep you calm enough to make good decisions, and also prepare the body to take action or cope with pain.

Brain
Blood flow to the brain increases for maximum processing speed.

Eyes
The pupils widen so you can spot danger better.

Lungs
Airways widen and the breathing rate increases to take in more oxygen.

Heart
The heart pumps faster and more strongly to increase the blood supply.

Muscles
The liver releases extra glucose into the blood for the muscles to use.

Sweat
The skin sweats to keep the body cool while it works extra hard.

Pain
Nerve signals for pain are blocked from traveling to the brain.

HORMONES FOR GROWING UP

The human body goes through many changes from birth to old age. The glands and organs of the endocrine system produce the hormones that trigger different stages of development. The most important period of change is adolescence—the transition from a child to an adult. During this stage of rapid growth, called puberty, the body changes shape and the reproductive system develops. A hormone in the brain triggers puberty, while other hormones regulate functions, such as growth, mood, and sleep.

HORMONES FOR PUBERTY

Hormones are the chemical messengers that travel between the body's organs and tissues. They can only instruct cells that have the right receptors to detect them, so many different hormones are involved in the chain of events of puberty.

The starting point

Puberty begins in the brain. Between the ages of about 9 and 12, an area of the brain called the hypothalamus sends messages to the pituitary gland to release hormones that start the process of puberty by instructing other glands to produce hormones.

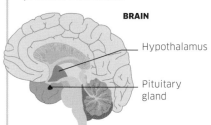

BRAIN

Hypothalamus

Pituitary gland

Growth hormone

The body grows very fast during puberty—and growth hormone (hGH) is the driver of growth spurts. It is released by the pituitary gland, and affects all parts of the body, making muscles and organs larger, and bones longer.

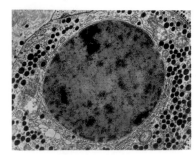

Hormone cell
Growth hormone is made by cells in the pituitary gland. The brown spots in the outer part of the cell are storing newly made growth hormone.

Getting ready to reproduce

This chart shows the chain of some of the hormones that turn children into adults capable of having their own children. Luteinizing hormone (LH) and follicle-stimulating hormone (FSH) play a major role, stimulating different hormones in boys and girls that control the necessary changes.

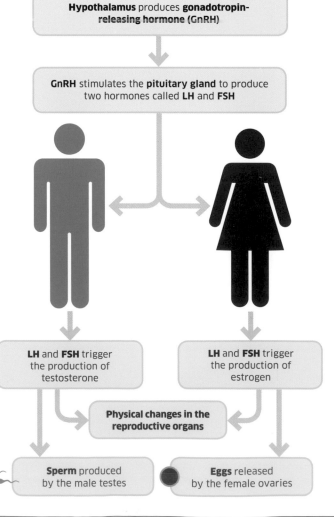

Hypothalamus produces **gonadotropin-releasing hormone (GnRH)**

GnRH stimulates the **pituitary gland** to produce two hormones called **LH** and **FSH**

LH and **FSH** trigger the production of testosterone

LH and **FSH** trigger the production of estrogen

Physical changes in the reproductive organs

Sperm produced by the male testes

Eggs released by the female ovaries

BODY TRANSFORMATION

Puberty marks the start of the process of preparing the body for reproduction later in life. In the reproductive organs, girls begin to produce eggs, while boys start to produce sperm. Puberty starts at different ages and takes different amounts of time to complete, so friends of the same age can often be very different heights and shapes.

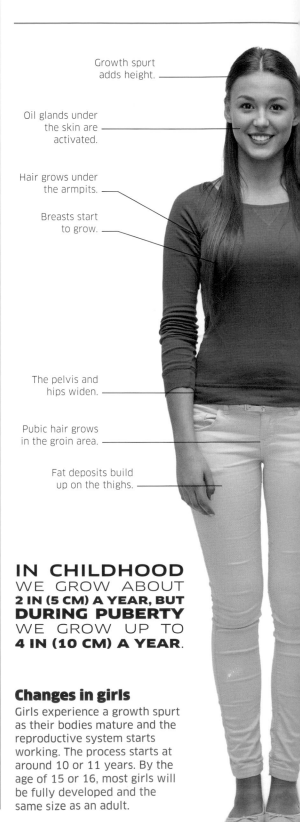

Growth spurt adds height.

Oil glands under the skin are activated.

Hair grows under the armpits.

Breasts start to grow.

The pelvis and hips widen.

Pubic hair grows in the groin area.

Fat deposits build up on the thighs.

IN CHILDHOOD
WE GROW ABOUT **2 IN (5 CM) A YEAR, BUT DURING PUBERTY** WE GROW UP TO **4 IN (10 CM) A YEAR**.

Changes in girls

Girls experience a growth spurt as their bodies mature and the reproductive system starts working. The process starts at around 10 or 11 years. By the age of 15 or 16, most girls will be fully developed and the same size as an adult.

Teenage acne

During puberty, hormones called androgens stimulate the skin's oily sebaceous glands. Before they settle down to normal production, the newly activated glands can produce too much oil. Skin pores become blocked, causing blackheads. If the trapped oil gets infected, the area becomes inflamed and pimples appear.

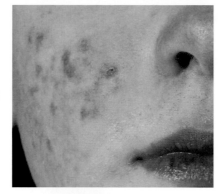

Pimples
Pimples and blackheads on the face, back, and chest are very common in puberty.

Changes in boys

Boys enter puberty between the ages of 9 to 12, and most have completed the stage by the time they are 17 or 18 years old.

Oil glands under the skin are activated.

Facial hair begins to grow.

The enlarged larynx produces a lump on the neck, called an Adam's apple.

Shoulders become broader.

Hair grows under the armpits.

Muscles build in the chest and limbs.

Pubic hair begins to grow.

Male genitals get bigger.

Hair grows on the legs.

Deeper sounds

The hormone testosterone affects boys' voices in adolescence. Vocal cords grow thicker, so they vibrate at a lower frequency and the voice sounds deeper. The larynx tilts and sticks out, forming the Adam's apple.

Breaking voices
As boys go through puberty, their voices can fluctuate between high and low as they learn to control their thicker vocal cords.

◉ MATURING BRAIN

As hormone levels go up and down, teenagers can experience emotional highs and lows. Adolescence is a time of great upheaval in the brain, too. It is clearing out millions of neural connections that are no longer needed, forming more efficient networks of nerve pathways, and learning to control rapidly growing limbs and muscles. These factors affect thinking and behavior, and many teenagers often feel clumsy and moody.

Gray to white

The brain is rewired dramatically during puberty, as these scans show. The red areas show the highest volume of gray matter, while blue and purple areas have lower gray matter volume. As unused brain circuits are pruned away, gray matter is reduced. With less gray matter and more white matter, the brain does not learn new skills so quickly, but it is much better at using the skills it already knows.

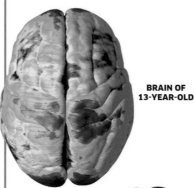

BRAIN OF 13-YEAR-OLD

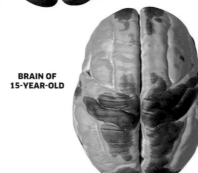

BRAIN OF 15-YEAR-OLD

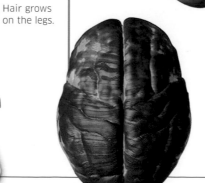

BRAIN OF 18-YEAR-OLD

Raging hormones

In addition to affecting the physical makeup of the brain, hormones alter the behavior of teenagers.

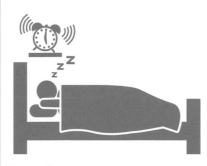

Sleep patterns
Teenagers need more sleep than children or adults. A hormone called melatonin helps people fall asleep. This is released later in the evening for teenagers, which is why they struggle to get up in the morning.

Taking risks
Teens sometimes do risky things without thinking of the consequences. They lack judgment because although the thrill-seeking part of the brain is fully formed, the decision-making area is still maturing.

Moodiness
Alterations in hormone levels, together with changes in parts of the brain that deal with emotions, can cause teenage mood swings and impulsive or aggressive behavior.

Clumsiness
Teens may feel clumsy and uncoordinated at times. This happens because their body shapes are changing, and the brain is struggling to make new neuron connections fast enough to keep up.

Cardiovascular system

The cardiovascular, or circulatory, system is the body's blood transport network. Blood delivers oxygen and nutrients to cells so they can convert them into energy. Then it carries away waste products created by this energy-making process.

Together, the heart, blood, and an intricate network of hollow tubes called blood vessels make up the circulatory system. The heart beats constantly to pump blood through the vessels to every part of the body.

Never-ending circuit
Blood travels round the body via blood vessels. Arteries, shown in red, carry blood from the heart, branching into smaller and smaller vessels to deliver oxygen-filled blood to the body's cells. Veins, shown in blue, deliver blood back to the heart. This process is called circulation because the same blood flows around and around.

External jugular vein
Blood is carried away from the face and scalp by this vein.

Common carotid artery
This large vessel supplies blood to the head and neck.

Subclavian artery
This is the main vessel supplying blood to the arm and hand.

Subclavian vein
Blood is drained from the arm and hand by this vein.

Axillary artery
Oxygen-rich blood reaches the upper arm via this artery.

Brachial vein
This blood vessel drains oxygen-poor blood from the arm.

Superior mesenteric vein
This vein drains blood from the small intestine.

Radial artery
The pulse can be taken where this artery passes through the wrist.

External iliac vein
This is the main vein carrying blood back from the thigh, leg, and foot.

External iliac artery
This is the main artery supplying the thigh, leg, and foot.

Aorta
As thick as an adult's thumb, this is the body's largest artery.

Heart
This muscular pump pushes blood around the body.

Descending aorta
This large artery runs down through the chest to the abdomen.

Inferior vena cava
Blood from the lower body is carried back to the heart by this vein.

Basilic vein
The basilic vein helps drain blood from the hand and forearm.

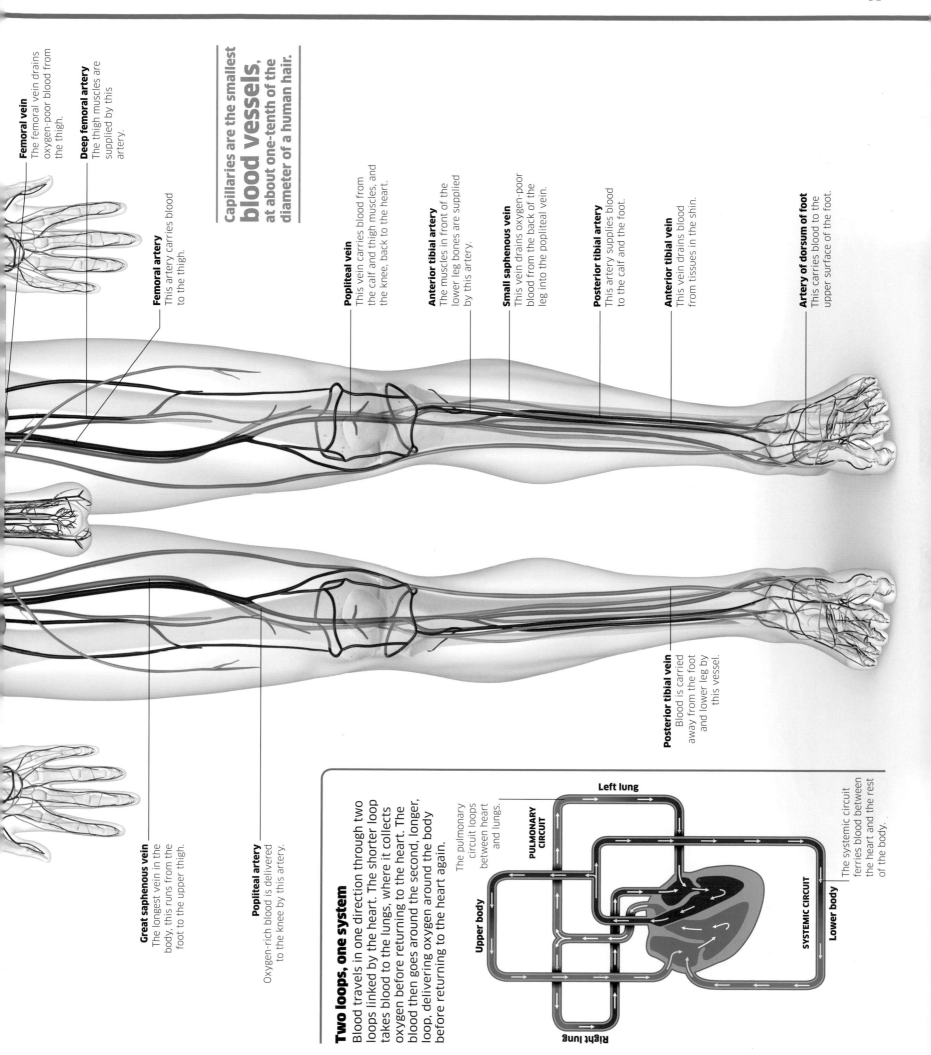

Femoral vein
The femoral vein drains oxygen-poor blood from the thigh.

Deep femoral artery
The thigh muscles are supplied by this artery.

Capillaries are the smallest **blood vessels**, at about one-tenth of the diameter of a human hair.

Femoral artery
This artery carries blood to the thigh.

Popliteal vein
This vein carries blood from the calf and thigh muscles, and the knee, back to the heart.

Anterior tibial artery
The muscles in front of the lower leg bones are supplied by this artery.

Small saphenous vein
This vein drains oxygen-poor blood from the back of the leg into the popliteal vein.

Posterior tibial artery
This artery supplies blood to the calf and the foot.

Anterior tibial vein
This vein drains blood from tissues in the shin.

Artery of dorsum of foot
This carries blood to the upper surface of the foot.

Posterior tibial vein
Blood is carried away from the foot and lower leg by this vessel.

Great saphenous vein
The longest vein in the body, this runs from the foot to the upper thigh.

Popliteal artery
Oxygen-rich blood is delivered to the knee by this artery.

Two loops, one system

Blood travels in one direction through two loops linked by the heart. The shorter loop takes blood to the lungs, where it collects oxygen before returning to the heart. The blood then goes around the second, longer, loop, delivering oxygen around the body before returning to the heart again.

The pulmonary circuit loops between heart and lungs.

Left lung

PULMONARY CIRCUIT

Upper body

Right lung

SYSTEMIC CIRCUIT

Lower body

The systemic circuit ferries blood between the heart and the rest of the body.

Lymphatic system

The lymphatic system collects and drains away excess fluid that has passed from the blood into tissues. It also carries cells that fight infection by helping to stop disease-causing germs, called pathogens, from spreading around the body.

All body tissues are bathed in a watery liquid that comes from the surrounding blood vessels. Most of it drains back into the veins, but the rest becomes a clear fluid called lymph. This is transported along a network of vessels, called lymphatics, back to the bloodstream. The lymph passes through lymph nodes, which contain cells that target and destroy germs in the lymph fluid.

The average human body returns

6½ pints (3 liters)

of lymph fluid back to the bloodstream every day.

Tonsils
Deep inside the throat, the tonsils help to destroy germs that come into the body through the nose and mouth.

Left subclavian vein
This drains blood from the left arm and collects lymph from the left side of the body and the lower half of the right side.

Right subclavian vein
This drains blood from the right arm and collects lymph from the upper half of the right side of the body.

Spleen
The largest organ in the lymphatic system, the spleen produces cells that help to fight infection.

Inguinal nodes
Lymph from the legs passes through these nodes.

Thoracic duct
Lymph drains into the left subclavian vein through this tube.

Rib cage
Red bone marrow in the ribs produces white blood cells.

Cysterna chyli
This collects lymph from the lower half of the body before it goes up into the thoracic duct.

Lymph node
Lymph is processed and cleaned as it passes through lymph nodes.

Lymph vessels

These tubes drain and transport lymph from body tissues.

Flowing fluid

The lymphatic system consists of a network of vessels (green), nodes, and organs, including the tonsils, spleen, and thymus gland. Unlike the vessels in the blood circulation system, lymphatics have no pump. Instead, lymph is pushed through the system by the movement of the surrounding muscles. Lymph eventually drains into two tubes, or ducts, in the chest that carry the fluid back to the bloodstream.

In the body there are around **650 lymph nodes,** with the largest clusters in **the groin and armpits.**

How lymph nodes work

The network of lymph vessels carries the lymph fluid through tiny, beanlike glands called lymph nodes. As lymph flows through the spongy tissue of the node, cells called lymphocytes and macrophages identify germs and attack them. The lymph nodes also work like a filter to clean the lymph. The cleaned fluid then flows out of the node and continues to the bloodstream.

Lymphocytes

Lymph flows in via lymph vessel

Valve keeps lymph flowing in one direction

Vein carries blood out

Artery carries blood in

Lymph flows out of node

BODY INVADERS

Pathogens are bacteria and viruses that cause disease. Most bacteria are simple and harmless, and some are helpful, such as those that live in the gut to help with digestion. However, some bacteria invade and damage body tissues. Viruses are chemical packages much smaller than bacteria that take control of body cells and multiply, causing illness and disease.

Cocci
These round bacteria can live in the body without a problem, or cause serious diseases such as scarlet fever and pneumonia.

Bacteria

Bacteria are simple, single-celled organisms that can multiply rapidly. A few can cause serious diseases by invading the body, and some release poisons called toxins.

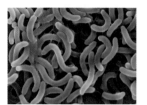

Bacilli
These rod-shaped bacteria often live harmlessly in the gut. Other bacilli cause illness, such as bladder infections and typhoid.

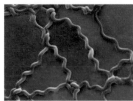

Spirilla
Small, spiral-shaped bacteria, called spirilla, come from uncooked shellfish or stale water. These cause stomach upsets and diarrhea.

ATTACK AND DEFENSE

Every day the human body comes under attack from a range of microscopic invaders that cause disease. All kinds of defensive measures are in place to stop them. Skin and membranes form physical barriers. Fluids such as saliva, tears, and mucus provide chemical warfare. If these lines are passed, the immune system fights back. Armies of special cells target and destroy enemy attackers to make the body healthy again.

Viruses

Viruses reproduce by invading a body cell. The hijacked cell is turned into a factory where more viruses are produced. These are then released to infect more and more cells.

Adenovirus
This virus can infect lungs to produce coughs, eyes to give conjunctivitis, and the digestive system to trigger diarrhea.

A large outbreak of a disease is called an **epidemic.** If it spreads worldwide, it is known as a pandemic.

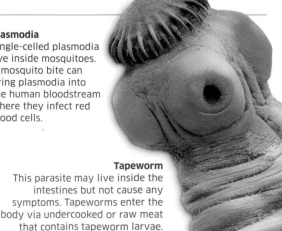

Influenza
There are three main types of influenza virus. Types A and B can cause flu, especially in the winter. Type C usually causes a milder respiratory illness.

Fungi, protists, and parasites

Although most fungi grow in soil or rotting food, some live on or inside humans. Protists are simple organisms, some of which cause human disease. Parasites are other living things that live on or in our bodies.

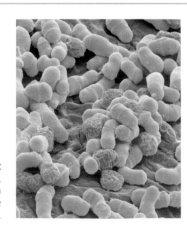

Athlete's foot
This fungus, called *Trichophyton*, grows as a network of threads in damp skin, especially between the toes. It causes an itchy infection.

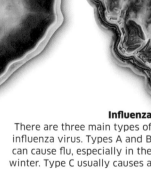

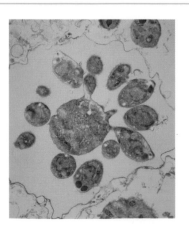

Plasmodia
Single-celled plasmodia live inside mosquitoes. A mosquito bite can bring plasmodia into the human bloodstream where they infect red blood cells.

Tapeworm
This parasite may live inside the intestines but not cause any symptoms. Tapeworms enter the body via undercooked or raw meat that contains tapeworm larvae.

BODY BARRIERS

Bacteria, viruses, and other pathogens face huge resistance from the human body. The first line of defense is the skin and the linings of the eyes, mouth, nose, throat, and stomach.

Inner defenses

Pathogens can enter the body through the food we eat or the air we breathe. To stop germs from gaining access, internal passageways are lined with protective fluids, such as saliva, mucus, and tears.

Tears
Salty tears form to wash away eye pathogens.

Mucus
The nose is lined with sticky mucus to trap germs.

Saliva
This slimy substance has chemicals to kill mouth bacteria.

Wax
Ears contain thick wax to deter invaders.

Skin
The body's outer covering is a barrier against infection.

Blood
Different types of white blood cells unite to attack invaders.

Stomach
Powerful acid in the stomach destroys germs in food.

IMMUNE SYSTEM

The body's collective defense measures are known as the immune system. This works by identifying and targeting pathogens. Over time, the body remembers some germs and gives immunity so the same diseases do not return.

Antibodies

The body makes weapons called antibodies. These defensive chemical proteins attach themselves to invaders to identify them as enemies for white blood cells to eat.

Armies of antibodies

When the body recognizes a pathogen, about 10,000 trillion antibodies are released into the bloodstream and attach themselves to the known germs.

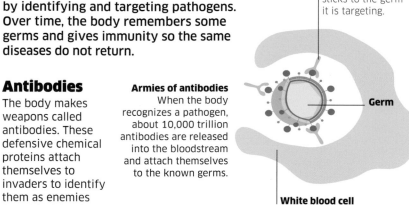

Antibody
The antibody sticks to the germ it is targeting.

Germ

White blood cell
This surrounds and eats the marked germ.

ALLERGIES

The immune system can go wrong when harmless substances that we swallow, breathe in, or touch are targeted by our body's defenses. This overreaction is called an allergy.

Allergens

Substances that trigger an allergic reaction are called allergens. Common allergens include nuts, pollen from flowers, and animal fur.

Automatic response
Common allergic reactions are sneezing; coughing; or red, itchy skin. Reactions are sometimes severe enough to cause breathing problems and be life-threatening.

FIGHTING BACK

Even if some pathogens manage to get past the body's first line of defense, they are unlikely to beat the many millions of white blood cells.

White blood cells

The immune system is run by white blood cells, which move through the bloodstream and other bodily fluids looking for bacteria and viruses to kill. Most white blood cells are made inside bone marrow tissue, and more are produced when germs are present.

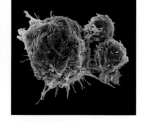
Macrophage
This type of white blood cell kills bacteria and other germs by engulfing them and eating them.

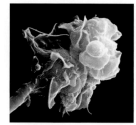
Lymphocyte
This type learns to attack only one type of germ by filling it with poison or releasing antibodies.

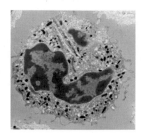
Neutrophil
This is the most common type of white blood cell. Neutrophils help to fight bacteria and fungi.

Appetite for destruction

Macrophages hunt invading bacteria by following the chemical trails they leave behind. If these hungry white blood cells track down an invader, they surround and swallow it. Each macrophage eats about 200 bacteria before it dies.

Macrophage

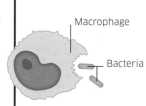
Bacteria

Bacteria being digested

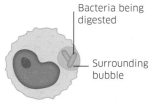
Surrounding bubble

Waste particles are released

1 PLAN OF ATTACK
A macrophage identifies bacteria as enemies and prepares to attack.

2 KILLER CHEMICALS
The bacteria are captured, surrounded, and digested by powerful chemicals.

3 HUNGRY HUNTER
The macrophage expels harmless waste and carries on hunting for invaders.

Fighting inflammation

When the skin is broken by a cut, the body's defense team responds at once. Damaged tissues release chemicals to attract white blood cells, ready to destroy pathogens. Blood vessels allow blood to leak out, so platelets and white blood cells can reach the site of the wound.

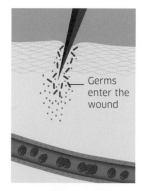
Germs enter the wound

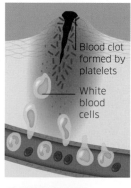
Blood clot formed by platelets

White blood cells

1 INJURY
The skin is pierced. Blood vessels respond by getting wider to increase blood flow to the site. Exposed tissue leaves germs and dirt free to enter.

2 BLOOD CLOT
Platelets thicken the blood to create a clot that seals the wound. White blood cells arrive, looking for pathogens to destroy.

3 GERM EATERS
The white blood cells consume the pathogens. The tissue and skin can now begin to repair itself.

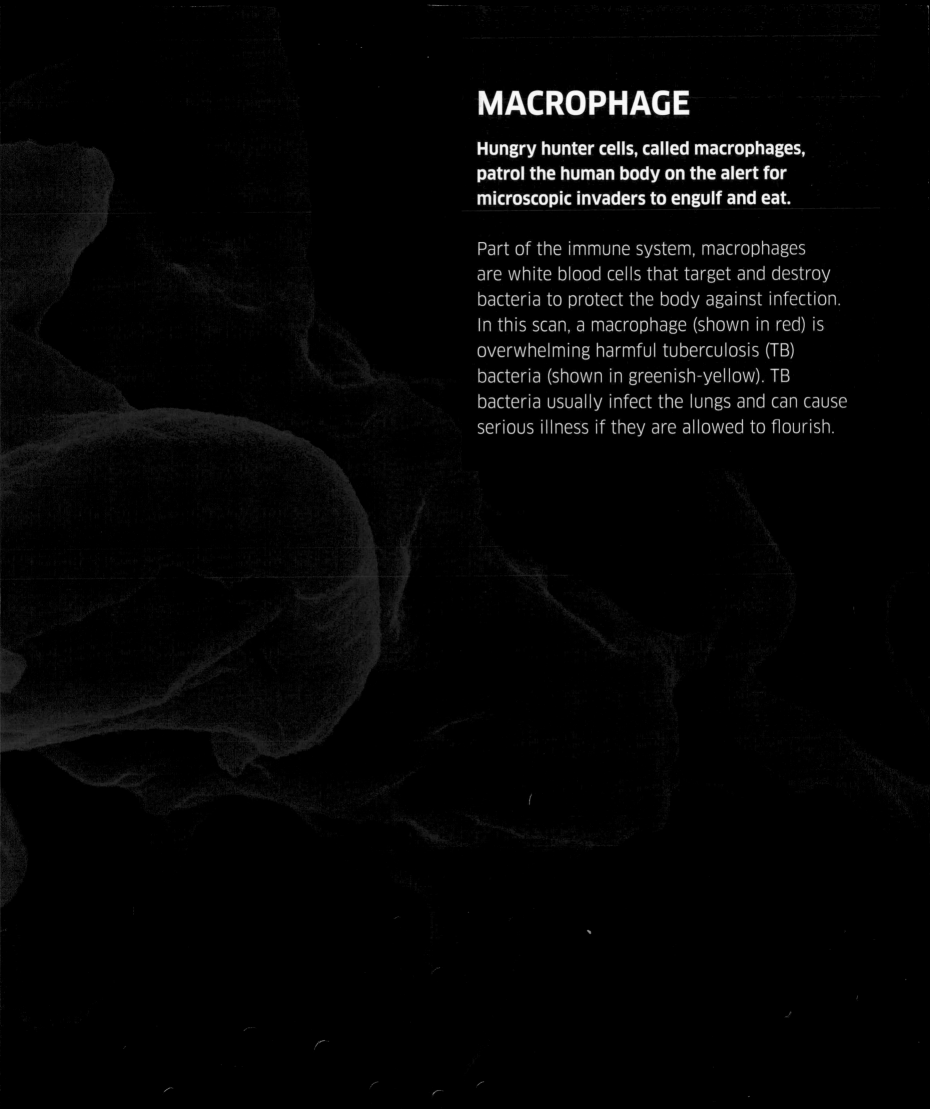

MACROPHAGE

Hungry hunter cells, called macrophages, patrol the human body on the alert for microscopic invaders to engulf and eat.

Part of the immune system, macrophages are white blood cells that target and destroy bacteria to protect the body against infection. In this scan, a macrophage (shown in red) is overwhelming harmful tuberculosis (TB) bacteria (shown in greenish-yellow). TB bacteria usually infect the lungs and can cause serious illness if they are allowed to flourish.

Respiratory system

Every cell in the human body needs a constant supply of oxygen to survive. The lungs and airways of the respiratory system deliver this oxygen and also expel waste carbon dioxide.

We take in air through the mouth and nose into the lungs. Oxygen from the air seeps through the lung membranes into the bloodstream, where it is carried to all the body's cells. These cells burn oxygen to make energy, in a process called cellular respiration. This process causes cells to release another gas—carbon dioxide. This is carried back in the blood to the lungs to be exhaled.

Air intake

The respiratory system is a vast network of millions of airways, spreading like the branches of a tree into the lungs. With each breath, air sucked in through the nose or mouth rushes down the windpipe, or trachea. This carries air to a fork deep inside the chest where the airways divide in two. One of the branches, or bronchi, leads to the left lung, while the other leads to the right. Air comes in when the lungs expand and is pushed out when they shrink back.

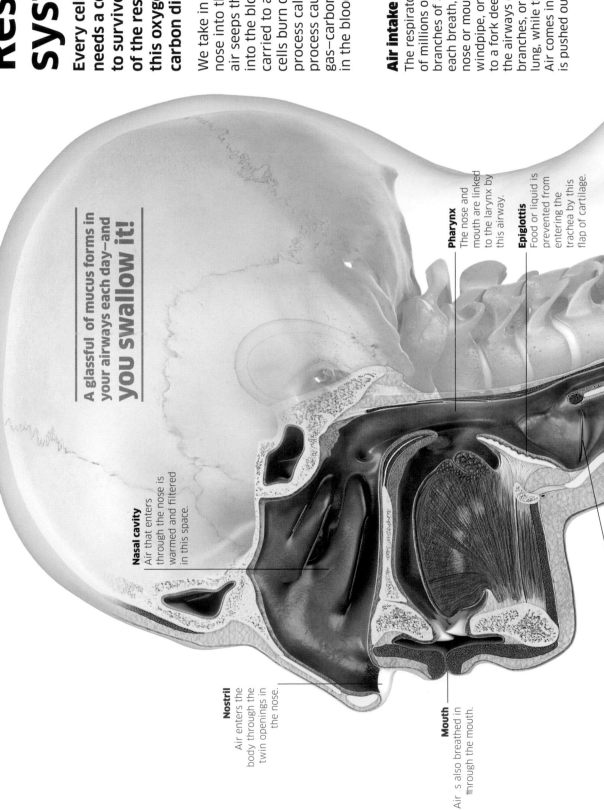

A glassful of mucus forms in your airways each day—and you swallow it!

Nasal cavity
Air that enters through the nose is warmed and filtered in this space.

Nostril
Air enters the body through the twin openings in the nose.

Mouth
Air is also breathed in through the mouth.

Larynx
This is the top part of the trachea. It has bands, called vocal cords, which contract and relax to create sounds.

Intercostal muscles
During breathing, muscles between the ribs pull the rib cage up and down.

Pharynx
The nose and mouth are linked to the larynx by this airway.

Epiglottis
Food or liquid is prevented from entering the trachea by this flap of cartilage.

Trachea
The windpipe, a strong tube of muscle and rings of cartilage, carries air from the larynx to the lungs.

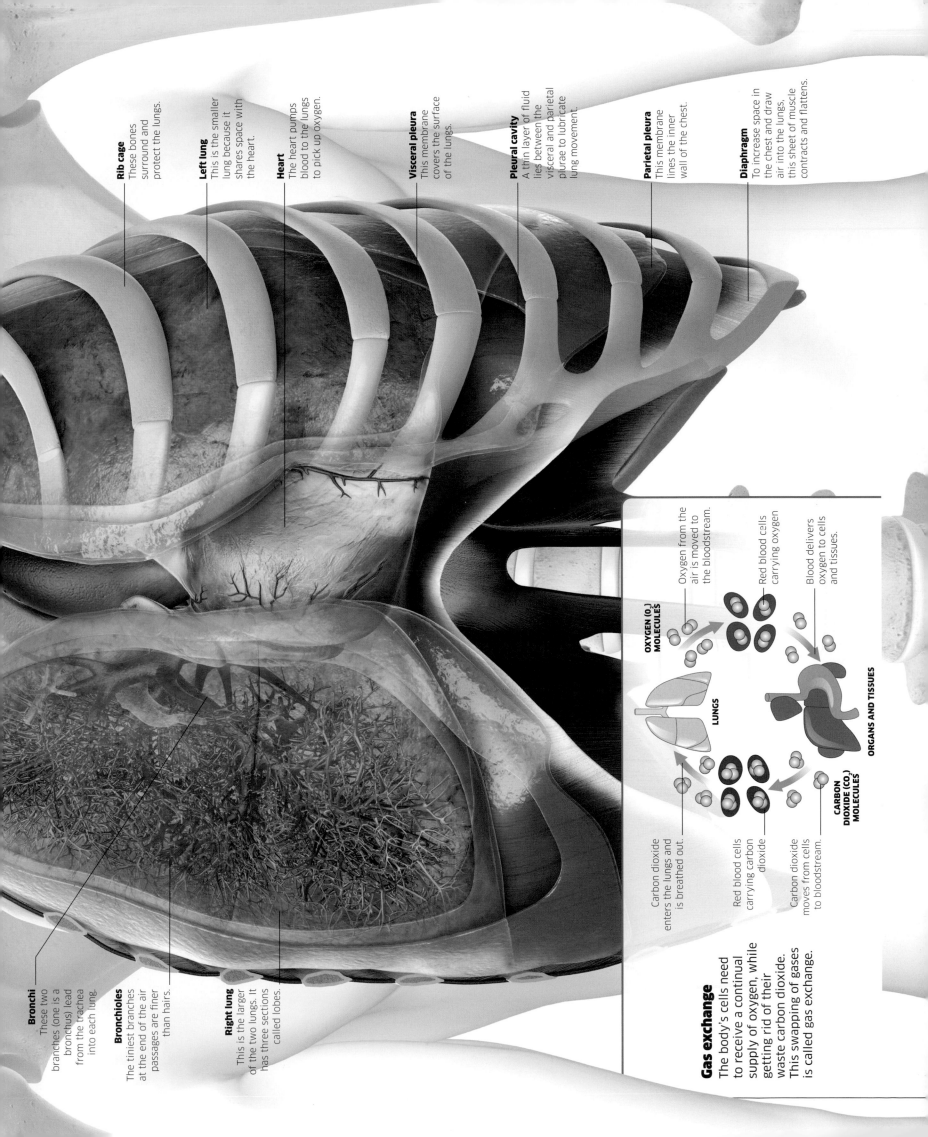

Rib cage
These bones surround and protect the lungs.

Left lung
This is the smaller lung because it shares space with the heart.

Heart
The heart pumps blood to the lungs to pick up oxygen.

Visceral pleura
This membrane covers the surface of the lungs.

Pleural cavity
A thin layer of fluid lies between the visceral and parietal plurae to lubricate lung movement.

Parietal pleura
This membrane lines the inner wall of the chest.

Diaphragm
To increase space in the chest and draw air into the lungs, this sheet of muscle contracts and flattens.

Bronchi
These two branches (one is a bronchus) lead from the trachea into each lung.

Bronchioles
The tiniest branches at the end of the air passages are finer than hairs.

Right lung
This is the larger of the two lungs. It has three sections called lobes.

Gas exchange

The body's cells need to receive a continual supply of oxygen, while getting rid of their waste carbon dioxide. This swapping of gases is called gas exchange.

Carbon dioxide enters the lungs and is breathed out.

Red blood cells carrying carbon dioxide

Carbon dioxide moves from cells to bloodstream.

CARBON DIOXIDE (CO₂) MOLECULES

OXYGEN (O₂) MOLECULES

Oxygen from the air is moved to the bloodstream.

Red blood cells carrying oxygen

Blood delivers oxygen to cells and tissues.

LUNGS

ORGANS AND TISSUES

Digestive system

Food gives the body the nutrients and energy it needs. The job of the digestive system is to break food down into simple substances the body can use. These are then absorbed into the bloodstream, while any indigestible waste is removed.

The main part of the digestive system is a long tube, called the digestive tract. It starts in the mouth, travels down the esophagus to the stomach, then runs through the small and large intestines to the anus. Other organs also play a role in digestion: these are the teeth, tongue, salivary glands, liver, pancreas, and gallbladder.

Stages of digestion

There are four main stages along the digestive tract. The first is the mouth, which cuts and chews food into small chunks. The second is the stomach, where food is churned into a liquid called chyme. Inside the small intestine, the chyme is broken down into nutrients that can be absorbed and carried to the body's cells. Finally, anything not used enters the large intestine, where it dries out to become feces.

From the mouth at one end to the anus at the other, an adult's digestive tract is around 23 ft (7 m) long.

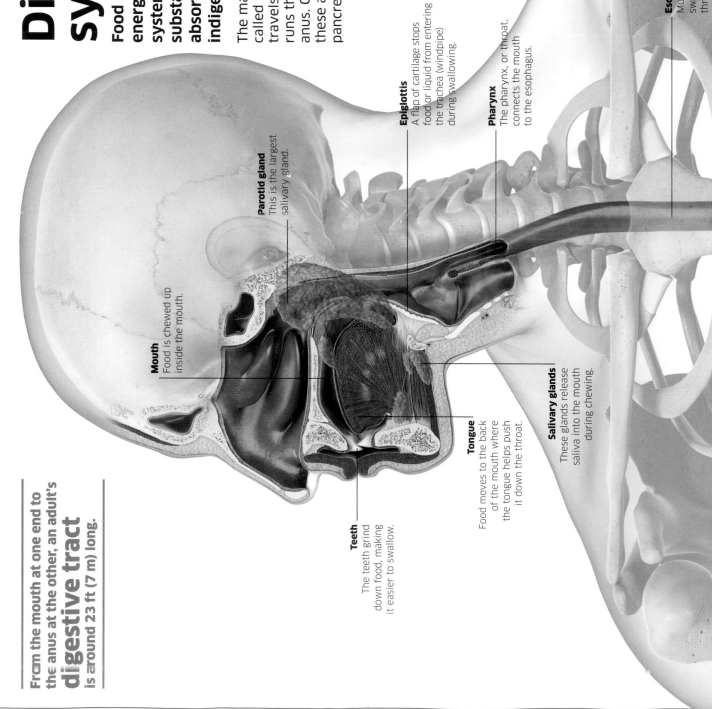

Parotid gland
This is the largest salivary gland.

Mouth
Food is chewed up inside the mouth.

Epiglottis
A flap of cartilage stops food or liquid from entering the trachea (windpipe) during swallowing.

Pharynx
The pharynx, or throat, connects the mouth to the esophagus.

Esophagus
Muscles in this tube push swallowed food from the throat to the stomach.

Tongue
Food moves to the back of the mouth where the tongue helps push it down the throat.

Teeth
The teeth grind down food, making it easier to swallow.

Salivary glands
These glands release saliva into the mouth during chewing.

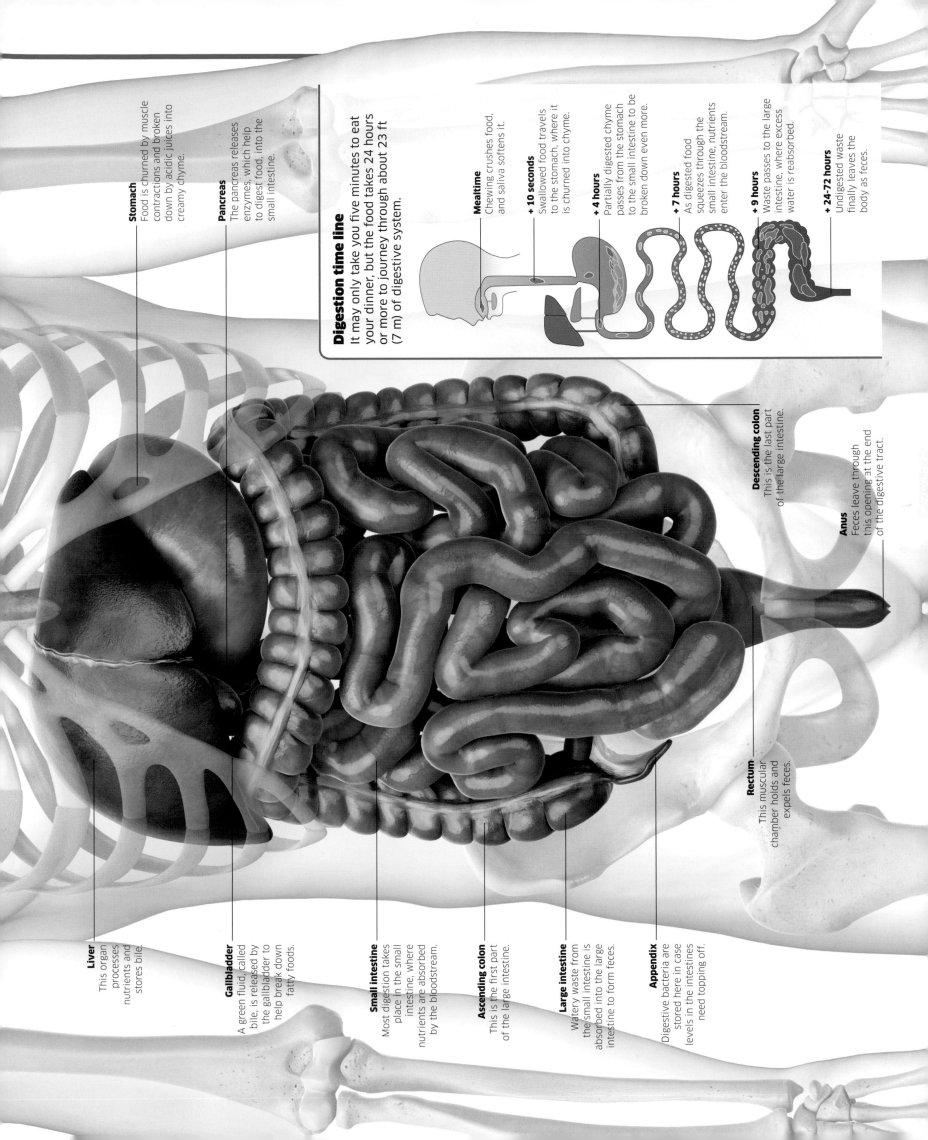

Stomach
Food is churned by muscle contractions and broken down by acidic juices into creamy chyme.

Pancreas
The pancreas releases enzymes, which help to digest food, into the small intestine.

Digestion time line

It may only take you five minutes to eat your dinner, but the food takes 24 hours or more to journey through about 23 ft (7 m) of digestive system.

Mealtime
Chewing crushes food, and saliva softens it.

+ 10 seconds
Swallowed food travels to the stomach, where it is churned into chyme.

+ 4 hours
Partially digested chyme passes from the stomach to the small intestine to be broken down even more.

+ 7 hours
As digested food squeezes through the small intestine, nutrients enter the bloodstream.

+ 9 hours
Waste passes to the large intestine, where excess water is reabsorbed.

+ 24-72 hours
Undigested waste finally leaves the body as feces.

Descending colon
This is the last part of the large intestine.

Anus
Feces leave through this opening at the end of the digestive tract.

Rectum
This muscular chamber holds and expels feces.

Appendix
Digestive bacteria are stored here in case levels in the intestines need topping off.

Large intestine
Watery waste from the small intestine is absorbed into the large intestine to form feces.

Ascending colon
This is the first part of the large intestine.

Small intestine
Most digestion takes place in the small intestine, where nutrients are absorbed by the bloodstream.

Gallbladder
A green fluid, called bile, is released by the gallbladder to help break down fatty foods.

Liver
This organ processes nutrients and stores bile.

Urinary system

In addition to delivering nutrients around the body, the blood also collects waste products from cells and delivers them to two hardworking organs called kidneys. There, waste and excess fluids are filtered out and processed into a liquid called urine, then passed out of the body.

The urinary system also keeps the volume and pressure of the blood stable by holding water back when there is a shortage, and making more urine when there is too much. This system also maintains a healthy balance of minerals and salts in the body.

You make up to 4.2 pints (2 liters) of urine every day, which would fill about **six coffee cups.**

Waste disposal

The urinary system consists of two kidneys, two ureters, a bladder, and a urethra. The kidneys process the blood's waste into urine, which passes through the ureters to the bladder. When the bladder is full, pressure sensors send signals to the brain. Humans are not born with the ability to control the urge to urinate. Children start to learn bladder control at around the age of two.

Left kidney
This is one of two bean-shaped organs that filters blood to make urine.

Renal vein
The two renal veins carry filtered blood to the heart, from where it can be pumped around the body again.

Left ureter
A one-way flow of urine is carried by the ureters from the kidneys to the bladder.

Abdominal aorta
This main artery carries oxygen-rich blood from the heart.

Inferior vena cava
Oxygen-poor blood is carried toward the heart in this large vein.

Right ureter

Renal artery
The renal arteries bring unfiltered blood to the kidneys.

Right kidney
This organ sits slightly lower than the left kidney, beneath the liver.

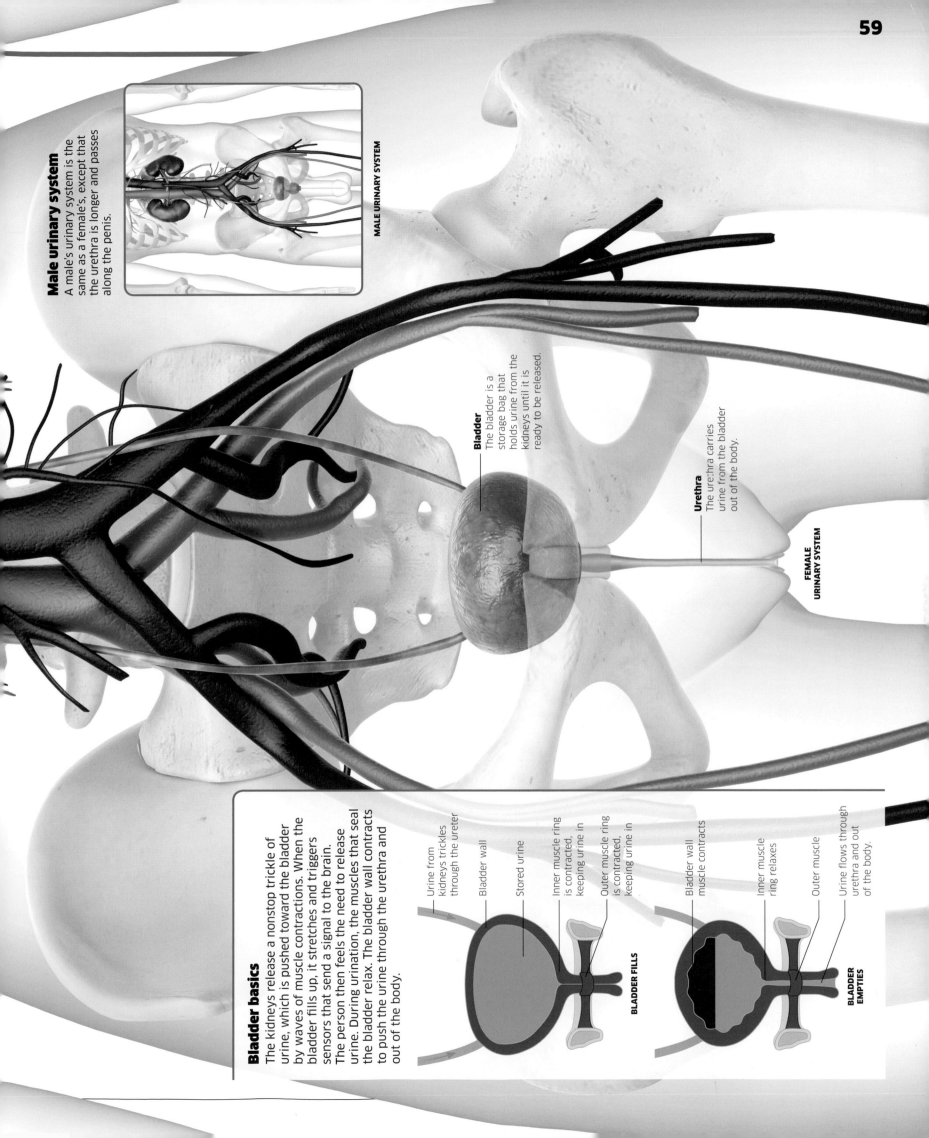

Male urinary system

A male's urinary system is the same as a female's, except that the urethra is longer and passes along the penis.

MALE URINARY SYSTEM

Bladder
The bladder is a storage bag that holds urine from the kidneys until it is ready to be released.

Urethra
The urethra carries urine from the bladder out of the body.

FEMALE URINARY SYSTEM

Bladder basics

The kidneys release a nonstop trickle of urine, which is pushed toward the bladder by waves of muscle contractions. When the bladder fills up, it stretches and triggers sensors that send a signal to the brain. The person then feels the need to release urine. During urination, the muscles that seal the bladder relax. The bladder wall contracts to push the urine through the urethra and out of the body.

Urine from kidneys trickles through the ureter

Bladder wall

Stored urine

Inner muscle ring is contracted, keeping urine in

Outer muscle ring is contracted, keeping urine in

BLADDER FILLS

Bladder wall muscle contracts

Inner muscle ring relaxes

Outer muscle

Urine flows through urethra and out of the body.

BLADDER EMPTIES

Reproductive system

The reproductive system consists of the body parts used to create new life. Humans cannot reproduce on their own—both male and female cells are needed to make a baby. The reproductive organs are different in men and women, as they have different roles in the reproductive process.

Adults have special sex cells called gametes. The creation of a new baby begins when a male sex cell (sperm) unites with a female sex cell (egg). This process is called fertilization. The male reproductive system makes the sperm to fertilize the female egg. The female system produces eggs and sustains the baby during its development in the uterus. After a baby is born, the mother's mammary glands, in the breasts, produce milk to feed the baby.

Reproductive organs

A woman's reproductive organs sit inside her body. They consist of the uterus, two ovaries and two fallopian tubes, the vagina, the breasts, and the milk-producing glands. The male reproductive system is much simpler, and most of it is outside the body. It manufactures and provides sperm to fertilize the female egg.

Secretory lobule
These tissues contain clusters of milk-producing glands called alveoli.

Milk duct
Many of these tiny tubes carry milk from the glands to the nipple.

Nipple
The nipple is the opening of the milk ducts, where the baby sucks out milk.

Every single day, about **353,000 babies** are born around the world.

Fimbriae
These feathery tails sweep the ovary and draw eggs into the fallopian tube.

Myometrium
The muscle of the uterus is smooth and strong.

Vas deferens
This muscular tube carries sperm from the testes to the urethra.

Endometrium
The lining of the uterus thickens to receive an egg, then sheds if the egg is not fertilized.

Penis
The penis transfers sperm to the woman's vagina.

Urethra
This tube carries sperm and urine out of the penis.

Testes
Also called testicles, they manufacture sperm, the male sex cells.

Seminal vesicle
Fluid released here mixes with sperm cells to make a liquid called semen.

Scrotum
This protective casing of skin and muscle covers the testes.

MALE REPRODUCTIVE SYSTEM

Fallopian tube
This tube connects the ovary to the body of the uterus. Eggs are fertilized here.

Uterus
The stretchy uterus is where fertilized eggs develop.

Cervix
This is the opening of the uterus.

Vagina
This muscular tube goes from the uterus to the outside of the body.

FEMALE REPRODUCTIVE SYSTEM

Ovary
The two ovaries are where eggs are stored and released.

Circle of life

Without reproduction, human life would die out. Each stage of the life cycle involves changes in the body. The cycle begins with an egg inside a woman's uterus, which is fertilized by a male sperm. An embryo results, which grows for about nine months until the woman gives birth. The baby becomes a child, experiences changes during puberty, and becomes an adult. At this stage, the body has matured enough to reproduce and create the next generation of life. The adult body ages and eventually dies, while the offspring experience the next circle of life.

CHILD

BABY

ADOLESCENT

SPERM

EGG

ADULT

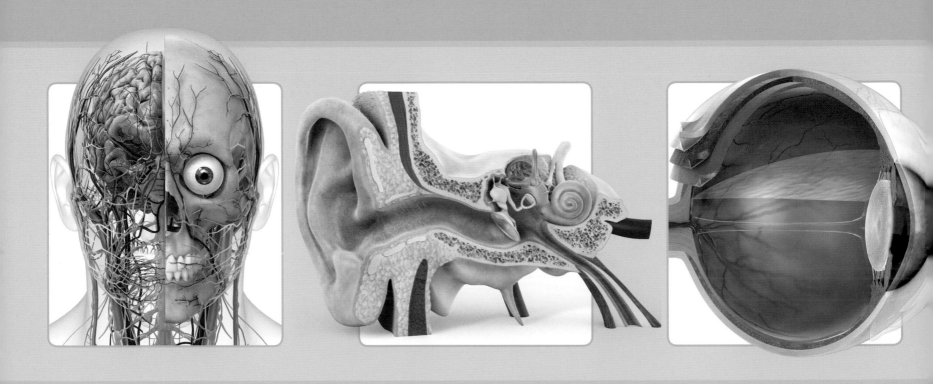

HEAD AND NECK

The control center of the body is the brain. It processes thoughts and interprets information from our surroundings. The skull protects this vital organ and the body's most important sensory organs. The neck supports the head, providing a communications highway between the brain and the body.

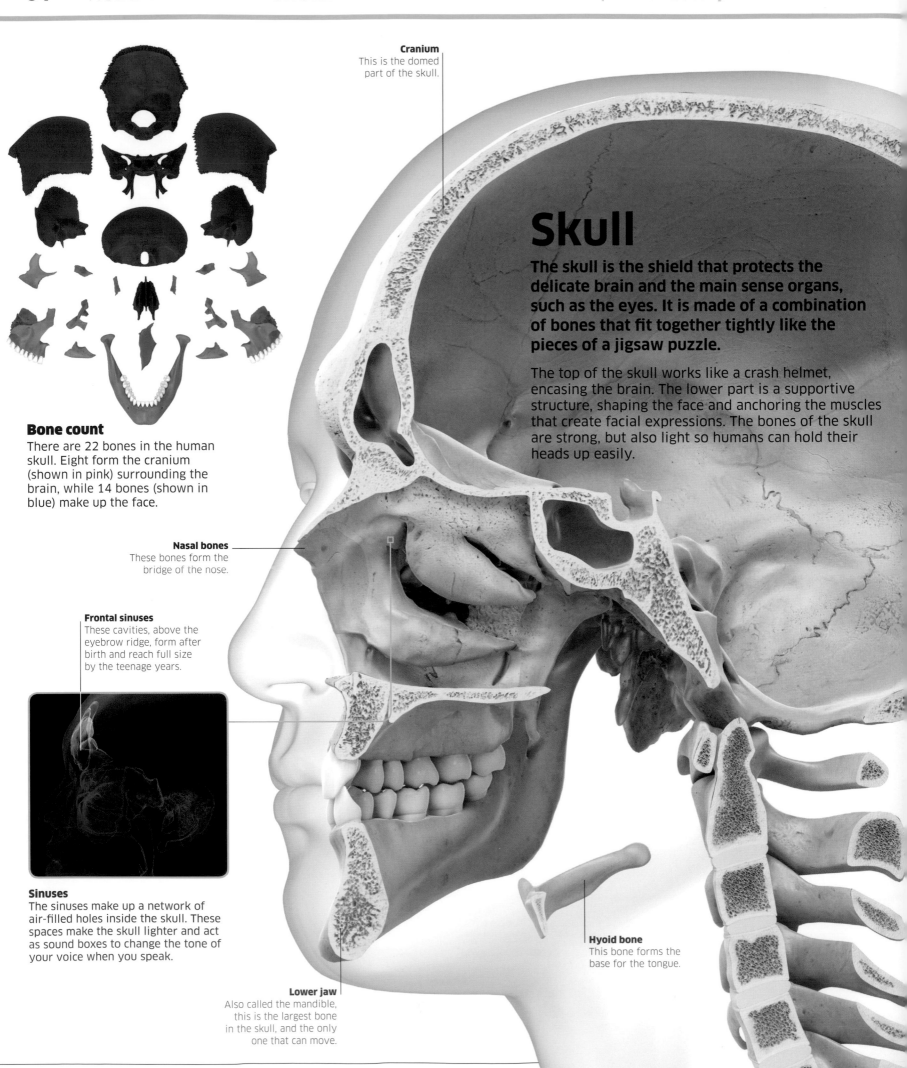

Cranium
This is the domed part of the skull.

Skull

The skull is the shield that protects the delicate brain and the main sense organs, such as the eyes. It is made of a combination of bones that fit together tightly like the pieces of a jigsaw puzzle.

The top of the skull works like a crash helmet, encasing the brain. The lower part is a supportive structure, shaping the face and anchoring the muscles that create facial expressions. The bones of the skull are strong, but also light so humans can hold their heads up easily.

Bone count
There are 22 bones in the human skull. Eight form the cranium (shown in pink) surrounding the brain, while 14 bones (shown in blue) make up the face.

Nasal bones
These bones form the bridge of the nose.

Frontal sinuses
These cavities, above the eyebrow ridge, form after birth and reach full size by the teenage years.

Sinuses
The sinuses make up a network of air-filled holes inside the skull. These spaces make the skull lighter and act as sound boxes to change the tone of your voice when you speak.

Lower jaw
Also called the mandible, this is the largest bone in the skull, and the only one that can move.

Hyoid bone
This bone forms the base for the tongue.

The **hyoid bone** anchors the root of the tongue; the bone is held in place purely by **muscles**.

The **rounded shape** of the skull gives it extra strength, similar to **the arch of a bridge**.

65

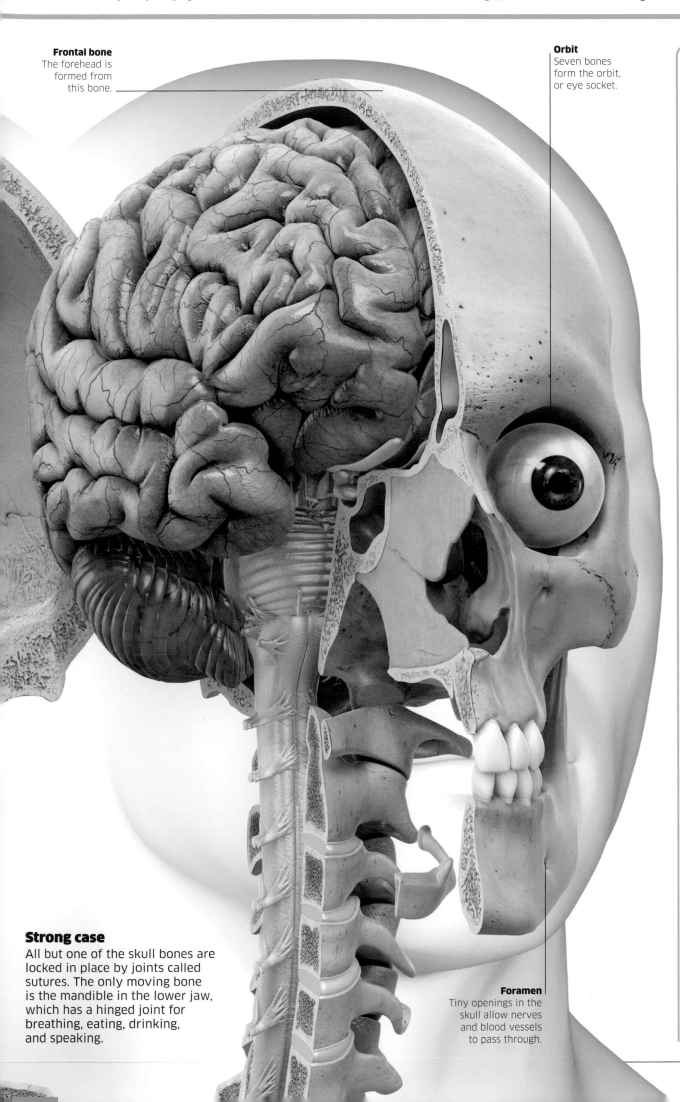

Frontal bone
The forehead is formed from this bone.

Orbit
Seven bones form the orbit, or eye socket.

Squishy skulls

Human babies have big heads compared to their bodies, but their heads are flexible enough to squeeze through the birth canal during birth. Newborns have gaps, called fontanels, between the skull bones. These spaces, loosely joined by soft tissue, allow the brain to grow fast—a baby's brain doubles in size in the first years after birth.

Fontanel
This gap allows the skull to change shape as the baby is being born.

SKULL OF A TWO-MONTH-OLD BABY

Hole in the head

The hole at the base of the skull is called the foramen magnum. The spinal column, which carries messages between the brain and the body, passes through it.

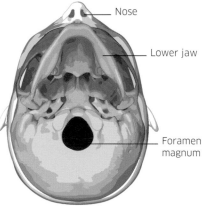

Nose

Lower jaw

Foramen magnum

SKULL FROM BELOW

Strong case

All but one of the skull bones are locked in place by joints called sutures. The only moving bone is the mandible in the lower jaw, which has a hinged joint for breathing, eating, drinking, and speaking.

Foramen
Tiny openings in the skull allow nerves and blood vessels to pass through.

THERE ARE NO BONES **SHAPING THE** NOSE OR EARS. **INSTEAD, THESE PARTS** ARE MADE OF **TOUGH, FLEXIBLE CARTILAGE.**

66 head and neck ∘ FACIAL MUSCLES

50 –the number of muscles you use to make facial expressions.

Facial muscles

The bones of the face are covered in layers of facial muscles. Flexing these muscles allows us to blink, talk, and eat, as well as make a range of facial expressions for communication.

The facial muscles are unique within the body because one end is usually attached to the skin rather than another bone. A small contraction of a facial muscle pulls the skin of the face to form a different expression. The ability to make—and understand—so many different facial expressions helps humans to communicate better.

Taking shape

The shape of a human face is mostly defined by its facial bones and muscles. Forensic sculptors can reconstruct a face from a skull to give a good idea of a person's appearance when they were alive. This can be achieved by modeling with clay or by using computer software programs.

New faces
Modelers use their knowledge of how muscles are arranged over the skull to re-create a face. The model face on the right has been built up, layer by layer, from the skull on the left.

Corrugator supercilii
When this short, narrow muscle is flexed it pulls the eyebrows together and down to form a frown.

Orbicularis oculi
The circular muscle around the eye socket closes the eye.

Zygomaticus
The zygomaticus muscles raise the corners of the mouth to smile.

Buccinator
This muscle keeps food in the mouth by holding the cheek close to the teeth during chewing.

Pulling faces

The facial muscles pull the skin and change the position of the eyes, eyebrows, and lips to make us smile and scowl. These expressions are hard to fake because we make them automatically.

Key

■ MUSCLE CONTRACTS

■ MUSCLE RELAXES

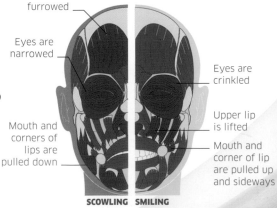

Brow is furrowed

Eyes are narrowed

Mouth and corners of lips are pulled down

Eyes are crinkled

Upper lip is lifted

Mouth and corner of lip are pulled up and sideways

SCOWLING   SMILING

Micro-expressions are facial muscles that last less than a second, and may tell us about a person's **true emotions**.

The word **"levator"** in a muscle's name means it pulls upward, while **"depressor"** tells us the muscle pulls downward.

67

Layered muscles

The facial muscles are arranged in thin layers. Superficial muscles lie just under the skin, and beneath them is a layer of deep muscles. In some parts of the face, these two layers are connected by dense fibers.

Only about 20% of humans can **wiggle their ears** voluntarily, using the auricularis muscles.

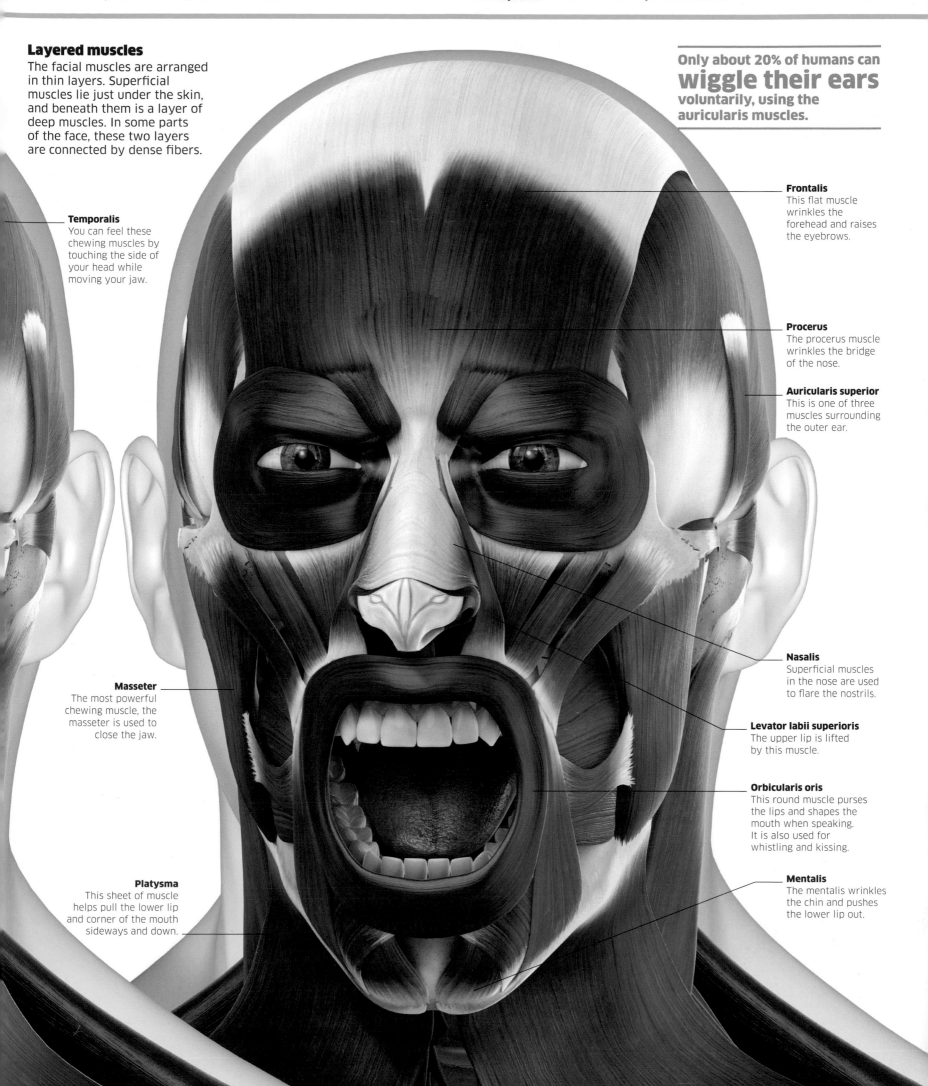

Temporalis
You can feel these chewing muscles by touching the side of your head while moving your jaw.

Frontalis
This flat muscle wrinkles the forehead and raises the eyebrows.

Procerus
The procerus muscle wrinkles the bridge of the nose.

Auricularis superior
This is one of three muscles surrounding the outer ear.

Masseter
The most powerful chewing muscle, the masseter is used to close the jaw.

Nasalis
Superficial muscles in the nose are used to flare the nostrils.

Levator labii superioris
The upper lip is lifted by this muscle.

Orbicularis oris
This round muscle purses the lips and shapes the mouth when speaking. It is also used for whistling and kissing.

Platysma
This sheet of muscle helps pull the lower lip and corner of the mouth sideways and down.

Mentalis
The mentalis wrinkles the chin and pushes the lower lip out.

Inside the head

Some of the body's most important—and delicate—organs are in the head and neck area. The brain is the center of operations for the body, and sits within the skull's protective case of bone. The head also houses the eyes, ears, mouth, and nose—our main sense organs.

The area is served by a complex network of blood vessels and nerves. Blood supplies the fuel needed to power the muscles, nerves, and organs in this part of the body. Nerves transmit messages between the brain and the sense organs in the head, enabling us to see, hear, smell, and taste.

Head and neck
This image shows the head and neck with the skin and muscles removed. One side shows the skull bones, while the other exposes the brain. The neck, through which the spinal cord passes, provides a communication channel between the brain and the rest of the body.

Temporal artery
This blood vessel provides a blood supply to the scalp.

Temporal vein
Blood is carried away from the scalp by this vessel.

Eye socket (orbit)
The two hollow eye sockets surround and protect the eyeballs.

Nasal cavity
This hollow area is filled with smell-detecting sensors.

Frontal bone
The front of the skull and the upper part of the eye sockets are formed by this bone.

Brain
The body's center of operations, this controls movement, thinking, emotions, and memory.

Eyeball
The eyes detect light and send signals to the brain, enabling us to see.

Brain stem
The brain stem controls automatic functions such as breathing.

Facial vein
This vein carries blood away from the face.

Buccal (cheek) nerve
This relays sensations from the cheek to the brain.

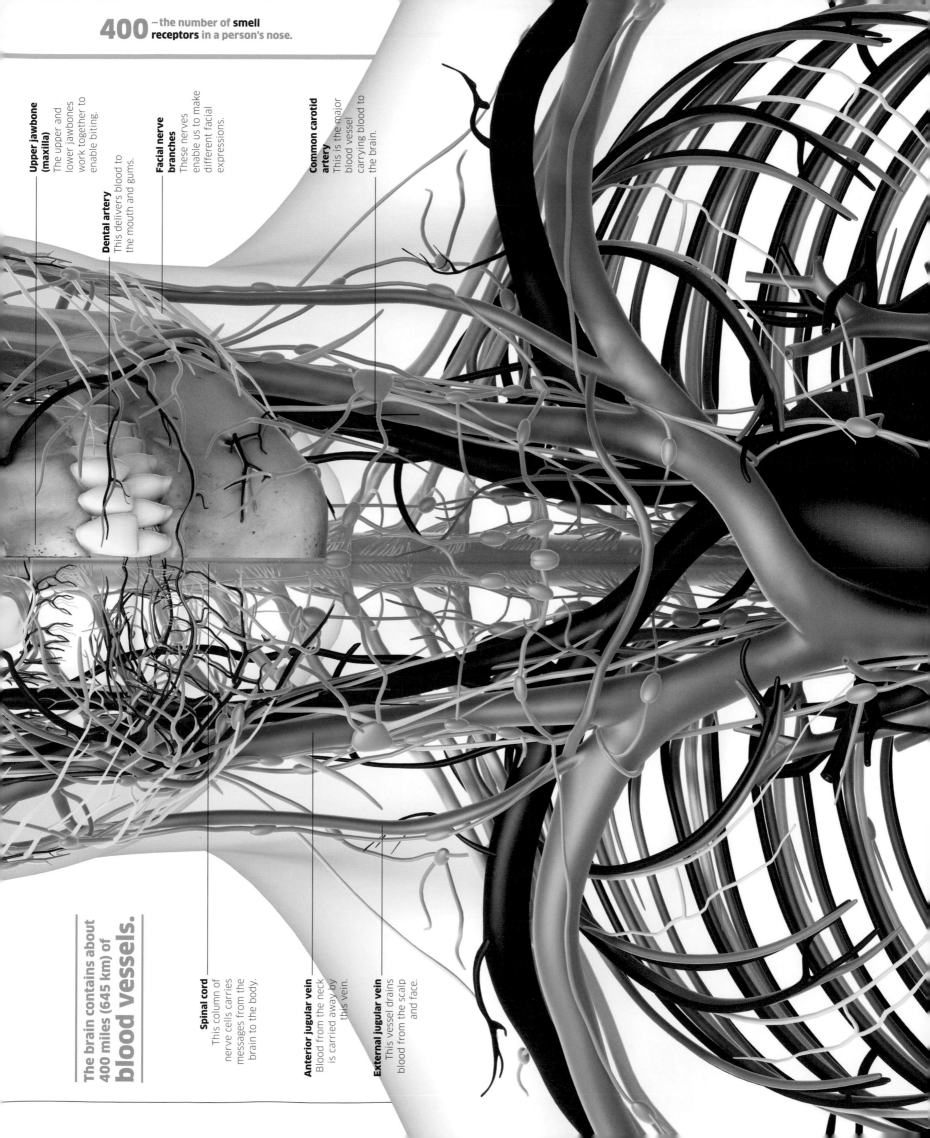

Upper jawbone (maxilla)
The upper and lower jawbones work together to enable biting.

Dental artery
This delivers blood to the mouth and gums.

Facial nerve branches
These nerves enable us to make different facial expressions.

Common carotid artery
This is the major blood vessel carrying blood to the brain.

The brain contains about 400 miles (645 km) of **blood vessels.**

Spinal cord
This column of nerve cells carries messages from the brain to the body.

Anterior jugular vein
Blood from the neck is carried away by this vein.

External jugular vein
This vessel drains blood from the scalp and face.

3 lb (1.5 kg)—the **average weight** of an adult's brain.

100 billion—the number of **nerve cells** in the human brain.

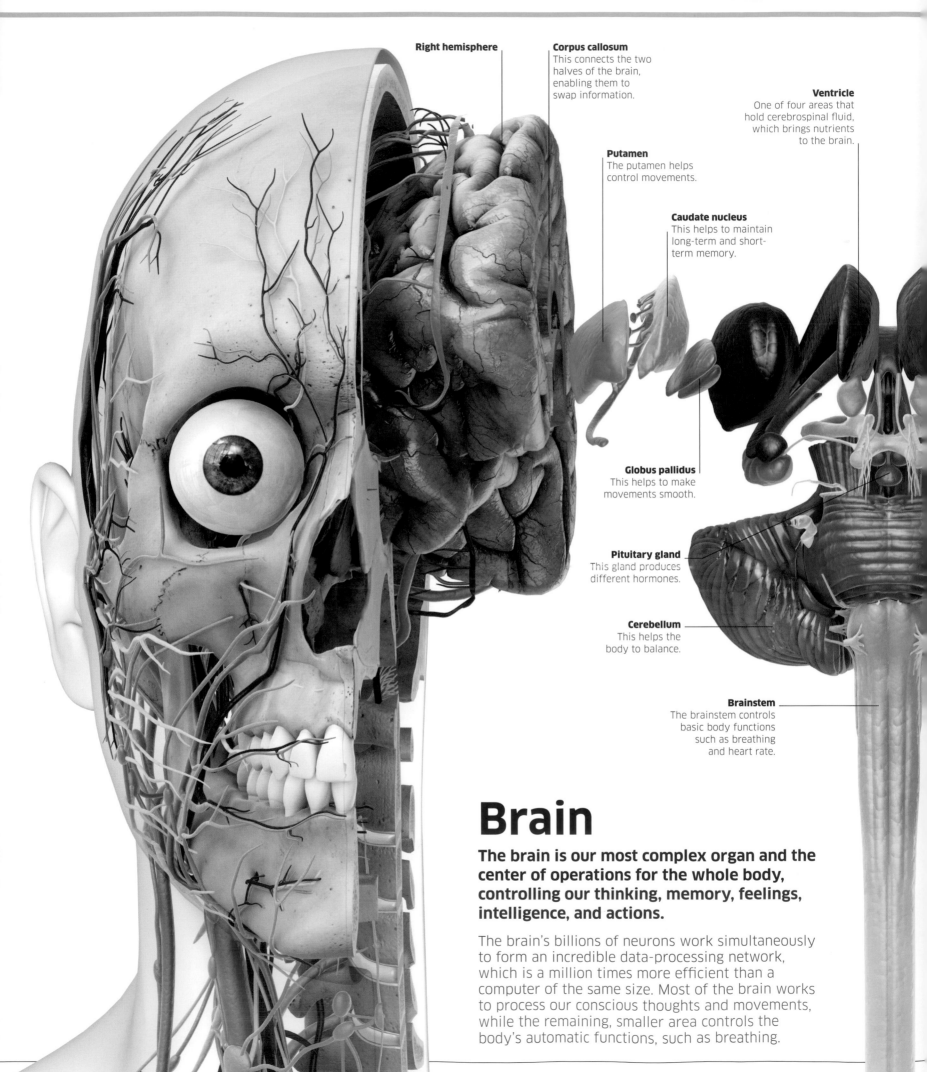

Right hemisphere

Corpus callosum
This connects the two halves of the brain, enabling them to swap information.

Ventricle
One of four areas that hold cerebrospinal fluid, which brings nutrients to the brain.

Putamen
The putamen helps control movements.

Caudate nucleus
This helps to maintain long-term and short-term memory.

Globus pallidus
This helps to make movements smooth.

Pituitary gland
This gland produces different hormones.

Cerebellum
This helps the body to balance.

Brainstem
The brainstem controls basic body functions such as breathing and heart rate.

Brain

The brain is our most complex organ and the center of operations for the whole body, controlling our thinking, memory, feelings, intelligence, and actions.

The brain's billions of neurons work simultaneously to form an incredible data-processing network, which is a million times more efficient than a computer of the same size. Most of the brain works to process our conscious thoughts and movements, while the remaining, smaller area controls the body's automatic functions, such as breathing.

A newborn baby's brain grows by **1% each day** until it is about 3 months old.

By the age of nine, a **child's brain is already 95%** of the size of an adult's.

71

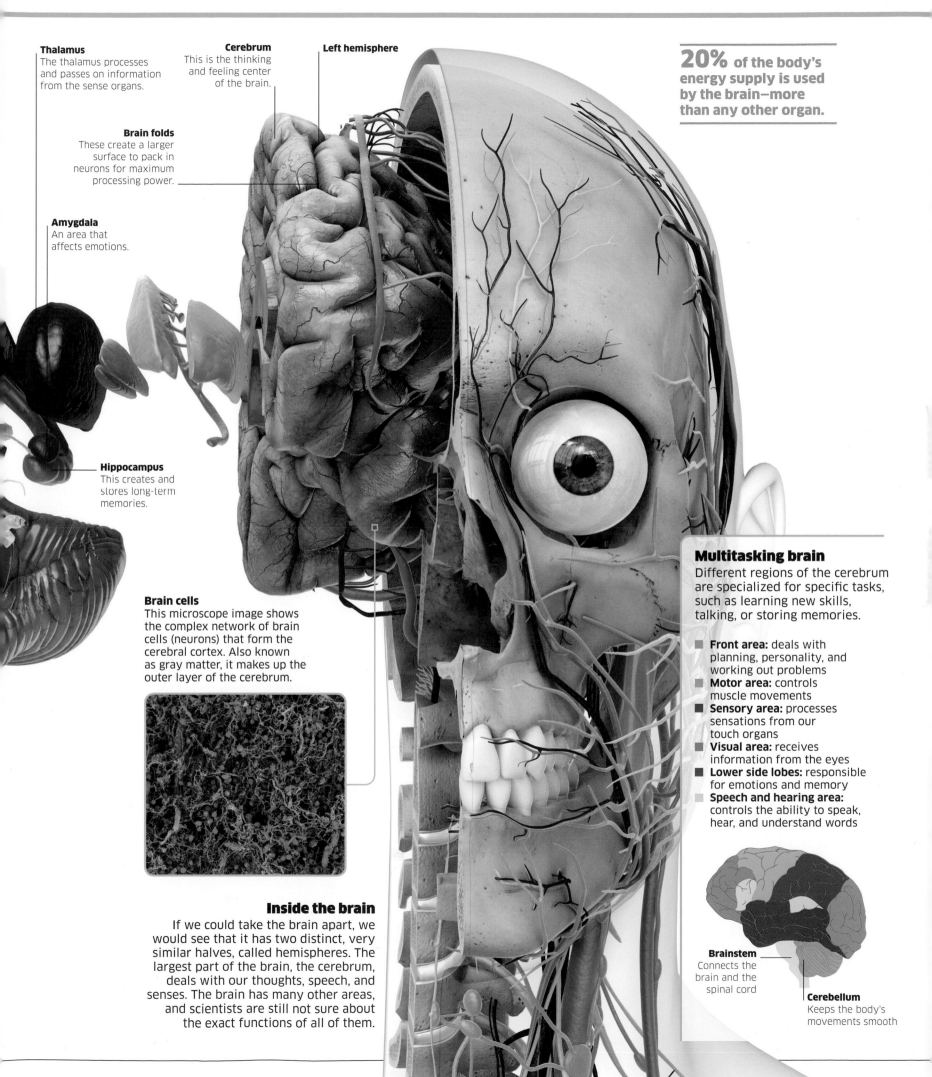

Thalamus
The thalamus processes and passes on information from the sense organs.

Cerebrum
This is the thinking and feeling center of the brain.

Left hemisphere

Brain folds
These create a larger surface to pack in neurons for maximum processing power.

Amygdala
An area that affects emotions.

Hippocampus
This creates and stores long-term memories.

20% of the body's energy supply is used by the brain—more than any other organ.

Brain cells
This microscope image shows the complex network of brain cells (neurons) that form the cerebral cortex. Also known as gray matter, it makes up the outer layer of the cerebrum.

Multitasking brain
Different regions of the cerebrum are specialized for specific tasks, such as learning new skills, talking, or storing memories.

- **Front area:** deals with planning, personality, and working out problems
- **Motor area:** controls muscle movements
- **Sensory area:** processes sensations from our touch organs
- **Visual area:** receives information from the eyes
- **Lower side lobes:** responsible for emotions and memory
- **Speech and hearing area:** controls the ability to speak, hear, and understand words

Inside the brain
If we could take the brain apart, we would see that it has two distinct, very similar halves, called hemispheres. The largest part of the brain, the cerebrum, deals with our thoughts, speech, and senses. The brain has many other areas, and scientists are still not sure about the exact functions of all of them.

Brainstem
Connects the brain and the spinal cord

Cerebellum
Keeps the body's movements smooth

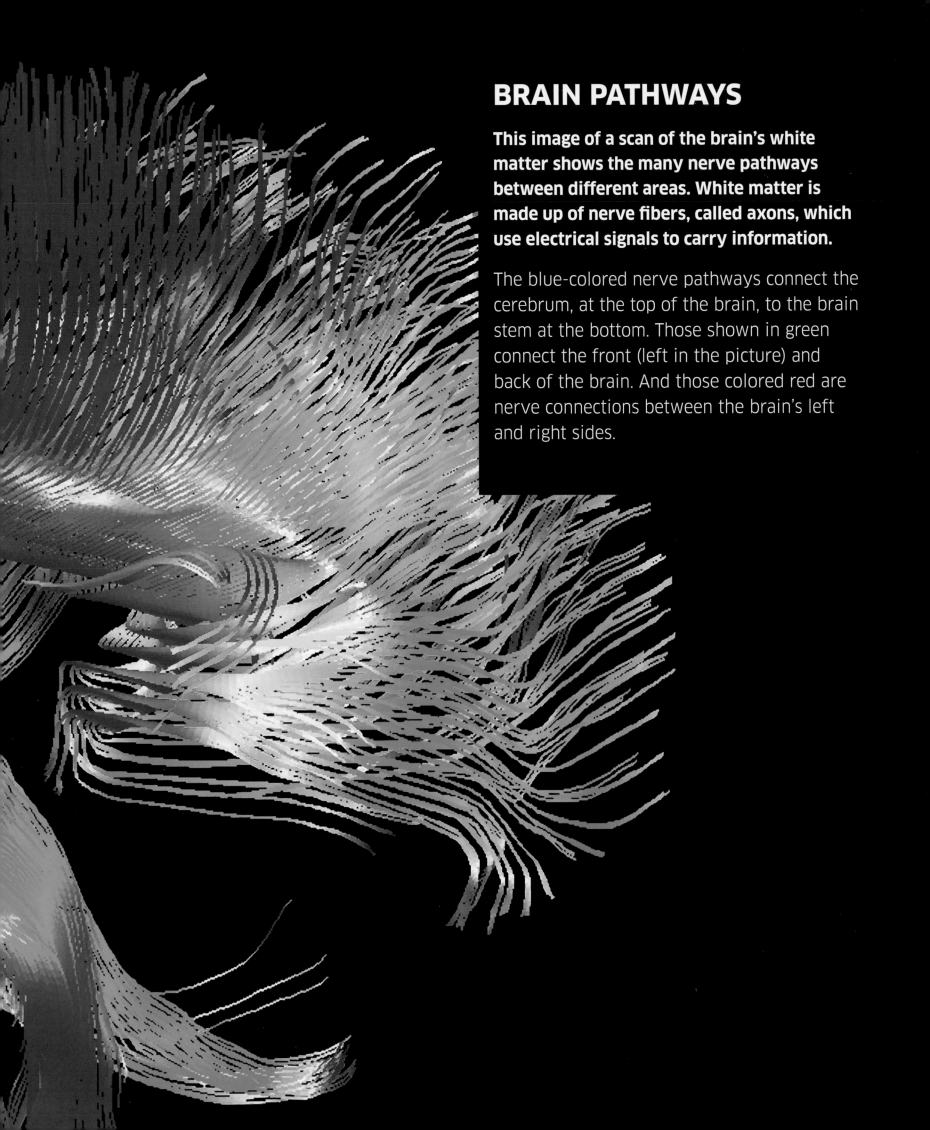

BRAIN PATHWAYS

This image of a scan of the brain's white matter shows the many nerve pathways between different areas. White matter is made up of nerve fibers, called axons, which use electrical signals to carry information.

The blue-colored nerve pathways connect the cerebrum, at the top of the brain, to the brain stem at the bottom. Those shown in green connect the front (left in the picture) and back of the brain. And those colored red are nerve connections between the brain's left and right sides.

CONTROL CENTER

The human brain is a million times more efficient than a computer the same size. This busy control center is responsible for our thoughts, movements, and memories. The brain needs a lot of energy to fuel its amazing processing power. Trillions of electrical impulses pass along the neural networks every second. These networks must be maintained and alternative routes planned, so if there is a problem, the signals can still get through.

MAKING MOVES

Body movement is stimulated by electrical impulses carried along nerve cells, called motor neurons. The impulse to move begins in the brain's cerebral cortex, travels down the spinal cord, along the motor neuron, and to the muscle. As muscles contract, the body moves.

Unconscious movement

Sometimes the body must respond so quickly to sensory information that it does not wait to involve the brain. This is an automatic reflex that protects the body in times of danger, such as touching something hot.

Conscious movement

Sometimes the body does not move until it receives specific sensory information. This prevents a player from swinging at a tennis ball before it reaches the racket. Nerves carry electrical impulses from the brain to the muscles to make sure the body moves at the right time.

Returning serve
As the tennis ball is coming, a signal is sent to the brain to predict where the ball will land and move the body into position.

RIGHT OR LEFT?

The cerebrum is divided into the right and left hemispheres. They communicate with each other through a thick bundle of nerve fibers called the corpus callosum. The right hemisphere controls the left side of the body, while the left hemisphere controls the right side.

Brain divide

The brain's left side tends to control verbal and written skills and logical thought. The right side tends to be where creative and emotional impulses come from. But the sides work together in a complex way that we don't yet fully understand.

LIFE EXPERIENCE

The brain organizes and stores experiences as memories. These put information into context, such as whether you have been somewhere before or met someone previously. They also repeat useful information, such as the way to school. The brain does not keep every memory. If a memory is unimportant or the memory is not revisited, it is soon forgotten.

Memory bank

Memories are not stored in a single part of the brain—in fact, recalling just one memory can involve several different parts of the brain.

Language
Fluency with spoken words is controlled by the left hemisphere.

Spatial skills
The right side of your brain deals with 3-D shapes and structures.

Writing
The left hemisphere controls your ability to express yourself in written words.

Imagination
Creativity and imaginative thoughts are fueled by your right side.

Logical thought
The left side is responsible for thinking logically and finding solutions to problems.

Music
The right hemisphere is more active when you listen to music or play an instrument.

Math and science
The left side handles numbers, problems, and scientific thought.

Art
Your artistic streak shows up on the right whenever you draw or paint.

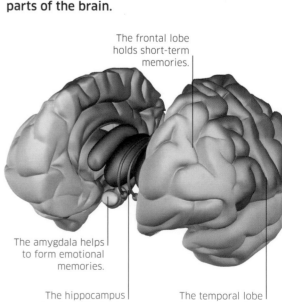

The frontal lobe holds short-term memories.

The amygdala helps to form emotional memories.

The hippocampus is where the brain stores long-term memories.

The temporal lobe stores data such as words and facts.

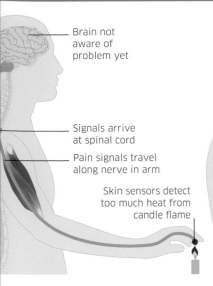

1 BURNING HOT
When you touch something very hot, the pain signal travels through the sensory nerve to the spinal cord.

- Brain not aware of problem yet
- Signals arrive at spinal cord
- Pain signals travel along nerve in arm
- Skin sensors detect too much heat from candle flame

2 AUTOMATIC RESPONSE
A nerve signal is sent from your spinal cord to your arm muscle, which contracts to pull the hand away.

- Pain registers in brain
- Brain still not aware of pain or movement
- Reflex link in spine
- Signals to arm muscle make it contract
- Hand withdraws to a safe distance

3 PAIN SIGNAL
The pain signal reaches the brain after the hand has moved away, and you now start to feel pain.

- Signals race to brain

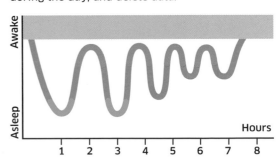

Setting a pattern
An experience will cause a certain set of brain cells to fire together. This creates a distinct neural pattern of activity in the brain. The information is bundled up and encoded as a memory.

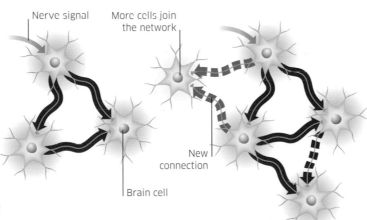

- Nerve signal
- More cells join the network
- New connection
- Brain cell

THE BRAIN
CAN STORE THE SAME AMOUNT OF INFORMATION AS 3 MILLION HOURS OF TELEVISION PROGRAMS.

1 NEURAL PATTERN
A new experience triggers a neuron to send signals to other brain cells, forming a connected neuron network.

2 STRONG CONNECTION
When this experience is remembered, the same network is used. It grows bigger and the connection becomes stronger.

Making memories
Experiencing a memorable moment stays in the memory because a unique pattern of neural activity is created and reinforced.

1 FORMATION
If you win a race, everything you experience—the way your body feels, the people around you, the weather on the day—combines to create a unique pattern of neural activity in the brain.

2 CONSOLIDATION
Afterward, when you talk about winning the race with a friend, you revisit the experience and add emotions, which makes the memory even stronger.

3 REVISITING
You replay the memory by looking at a photograph from the day. The more often you revisit this memory, the stronger the neural connections become, ensuring you don't forget it.

ENERGY RUSH
Although the brain makes up less than three percent of our body weight, it uses 20 percent of our total daily energy supply. Energy is required to fire neurons, and the brain has more than 100 billion of them. Two-thirds of the energy used by the brain fuels this neuron activity. The remaining third is used to repair and maintain neurons.

Full power
Scientists have found that the best way to maintain a healthy brain is to keep using it. Activities can be intellectual, such as learning a new language, or physical, such as running a race. Providing the brain with different kinds of challenges helps the growth, maintenance, and regeneration of neurons.

Cube challenge
A Rubik's cube stimulates neuron activity. Challenging the brain lifts the mood, reduces stress, and speeds up thinking.

A good night's sleep
Nobody knows exactly how and why we sleep, but most experts agree that sleep is probably important for the health of the brain. Sleeping and dreaming may give the brain the chance to store memories, process information taken in during the day, and delete data.

Awake — Asleep

Hours
1 2 3 4 5 6 7 8

Sleep cycle
We pass through the different stages of sleep several times a night, from light to deep sleep and back again.

- Light sleep—Body processes slow down; waking up is easy.
- REM sleep—The eyes flicker under the eyelids; dreams occur at this stage.
- Deep sleep—Body systems slow even more; waking is more difficult.

Mouth and throat

The mouth is the gateway for food and drink to enter the body. It also helps to carry air in and out, and we shape the mouth to produce different sounds when we speak.

The mouth is bounded by the lips, the roof and floor of the mouth, and the cheek muscles. It opens into the throat, a muscular tube that runs down the neck. Only air travels in the top section, which connects to the nose. Both air and food pass through the middle section, but not at the same time. The bottom section divides into two branches—the esophagus, which carries food to the stomach, and the windpipe, which channels air to the lungs.

More than 700

species of bacteria have been found in the mouth, but most healthy people host about 70 different varieties.

Inside the oral cavity

This cross section through a head shows the mouth, the oral cavity (space inside the mouth), and throat. At the back of the throat are the tonsils, which help destroy harmful bacteria that are carried into the mouth with food or in the air. The tongue is not shown, so the other organs can be seen more clearly.

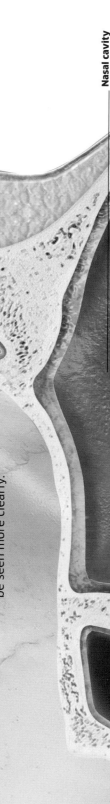

Nasal cavity Air is carried through this space between the nostrils and throat.

Swallowing food

When we eat, it's important that food does not enter our airways and make us choke. So as we swallow, the body automatically closes off the airways in the throat and nose. A flap of tissue called the epiglottis drops over the entrance to the windpipe. The soft palate lifts up to block access to the nasal cavity, too.

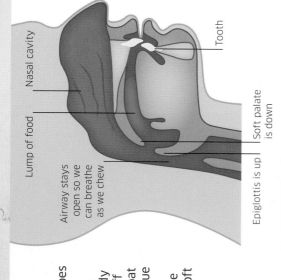

1 Chewing food
While we chew food, we can still breathe because the positions of the epiglottis and soft palate allow air in through the nose. As we prepare to swallow, the tongue pushes the food back into the throat.

Nasal cavity

Lump of food

Airway stays open so we can breathe as we chew

Tooth

Soft palate is down

Epiglottis is up

2 Swallowing
As the food hits the back of the throat, it triggers a reflex action in the body. The soft palate rises to block the nasal cavity, while the epiglottis folds down to cover the windpipe. The food is directed safely down the esophagus, toward the stomach.

Soft palate moves up to close the nasal airway

Windpipe

Esophagus

Epiglottis moves down to block entrance to the windpipe

7 **seconds** is how long it takes food to travel **from your mouth** to your stomach.

The salivary glands produce **less saliva at night** than they do during the day.

77

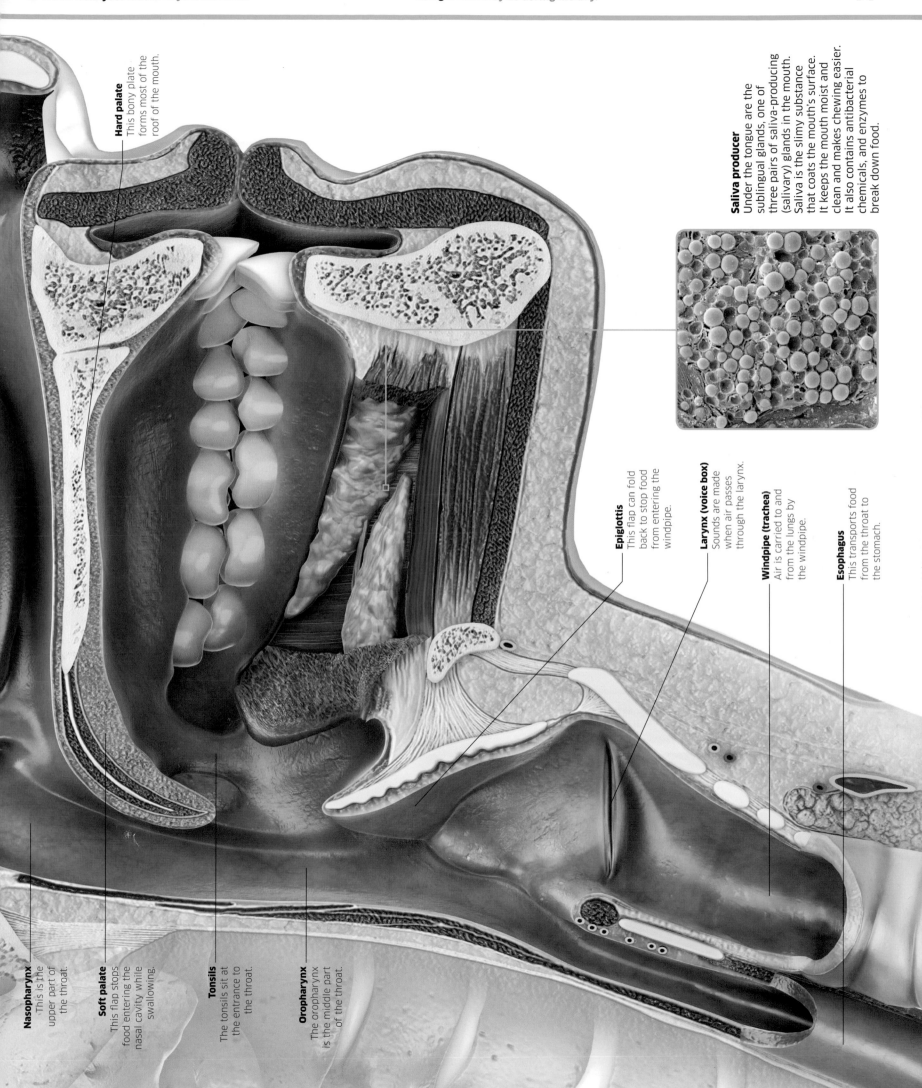

Hard palate
This bony plate forms most of the roof of the mouth.

Saliva producer
Under the tongue are the sublingual glands, one of three pairs of saliva-producing (salivary) glands in the mouth. Saliva is the slimy substance that coats the mouth's surface. It keeps the mouth moist and clean and makes chewing easier. It also contains antibacterial chemicals, and enzymes to break down food.

Epiglottis
This flap can fold back to stop food from entering the windpipe.

Larynx (voice box)
Sounds are made when air passes through the larynx.

Windpipe (trachea)
Air is carried to and from the lungs by the windpipe.

Esophagus
This transports food from the throat to the stomach.

Nasopharynx
This is the upper part of the throat.

Soft palate
This flap stops food entering the nasal cavity while swallowing.

Tonsils
The tonsils sit at the entrance to the throat.

Oropharynx
The oropharynx is the middle part of the throat.

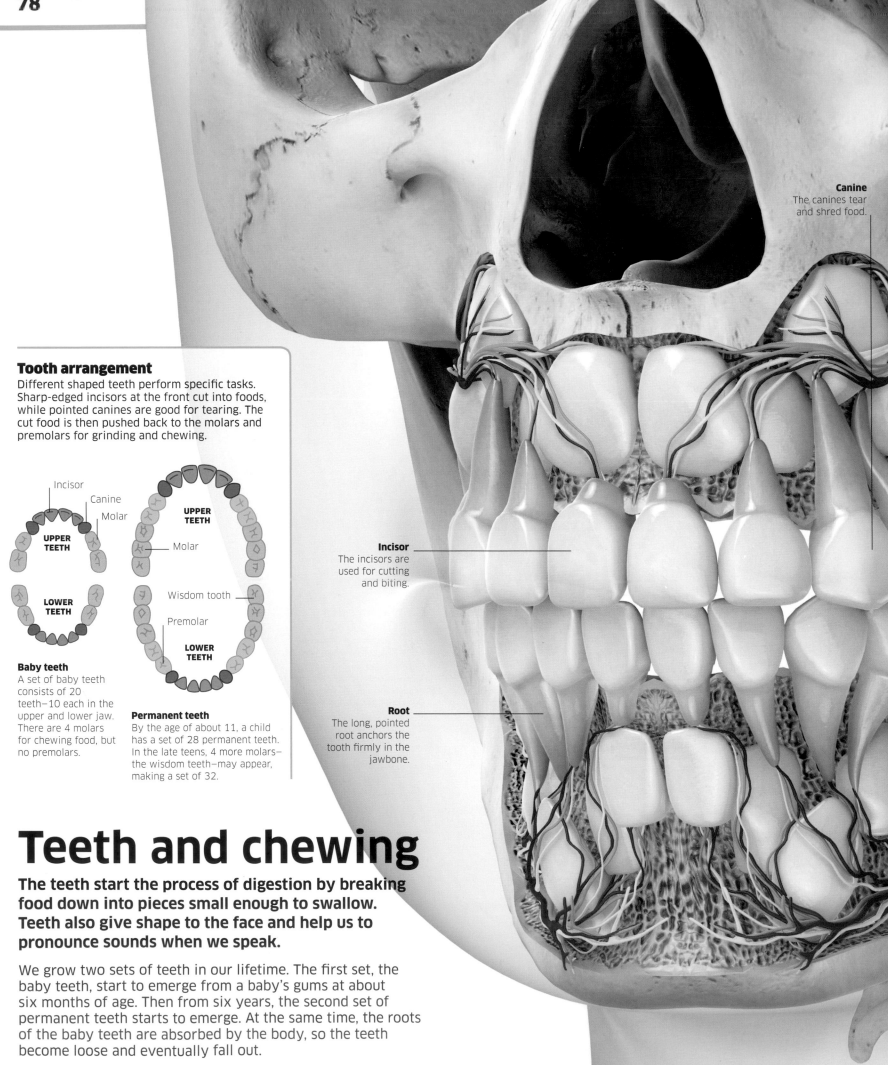

Tooth arrangement

Different shaped teeth perform specific tasks. Sharp-edged incisors at the front cut into foods, while pointed canines are good for tearing. The cut food is then pushed back to the molars and premolars for grinding and chewing.

Incisor
Canine
Molar
UPPER TEETH

UPPER TEETH

Molar

LOWER TEETH

Wisdom tooth

Premolar

LOWER TEETH

Baby teeth
A set of baby teeth consists of 20 teeth–10 each in the upper and lower jaw. There are 4 molars for chewing food, but no premolars.

Permanent teeth
By the age of about 11, a child has a set of 28 permanent teeth. In the late teens, 4 more molars– the wisdom teeth–may appear, making a set of 32.

Canine
The canines tear and shred food.

Incisor
The incisors are used for cutting and biting.

Root
The long, pointed root anchors the tooth firmly in the jawbone.

Teeth and chewing

The teeth start the process of digestion by breaking food down into pieces small enough to swallow. Teeth also give shape to the face and help us to pronounce sounds when we speak.

We grow two sets of teeth in our lifetime. The first set, the baby teeth, start to emerge from a baby's gums at about six months of age. Then from six years, the second set of permanent teeth starts to emerge. At the same time, the roots of the baby teeth are absorbed by the body, so the teeth become loose and eventually fall out.

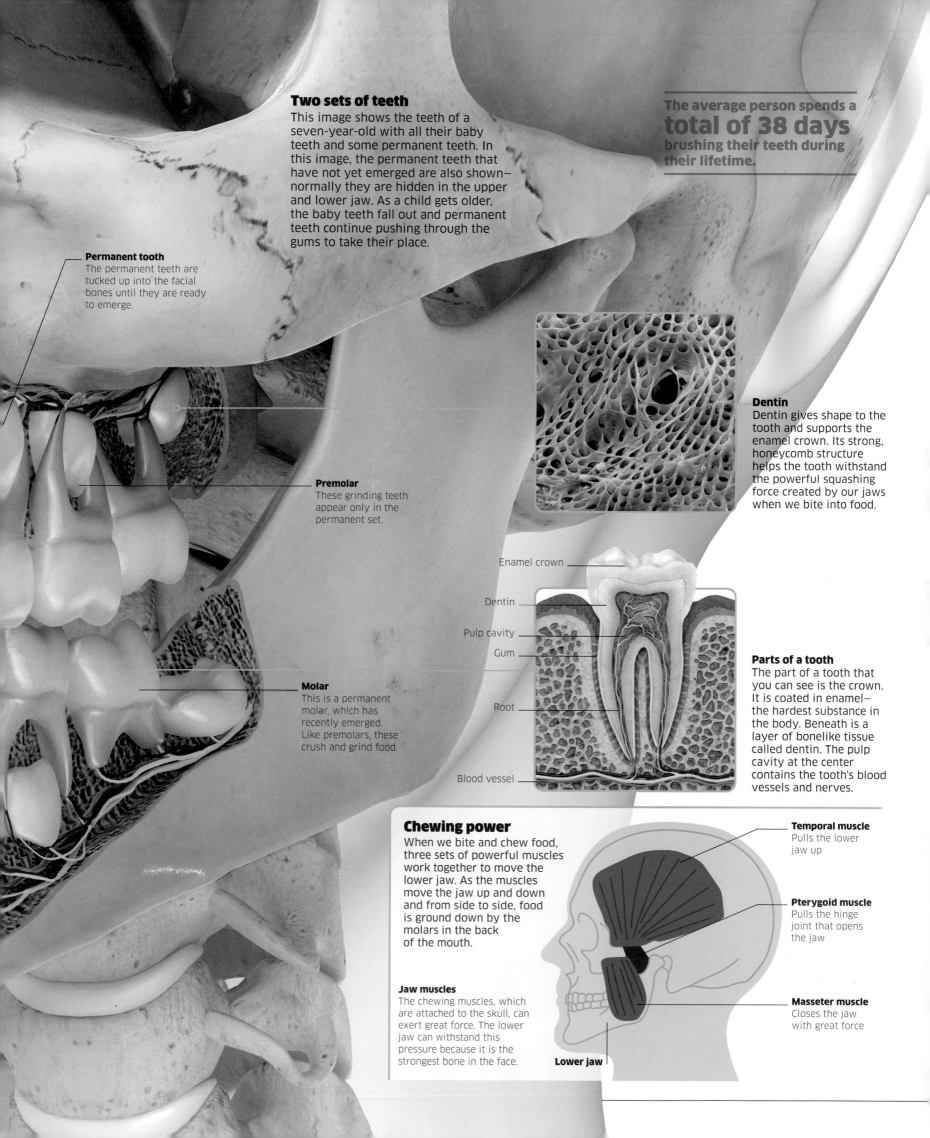

Two sets of teeth

This image shows the teeth of a seven-year-old with all their baby teeth and some permanent teeth. In this image, the permanent teeth that have not yet emerged are also shown—normally they are hidden in the upper and lower jaw. As a child gets older, the baby teeth fall out and permanent teeth continue pushing through the gums to take their place.

Permanent tooth
The permanent teeth are tucked up into the facial bones until they are ready to emerge.

Premolar
These grinding teeth appear only in the permanent set.

Molar
This is a permanent molar, which has recently emerged. Like premolars, these crush and grind food.

Dentin
Dentin gives shape to the tooth and supports the enamel crown. Its strong, honeycomb structure helps the tooth withstand the powerful squashing force created by our jaws when we bite into food.

Enamel crown
Dentin
Pulp cavity
Gum
Root
Blood vessel

Parts of a tooth
The part of a tooth that you can see is the crown. It is coated in enamel—the hardest substance in the body. Beneath is a layer of bonelike tissue called dentin. The pulp cavity at the center contains the tooth's blood vessels and nerves.

Chewing power

When we bite and chew food, three sets of powerful muscles work together to move the lower jaw. As the muscles move the jaw up and down and from side to side, food is ground down by the molars in the back of the mouth.

Temporal muscle
Pulls the lower jaw up

Pterygoid muscle
Pulls the hinge joint that opens the jaw

Masseter muscle
Closes the jaw with great force

Jaw muscles
The chewing muscles, which are attached to the skull, can exert great force. The lower jaw can withstand this pressure because it is the strongest bone in the face.

Lower jaw

Taste test

The tongue has thousands of taste buds, but these receptors can recognize only five different basic tastes.

Bitter
Tasting something bitter can stop us from eating harmful food. But some people enjoy bitter tastes like coffee.

Salty
This taste comes from sodium, which helps regulate muscle contractions, nerve signals, and keeping the right balance of water.

Sour
Acidic foods, such as lemons and vinegar, taste sour. Humans are the only animals to enjoy sour food.

Sweet
Sweetness is naturally attractive as it indicates the presence of sugar, which provides a swift energy boost.

Umami
This is a mouthwatering savory taste, found in foods such as grilled meat, mushrooms, or soy sauce.

Sensing danger

We use our senses of smell and taste to ensure we don't eat harmful things. Our sense of smell can also detect other potentially dangerous substances, such as smoke or toxic chemicals. The brain processes these smells and warns the body to steer clear.

Warning signal!
When fresh foods such as milk spoil, the sour smell quickly lets us know. Wrinkling the nose in disgust partly blocks off unpleasant, potentially harmful odors.

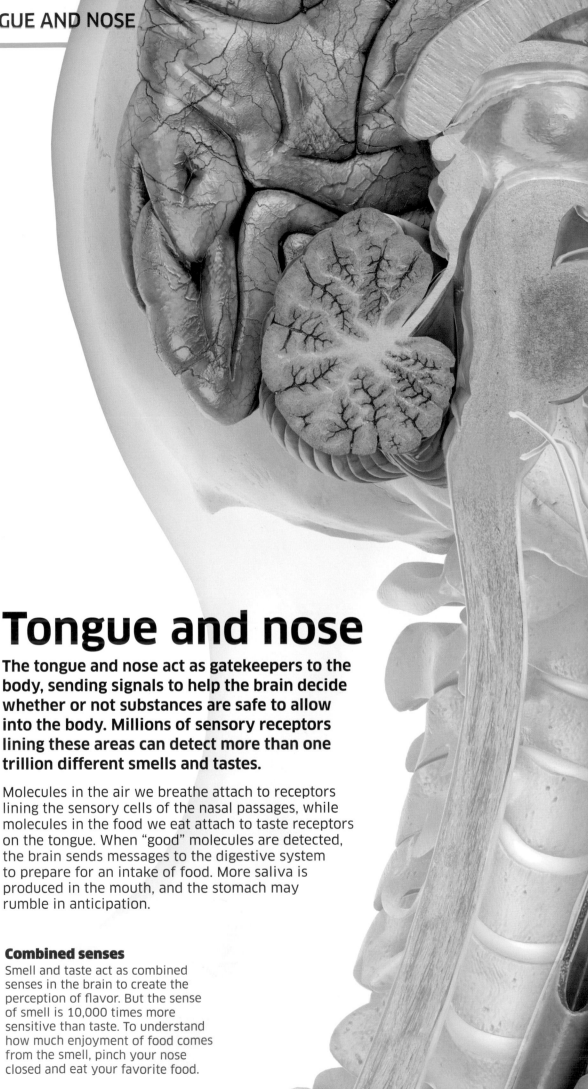

Tongue and nose

The tongue and nose act as gatekeepers to the body, sending signals to help the brain decide whether or not substances are safe to allow into the body. Millions of sensory receptors lining these areas can detect more than one trillion different smells and tastes.

Molecules in the air we breathe attach to receptors lining the sensory cells of the nasal passages, while molecules in the food we eat attach to taste receptors on the tongue. When "good" molecules are detected, the brain sends messages to the digestive system to prepare for an intake of food. More saliva is produced in the mouth, and the stomach may rumble in anticipation.

Combined senses

Smell and taste act as combined senses in the brain to create the perception of flavor. But the sense of smell is 10,000 times more sensitive than taste. To understand how much enjoyment of food comes from the smell, pinch your nose closed and eat your favorite food.

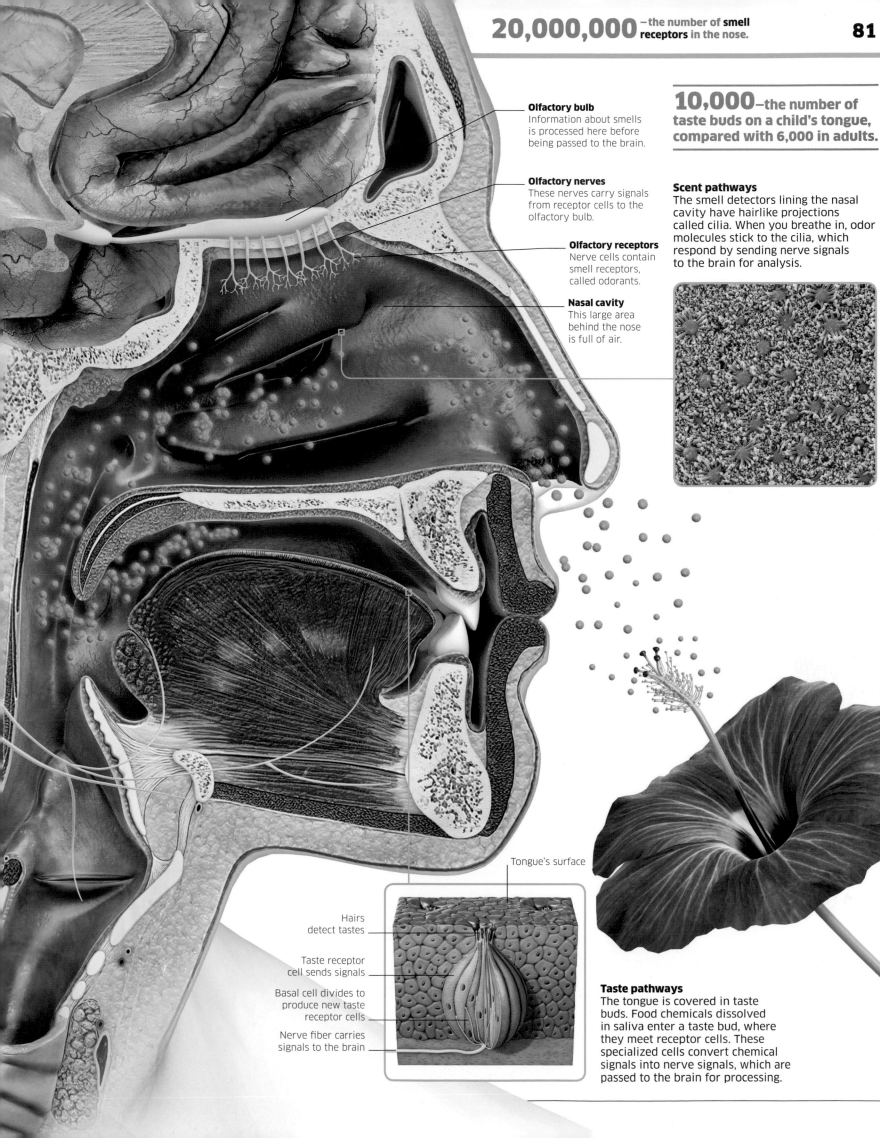

20,000,000—the number of **smell receptors** in the nose.

81

Olfactory bulb
Information about smells is processed here before being passed to the brain.

Olfactory nerves
These nerves carry signals from receptor cells to the olfactory bulb.

Olfactory receptors
Nerve cells contain smell receptors, called odorants.

Nasal cavity
This large area behind the nose is full of air.

10,000—the number of taste buds on a child's tongue, compared with 6,000 in adults.

Scent pathways
The smell detectors lining the nasal cavity have hairlike projections called cilia. When you breathe in, odor molecules stick to the cilia, which respond by sending nerve signals to the brain for analysis.

Tongue's surface

Hairs detect tastes

Taste receptor cell sends signals

Basal cell divides to produce new taste receptor cells

Nerve fiber carries signals to the brain

Taste pathways
The tongue is covered in taste buds. Food chemicals dissolved in saliva enter a taste bud, where they meet receptor cells. These specialized cells convert chemical signals into nerve signals, which are passed to the brain for processing.

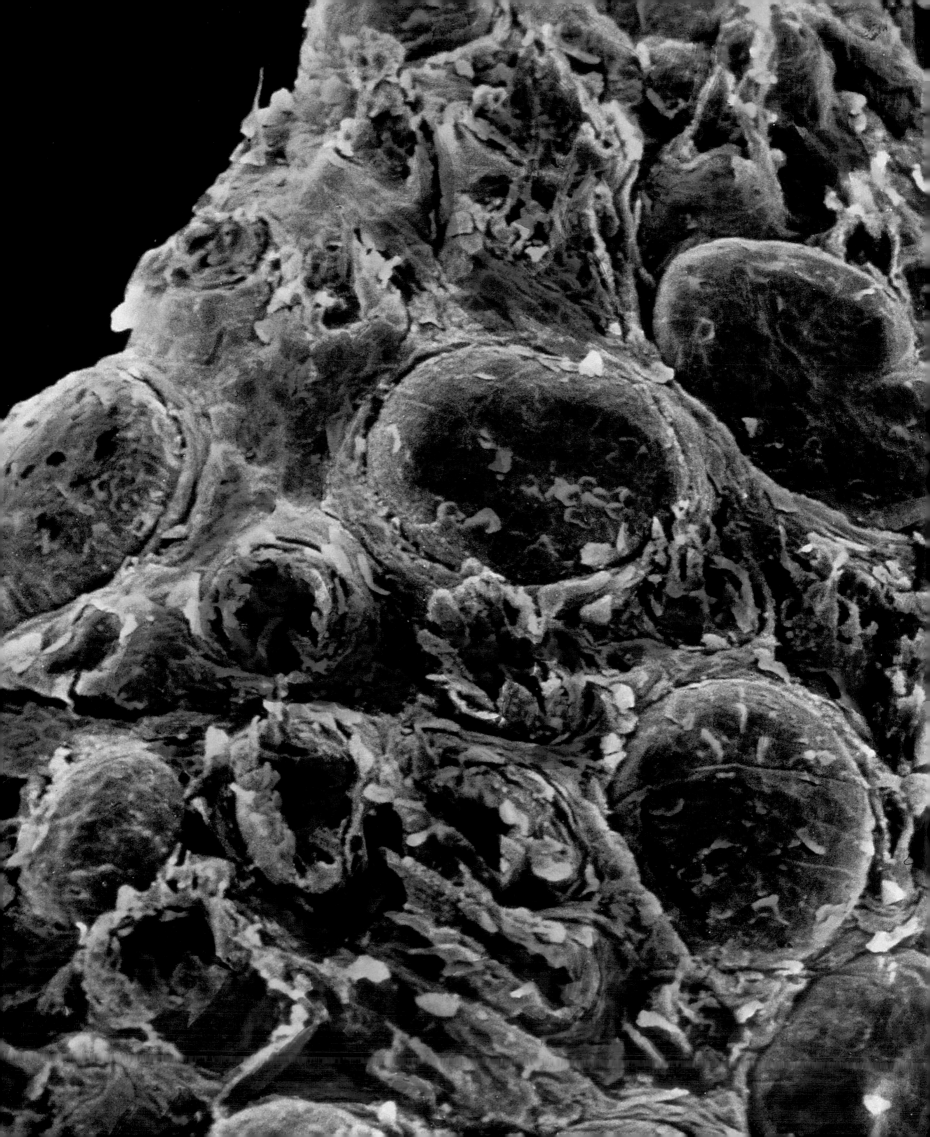

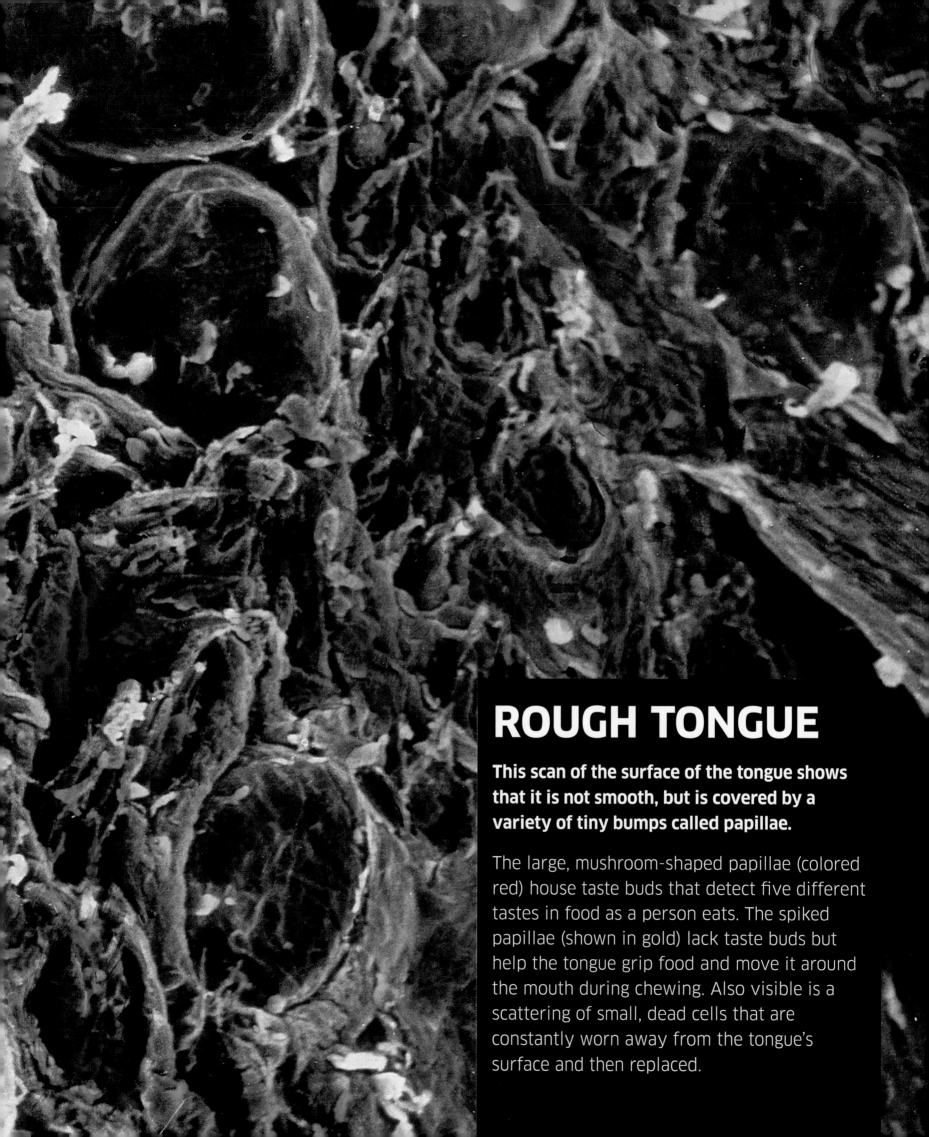

ROUGH TONGUE

This scan of the surface of the tongue shows that it is not smooth, but is covered by a variety of tiny bumps called papillae.

The large, mushroom-shaped papillae (colored red) house taste buds that detect five different tastes in food as a person eats. The spiked papillae (shown in gold) lack taste buds but help the tongue grip food and move it around the mouth during chewing. Also visible is a scattering of small, dead cells that are constantly worn away from the tongue's surface and then replaced.

84 head and neck ○ EYE

8 million—the **number of different colors** that the eye can recognize.

Eye muscles

Three pairs of muscles control the movements of each eye, allowing it to swivel and roll to look up, down, or from side to side. The muscles are fast-acting, so the eye can easily follow a moving object.

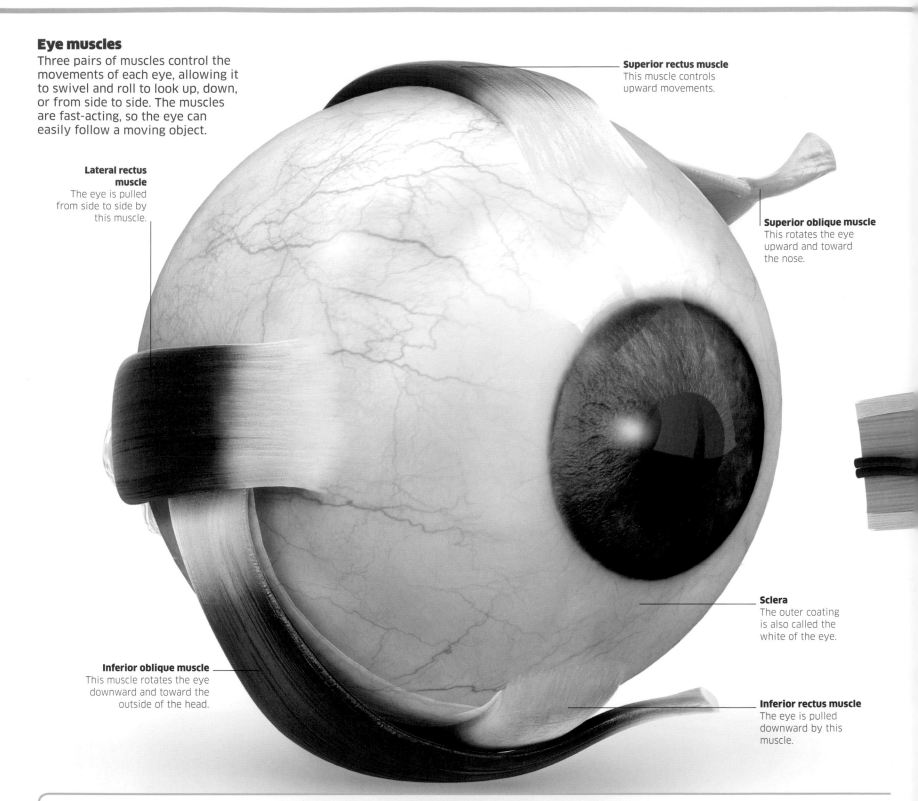

Superior rectus muscle
This muscle controls upward movements.

Lateral rectus muscle
The eye is pulled from side to side by this muscle.

Superior oblique muscle
This rotates the eye upward and toward the nose.

Sclera
The outer coating is also called the white of the eye.

Inferior oblique muscle
This muscle rotates the eye downward and toward the outside of the head.

Inferior rectus muscle
The eye is pulled downward by this muscle.

How vision works

When rays of light from an object hit the cornea (outer shell of the eye) they are bent (refracted). The rays then refract more as they pass through the transparent lens. With distant objects, light is refracted mainly by the cornea—the thin lens only refracts light a little. With nearer objects, the lens becomes wider and it does more of the refraction.

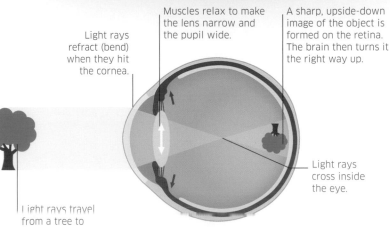

Light rays refract (bend) when they hit the cornea.

Muscles relax to make the lens narrow and the pupil wide.

A sharp, upside-down image of the object is formed on the retina. The brain then turns it the right way up.

Light refracts as it passes through the cornea.

Once it receives this image, the brain will flip the image the right way up.

Light rays cross inside the eye.

Light rays travel from a tree to the eye.

SEEING A DISTANT OBJECT

Light from a nearer object is refracted more through the wider lens.

SEEING A NEAR OBJECT

415 million—the number of times an **eye blinks** in an average lifetime.

The cornea is the only tissue in the human body that **doesn't contain blood vessels.**

130 million—the number of **light-sensitive** cells in the retina.

85

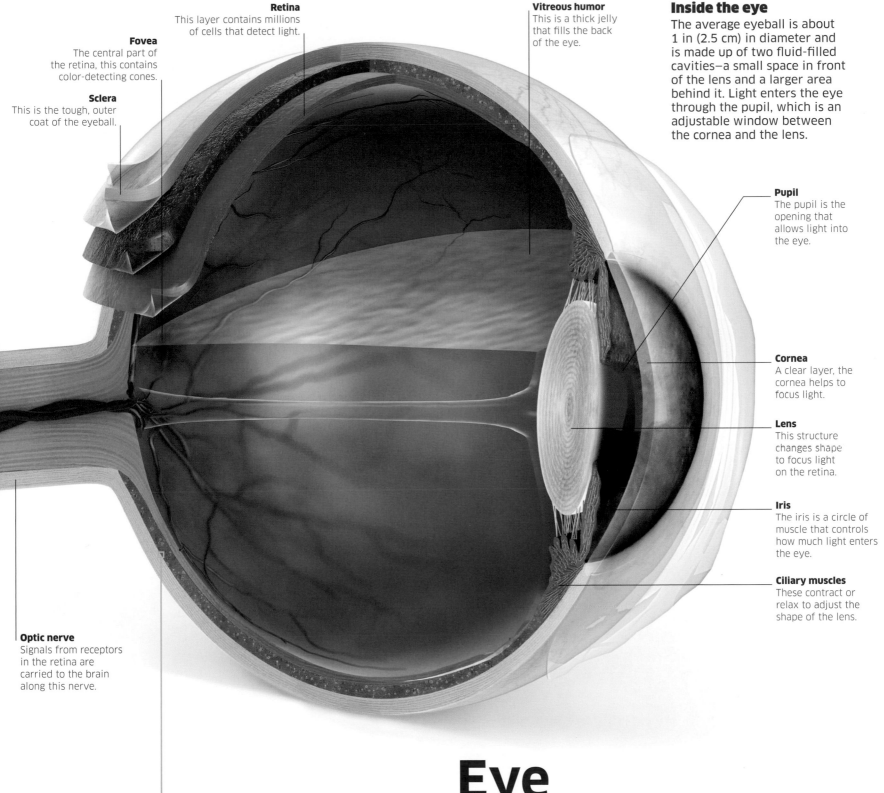

Retina
This layer contains millions of cells that detect light.

Fovea
The central part of the retina, this contains color-detecting cones.

Sclera
This is the tough, outer coat of the eyeball.

Vitreous humor
This is a thick jelly that fills the back of the eye.

Inside the eye
The average eyeball is about 1 in (2.5 cm) in diameter and is made up of two fluid-filled cavities—a small space in front of the lens and a larger area behind it. Light enters the eye through the pupil, which is an adjustable window between the cornea and the lens.

Pupil
The pupil is the opening that allows light into the eye.

Cornea
A clear layer, the cornea helps to focus light.

Lens
This structure changes shape to focus light on the retina.

Iris
The iris is a circle of muscle that controls how much light enters the eye.

Ciliary muscles
These contract or relax to adjust the shape of the lens.

Optic nerve
Signals from receptors in the retina are carried to the brain along this nerve.

Light detectors
This microscope image shows rods (green) and cones (blue)—the two types of light receptor cell on the retina. Rods pick up dim light, while cones detect color and detail. Then they send information about what they record to the brain via the optic nerve.

Eye

The role of the eyes is to collect vast amounts of visual information, which the brain turns into 3-D pictures of the world around us.

Each eye has a built-in lens to give a picture of the world and a bank of sensors to record it. Human eyes can focus on anything from a close-up speck of dust to a galaxy across the universe, and work in both faint moonlight and dazzling sunshine. The lens in each eye focuses light rays together on the back of the eyeball. Receptors record the patterns of light, shade, and colors, then send them to the brain to make an image.

VISION

The human eye is excellent at picking up different colours and fine details. The position of the two eyes also means they can provide a tremendous range of visual information about what is being looked at. The powerful vision-processing areas of the brain then interpret this torrent of data into highly detailed mental images—which your memory then helps you to recognize.

COLOR VISION

Human eyes can see in color thanks to 127 million light-sensitive cells on the back of the retina. These light detectors, called rods and cones, capture light rays from the lenses to create colored images.

Rods and cones

About 120 million rods are sensitive to low light. They see in black and white and provide only minimal detail. About 7 million cones see color and detail, but only in bright light.

Rod cells
The rods work well in dim light. They provide information about the whole image in shades of gray.

Cone cells
The cones detect color and detail at the center of the image, but only work in bright light.

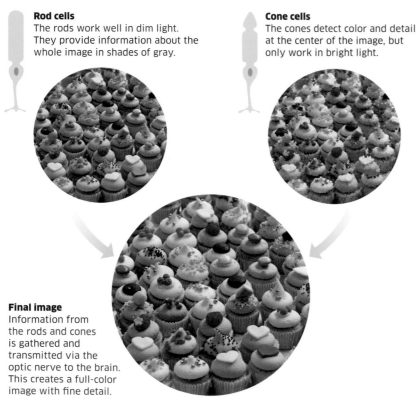

Final image
Information from the rods and cones is gathered and transmitted via the optic nerve to the brain. This creates a full-color image with fine detail.

Three colors

There are three types of color-detecting cones inside the eyes. They are sensitive to red, blue, or green. But combined, they can detect millions of colors, all made of mixtures of these three basic colors.

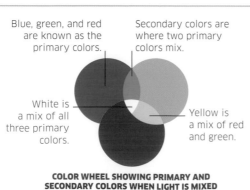

Blue, green, and red are known as the primary colors.

Secondary colors are where two primary colors mix.

White is a mix of all three primary colors.

Yellow is a mix of red and green.

COLOR WHEEL SHOWING PRIMARY AND SECONDARY COLORS WHEN LIGHT IS MIXED

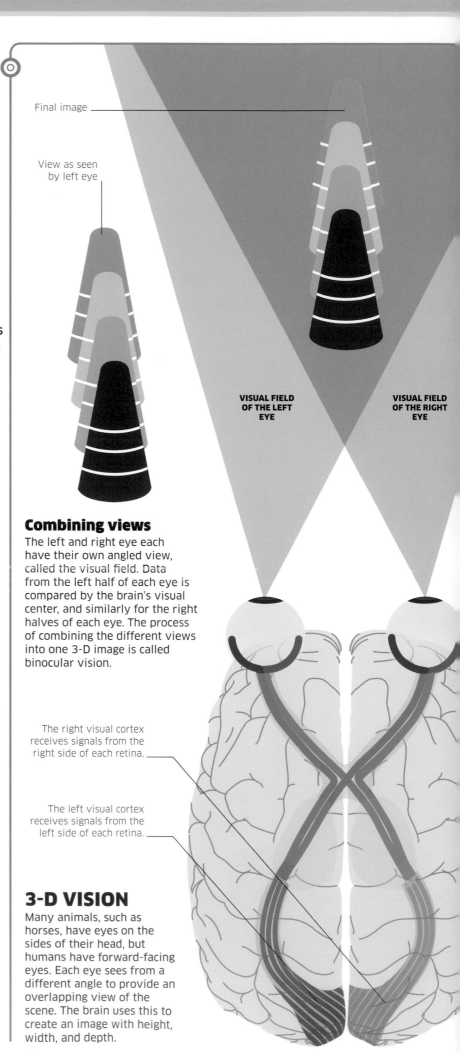

Final image

View as seen by left eye

VISUAL FIELD OF THE LEFT EYE

VISUAL FIELD OF THE RIGHT EYE

Combining views

The left and right eye each have their own angled view, called the visual field. Data from the left half of each eye is compared by the brain's visual center, and similarly for the right halves of each eye. The process of combining the different views into one 3-D image is called binocular vision.

The right visual cortex receives signals from the right side of each retina.

The left visual cortex receives signals from the left side of each retina.

3-D VISION

Many animals, such as horses, have eyes on the sides of their head, but humans have forward-facing eyes. Each eye sees from a different angle to provide an overlapping view of the scene. The brain uses this to create an image with height, width, and depth.

View as seen
by right eye

THE FARTHEST OUR EYES CAN SEE IS THE **ANDROMEDA GALAXY,** ABOUT 2.5 MILLION LIGHT-YEARS AWAY.

Movie magic
The ultimate cinematic experience is a 3-D movie. The film is made by copying what the eyes do. Scenes are shot with two cameras, then special glasses are worn to put the images together. The result makes the audience feel as though they are in the movie.

OPTICAL ILLUSIONS
The brain's task is to make sense of what the eyes see, and it usually gets it right. However, optical illusions can play tricks on the brain because it tries to fill any gaps in the visual information it receives.

Sidewalk painting
Artists can create the illusion of depth by skillful use of techniques such as shading and perspective (making lines meet as if they would in the distance). The brain uses past experience to interpret this scene—wrongly—as a huge chasm in the road.

Moving image
As you look at this image, parts of it seem to move. This is caused by the eyes' light-sensitive cells turning on and off as they react to different parts of the pattern. This fools the eye into thinking it is seeing movement.

EYE PROBLEMS
Sight is a key sense, so maintaining good vision is important to humans. Eyesight often deteriorates as the body ages and the number of light-sensitive rods and cones decreases. Two of the most common eye conditions are problems with focussing and with seeing certain colors.

Out of sight
The most common eye problems are nearsightedness and farsightedness, where distant or near objects can appear blurred. Glasses or contact lenses can help the light to focus in the right place within the eye and make images sharp again.

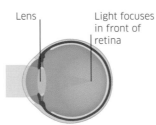

Lens

Light focuses in front of retina

Nearsightedness
Nearsighted people can focus on things that are close, but not on things that are farther away.

Lens

Light focuses behind retina

Farsightedness
Farsighted people can focus on things at a distance but not on near objects.

Color-blindness
Most eyes can see millions of different colors, but some people cannot distinguish between colors because of injury, illness, or an inherited condition. More boys than girls have color-blindness.

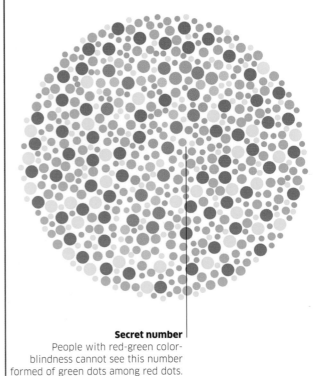

Secret number
People with red-green color-blindness cannot see this number formed of green dots among red dots.

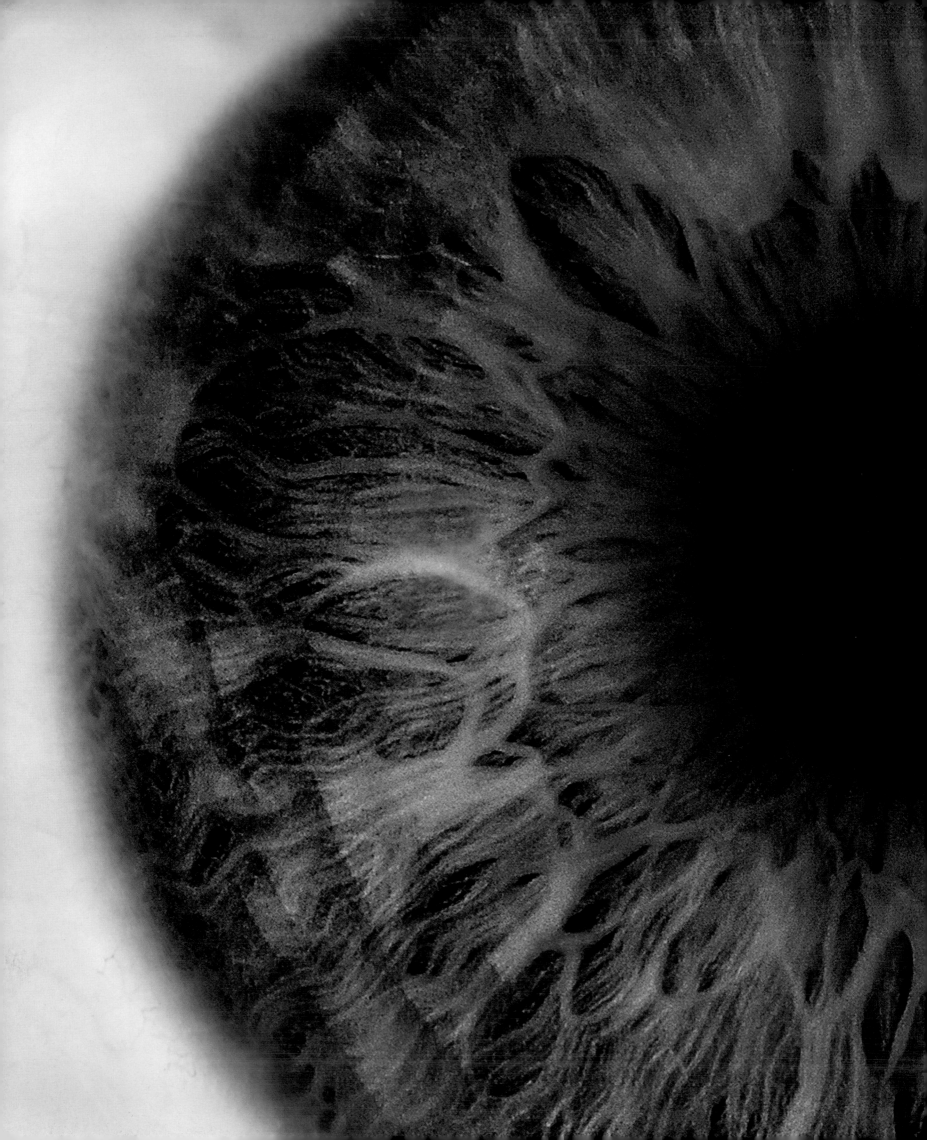

IRIS

This close-up image of an eye shows the colored ring of muscle called the iris. Every human has a unique iris pattern, which is why many modern security systems use iris recognition technology.

Two sets of muscles in the iris contract and relax to control the amount of light entering the eye through the hole in its center—the pupil. Circular muscles contract in bright light, making the pupil smaller to prevent a dazzling effect. In dim light, radial muscles (like spokes on a wheel) contract to make the pupil bigger so it allows in more light. Different amounts of melanin pigment inside the iris give eyes their different colors. Brown is the most common color, making up more than half the world's population.

The ear canal is ⅜ in (7 mm) wide, about the **width of a pencil**.

The inner ear sits within the temporal bone, the **hardest bone in the body**.

How hearing works

All sounds make invisible ripples, or waves, in the air. The ear collects sound waves and converts them first into vibrations, then into signals that the brain interprets as sounds.

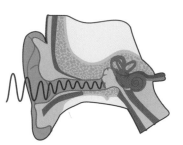

1 Outer ear
Sound waves travel along the ear canal until they hit the eardrum and make it vibrate.

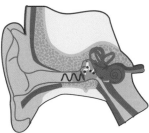

2 Middle ear
The vibrations pass through a series of bones, through the oval window, and into the cochlea.

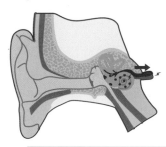

3 Inner ear
Microscopic hairs inside the cochlea convert the vibrations into nerve signals, which are sent to the brain.

Loud and clear

The louder the sound, the bigger the vibrations it makes. Our ears are so sensitive that we can detect even the smallest sound, such as a paper clip dropping on the floor. We measure the loudness of sounds in decibels (dB).

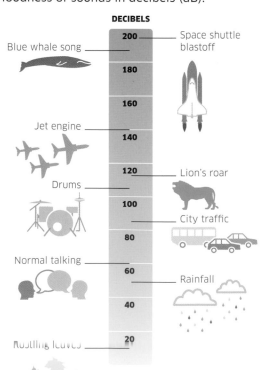

DECIBELS

Blue whale song — 200 — Space shuttle blastoff

180

160

Jet engine — 140

120 — Lion's roar

Drums — 100

City traffic

80

Normal talking — 60

40 — Rainfall

20

Rustling leaves —

Parts of the ear

The ear has three zones, each with different roles. The outer ear collects sounds and funnels them toward the middle ear, where they are converted into vibrations. In the inner ear, the vibrations are transformed again, into signals to send to the brain.

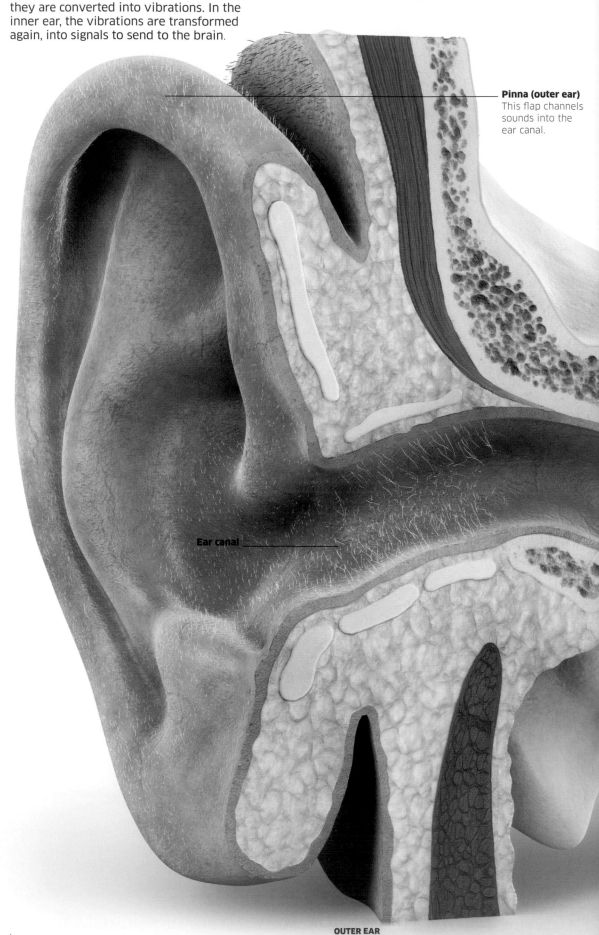

Pinna (outer ear)
This flap channels sounds into the ear canal.

Ear canal

OUTER EAR

The outer ear **continues growing** throughout a person's lifetime.

15,000 –the number of **sound-detecting hair cells** in the cochlea.

91

Eardrum
The eardrum is a thin film, about ⅜ in (9 mm) wide, which sits at the entrance to the middle ear and vibrates when sound waves hit it. The eardrum also helps to stop debris from getting inside the ear and damaging it.

Stirrup (stapes)
The tiny stirrup bone vibrates and moves the oval window in the cochlea.

Hammer (malleus)
Vibrations from the eardrum are picked up by this bone.

Oval window

Ear

The ear is the body's organ of hearing. It is larger than it looks—only a skin-covered flap is visible on the outside of the head, with the rest of the ear lying hidden from view inside the skull.

The ears collect sound waves and convert them into nerve signals for our brains to decode. Human ears can detect a huge range of different sounds, from high-pitched birdsong to the low rumble of thunder, and from the faintest whisper to the loud roar of a lion.

Semicircular canals
These three fluid-filled tubes contain sensors that detect movement.

Cochlea
The snail-shaped cochlea is filled with liquid and lined with tiny hair cells that detect vibrations.

Hair cells
Each hair cell in the cochlea is topped by groups of microscopic hairs. Incoming vibrations bend the hairs by different amounts. These vibration patterns are turned into nerve messages and sent to the brain.

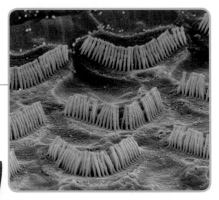

Anvil (incus)
Vibrations from the hammer to the stirrup are transmitted through the anvil.

Anvil

Smallest bones
The ear contains three of the tiniest bones in the human body. The stirrup bone is the smallest of all, at about the size of a grain of rice.

Stirrup | **Hammer**

MIDDLE EAR

INNER EAR

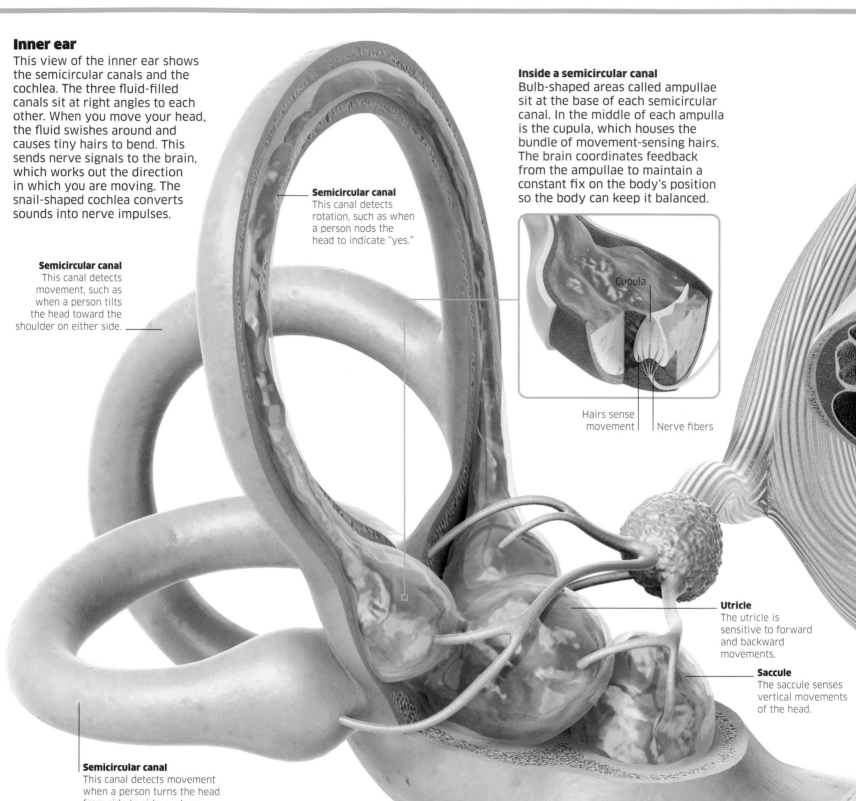

Inner ear
This view of the inner ear shows the semicircular canals and the cochlea. The three fluid-filled canals sit at right angles to each other. When you move your head, the fluid swishes around and causes tiny hairs to bend. This sends nerve signals to the brain, which works out the direction in which you are moving. The snail-shaped cochlea converts sounds into nerve impulses.

Semicircular canal
This canal detects movement, such as when a person tilts the head toward the shoulder on either side.

Semicircular canal
This canal detects rotation, such as when a person nods the head to indicate "yes."

Inside a semicircular canal
Bulb-shaped areas called ampullae sit at the base of each semicircular canal. In the middle of each ampulla is the cupula, which houses the bundle of movement-sensing hairs. The brain coordinates feedback from the ampullae to maintain a constant fix on the body's position so the body can keep it balanced.

Cupula

Hairs sense movement

Nerve fibers

Utricle
The utricle is sensitive to forward and backward movements.

Saccule
The saccule senses vertical movements of the head.

Semicircular canal
This canal detects movement when a person turns the head from side to side, such as when indicating "no."

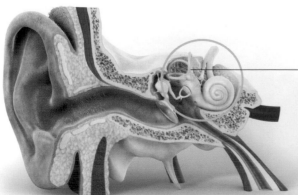

Inner ear
The semicircular canals and cochlea are part of the inner ear. They sit within a hollow in the temporal bone of the skull.

Oval window
The stapes, or stirrup bone, fits here to pass sound waves to the cochlea.

In an adult, the cochlea is roughly the **same size as a pea**.

1¼ in (31.5 mm)—the length of the **tubes of the cochlea** if they were unrolled.

93

Organ of Corti
Running through the middle of the cochlea is the organ of Corti, the main receptor for hearing. Sound waves create vibrations that make wavelike movements in the fluid inside the organ of Corti. These bend the hairs, producing nerve signals, which are sent to the brain to be registered as sounds.

Sensory hair

Nerve fiber

Hair cell

Balance and hearing

In addition to providing our sense of hearing, the ears help us to keep our balance and send vital information to the brain when we move.

The inner ear is the part deepest inside the head. It contains three fluid-filled tubes called semicircular canals. As we move, the fluid inside the canals moves, sending messages to the brain to help us keep our balance. Also in the inner ear is the cochlea, which converts sounds to hearing.

Cochlea
This snail-shaped organ turns vibrations into audible sounds.

Auditory nerve
This nerve carries signals from the ear to the brain.

Balancing act
Different body systems work to keep you balanced. Signals from the inner ear combine with visual signals from the eyes, pressure sensors in the skin, and stretch sensors in the muscles to reveal the body's position. The brain processes this and makes any adjustments to stop the body falling over.

Utricle and saccule
Inside the inner ear are two tiny organs that sense movement of the head in a straight line. The utricle detects forward and backward movement, and the saccule detects up-and-down movement.

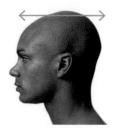

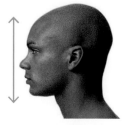

The brain takes
0.03 seconds
to send messages to the muscles to correct the body if you start to lose your balance.

Forward and backward movement, such as traveling in a car, are detected by the utricle.

Up-and-down motion, such as riding in an elevator, is sensed by the saccule.

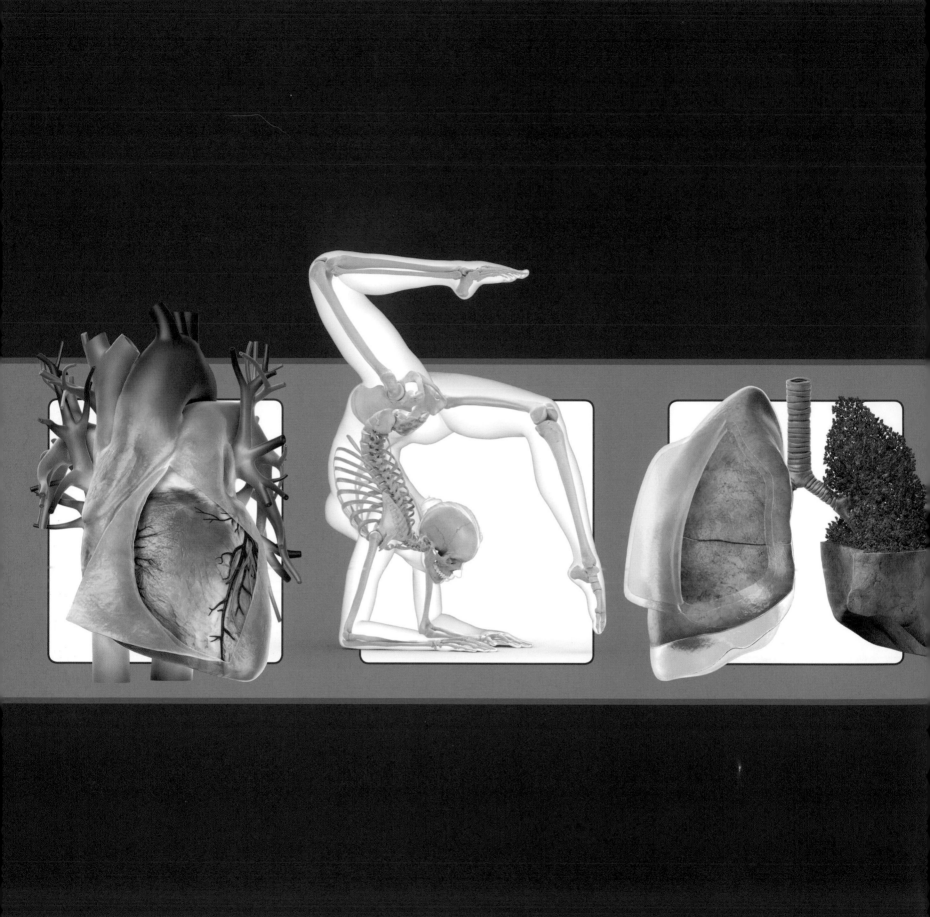

CHEST AND BACK

The chest houses the two powerhouse organs that keep the body running—the heart and lungs. All the body's cells are supplied with essential blood and oxygen thanks to these vital organs. The backbone supports the body and protects the spinal column, which carries messages to and from the brain.

There are 12 pairs
of ribs in a human's rib cage.

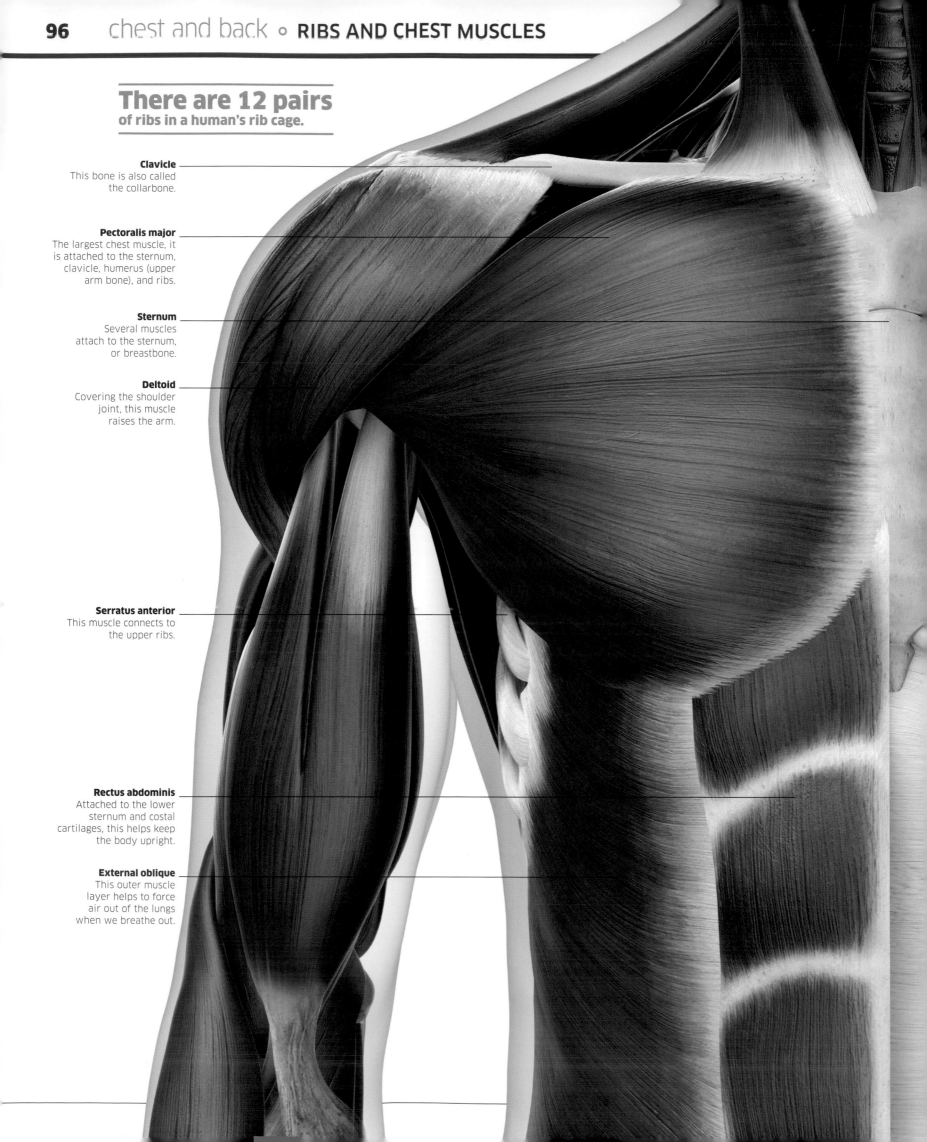

Clavicle
This bone is also called the collarbone.

Pectoralis major
The largest chest muscle, it is attached to the sternum, clavicle, humerus (upper arm bone), and ribs.

Sternum
Several muscles attach to the sternum, or breastbone.

Deltoid
Covering the shoulder joint, this muscle raises the arm.

Serratus anterior
This muscle connects to the upper ribs.

Rectus abdominis
Attached to the lower sternum and costal cartilages, this helps keep the body upright.

External oblique
This outer muscle layer helps to force air out of the lungs when we breathe out.

With every inhale, your **rib cage expands by up to 2 in (5 cm)**.

The two lowest pairs of ribs are called **floating ribs** because they attach only to vertebrae and not to the sternum.

97

Ribs and chest muscles

The chest, or thorax, lies between the neck and the abdomen. Inside the thorax lie the heart, lungs, and major blood vessels. The rib cage surrounding them is formed by the backbone, ribs, costal cartilages, and sternum (breastbone).

The rib cage is strong enough to protect the vital organs, but flexible enough to expand and contract for breathing. Attached to the rib cage are the muscles of the chest. Together with the diaphragm, many of these muscles help with breathing.

Costal cartilage
Tough, springy tissue connects the sternum to the ribs.

Internal muscle
When you breathe out, this muscle pulls the rib cage down and out.

Innermost muscle
This muscle lowers the ribs when breathing out.

External muscle
This muscle pulls the rib cage up and out when breathing in.

Intercostal muscles
Between the ribs are three layers of intercostal muscles ("intercostal" simply means "between the ribs"). The muscle fibers run in different directions so the ribs can be pulled in different ways.

Rib
Each rib is thin and curved, with an inside groove for veins, arteries, and nerves.

Internal oblique muscles
These help to push air out of the lungs when we breathe out.

Muscle movements

The muscles of the chest help with the process of breathing. They pull the ribs up and out, making more space for the lungs to expand as we breathe in. When they relax, the space gets smaller and the air is forced out again.

Back support

The muscles of the neck and back provide a strong support system for the spine—the long line of interlocking bones that helps to keep the upper body stable and upright. Some muscles also help with breathing by lifting and lowering the ribs.

Back muscles pull the spine backward, bend it sideways, or rotate it, allowing the back to perform a wide range of bending and turning movements. Layers of muscle packed around the spine also protect it against injury from pressure or knocks.

Stability and movement

The back has three main muscle layers, which work together to stabilize and move the torso and help with breathing. The deeper layer, shown here, sometimes called the core muscles, holds the body up and keeps you from flopping forward when you bend at the waist.

Developing strength

The layer of stabilizing back muscles plays an important role in a baby's developing ability to sit and move around independently.

Push-ups
Babies begin to build strength in their stabilizing muscles from about three months old. They lie on their tummies and lift their arms in the air to flex these muscles.

Stabilizing muscles get stronger

Sitting up
By nine months old, most babies have developed their stabilizing muscles enough to be able to sit up on their own.

First steps
At around a year old, a baby can stand on her feet and start to walk without help. Stabilizing muscles are still gaining strength, so early attempts can be wobbly.

Serratus posterior superior
During breathing, this muscle helps lift the ribs.

External intercostal muscle
This is one of a set of muscles that raises the ribs and expands the chest.

Rotatores
These small muscles run all the way up either side of the spine.

Psoas major
This muscle helps to move the hip.

Gluteal muscles
These muscles stabilize the hip, pelvis, and back.

Larger muscles in the back control movement, while smaller muscles help with posture.

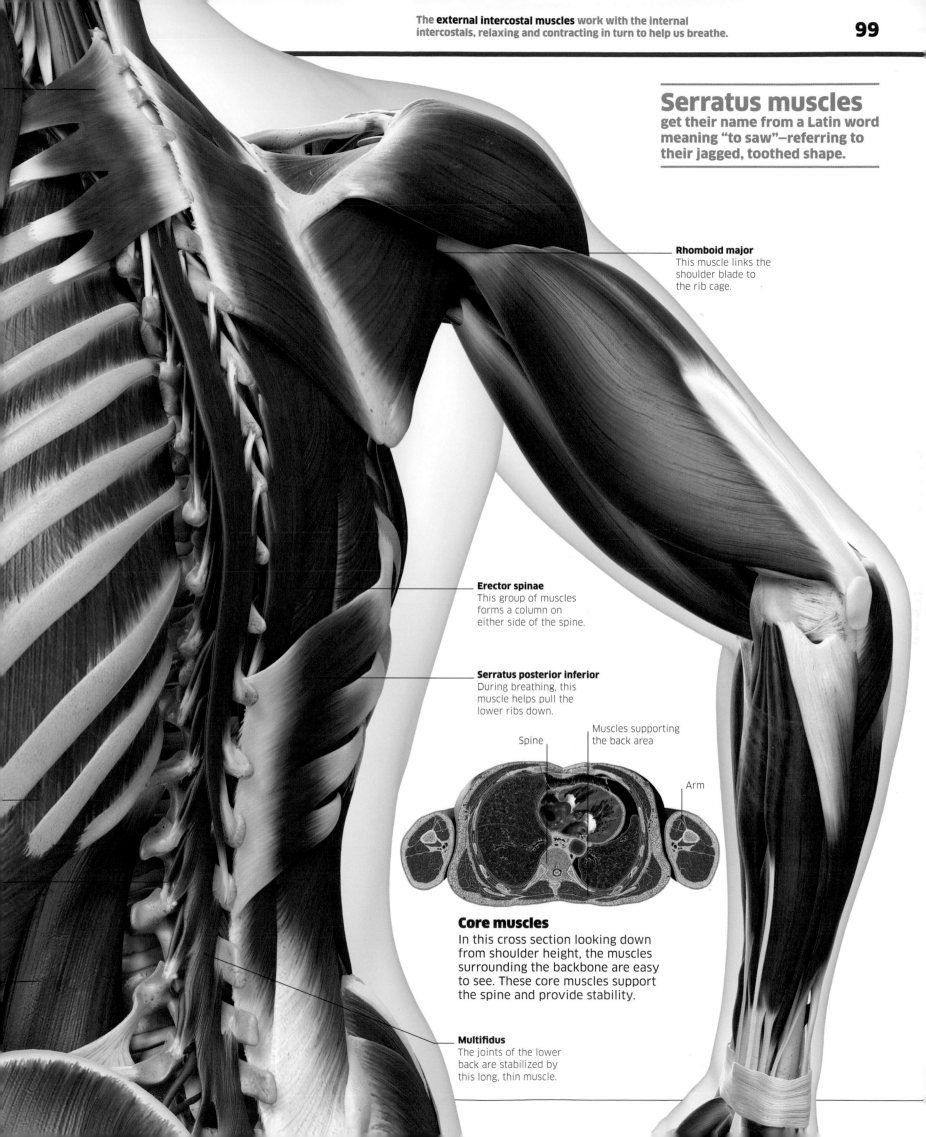

The **external intercostal muscles** work with the internal intercostals, relaxing and contracting in turn to help us breathe.

99

Serratus muscles

get their name from a Latin word meaning "to saw"—referring to their jagged, toothed shape.

Rhomboid major
This muscle links the shoulder blade to the rib cage.

Erector spinae
This group of muscles forms a column on either side of the spine.

Serratus posterior inferior
During breathing, this muscle helps pull the lower ribs down.

Spine

Muscles supporting the back area

Arm

Core muscles

In this cross section looking down from shoulder height, the muscles surrounding the backbone are easy to see. These core muscles support the spine and provide stability.

Multifidus
The joints of the lower back are stabilized by this long, thin muscle.

Backbone

The backbone, also called the spine, runs down the back of the body, from the base of the skull to the coccyx. It provides strong support for the head and body, while allowing the body to twist and bend. It also protects the spinal cord—the thick bundle of nerves that carries messages between the brain and the body.

The human backbone is formed by small, pillar-shaped bones called vertebrae (one is called a vertebra). These stack together to form a strong, flexible, S-shaped column. This shape makes the backbone springy enough to absorb shock during movement, while larger vertebrae in the lower back help to support the upper body's weight. Each vertebra slots into its neighbor to form a flexible but secure tunnel surrounding the spinal cord.

Regions of the backbone

The vertebrae that make up the backbone are often divided into five regions:

- **Cervical vertebrae**
  The seven cervical vertebrae support the head, with the top two vertebrae, the atlas and axis, enabling the head to nod and turn.

- **Thoracic vertebrae**
  The 12 thoracic vertebrae connect with the ribs, forming the back of the rib cage.

- **Lumbar vertebrae**
  There are five lumbar vertebrae, which support most of the body's weight.

- **Fused bones of the sacrum**
  A group of five bones connect the backbone to the pelvic girdle.

- **Fused bones of the coccyx**
  These four bones are an attachment point for muscles, tendons, and ligaments.

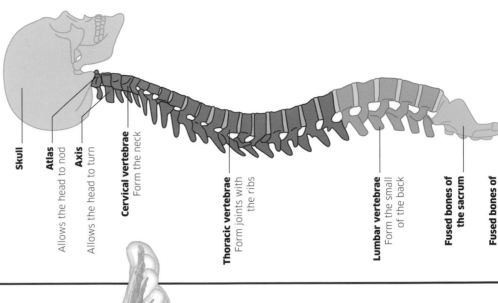

Skull

Atlas
Allows the head to nod

Axis
Allows the head to turn

Cervical vertebrae
Form the neck

Thoracic vertebrae
Form joints with the ribs

Lumbar vertebrae
Form the small of the back

Fused bones of the sacrum

Fused bones of the coccyx

Spine joints

The spurs of bone on the back of each vertebra slot together to form joints that glide back and forth as the spine moves, called facet joints. The shapes of the bones limit how much each joint can move. Disks of cartilage between the bones absorb shock by squishing slightly. They also stop the bones from grinding painfully against each other as they move.

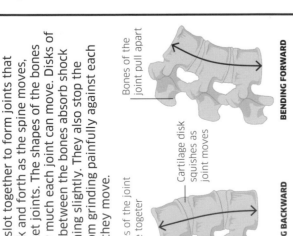

Bones of the joint pull apart

BENDING FORWARD

Cartilage disk squishes as joint moves

Bones of the joint come togeter

BENDING BACKWARD

33

—the number of bones in the spine, with 9 of them fused together.

Surprisingly flexible

To ensure that the spinal column is well protected, the joints between each vertebra only allow limited movement. But all the small movements add up, allowing the spine to bend backward and forward and side to side, as well as twist and turn.

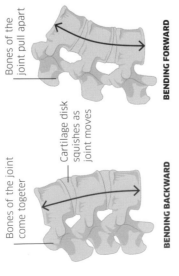

Hip bone

7 – the number of **vertebrae** in a human's neck, the same number as in a **giraffe's** neck.

25% of the backbone's total length is made up from the **cartilage disks** between the vertebrae.

101

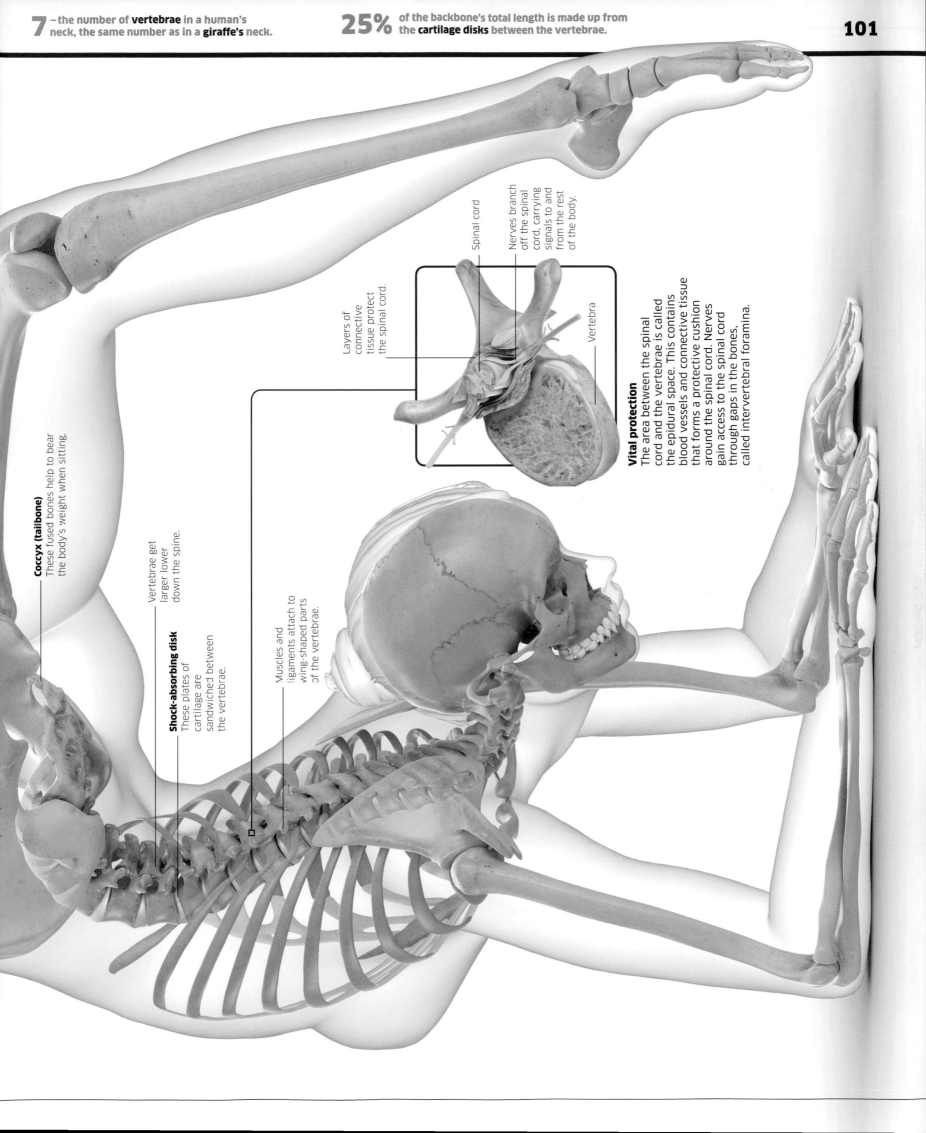

Spinal cord

Nerves branch off the spinal cord, carrying signals to and from the rest of the body.

Vertebra

Layers of connective tissue protect the spinal cord.

Vital protection
The area between the spinal cord and the vertebrae is called the epidural space. This contains blood vessels and connective tissue that forms a protective cushion around the spinal cord. Nerves gain access to the spinal cord through gaps in the bones, called intervertebral foramina.

Coccyx (tailbone)
These fused bones help to bear the body's weight when sitting.

Vertebrae get larger lower down the spine.

Shock-absorbing disk
These plates of cartilage are sandwiched between the vertebrae.

Muscles and ligaments attach to wing-shaped parts of the vertebrae.

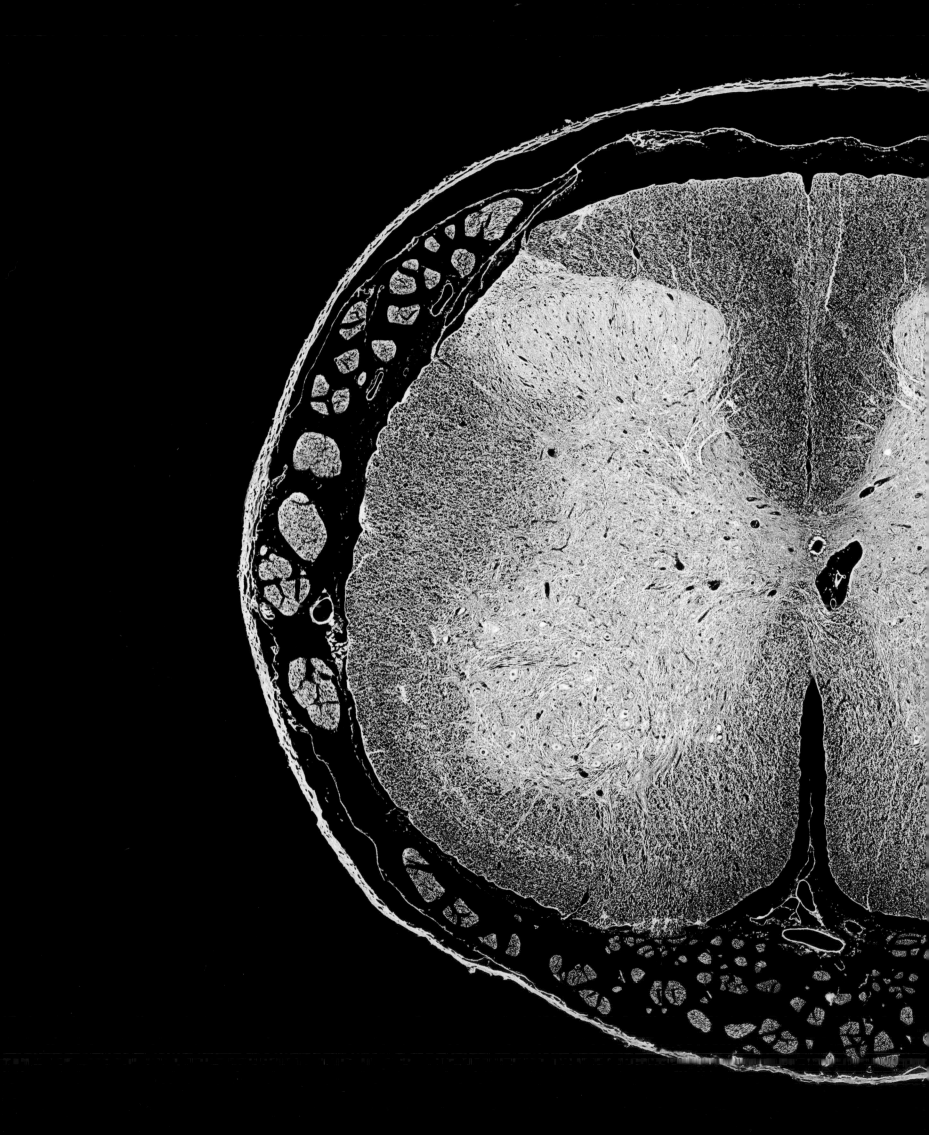

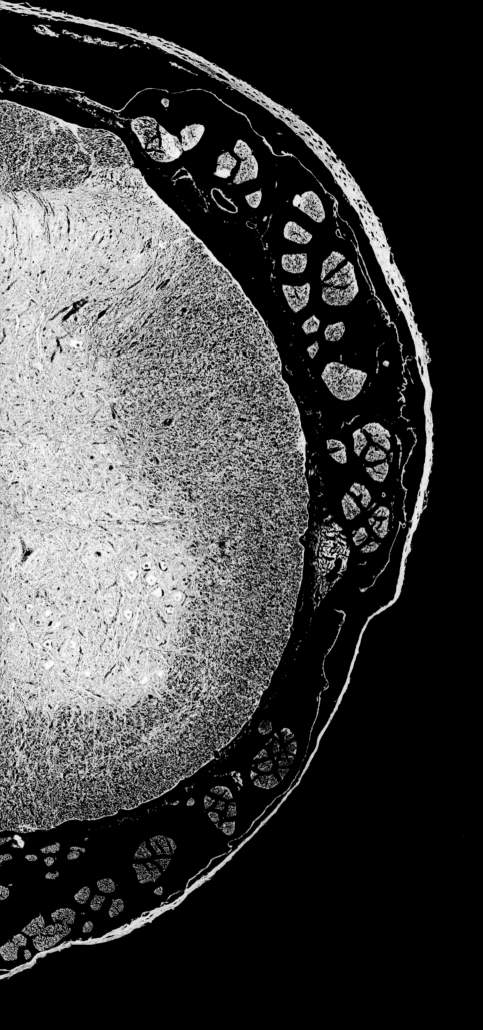

SPINAL CORD

This scan shows a cross-section of the spinal cord in the lower back region. The spinal cord is the body's information superhighway, along which billions of nerve cells carry messages that enable the body to move and function.

It has two main sections: a butterfly-shaped inner mass of gray matter (shown in yellow here) surrounded by outer white matter (shown in pink). White matter is made up of nerve fibers that relay signals to and from the brain. Gray matter contains neurons that receive signals from receptors around the body and send instructions to the muscles.

Heart rate

The heart rate is the number of beats per minute (bpm) that the heart makes. A person's average heart rate varies according to different factors, such as age, gender, and level of fitness.

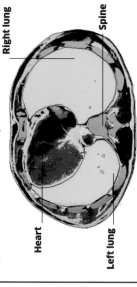

Adult man

Adult woman

10-year-old

Newborn
130 bpm

> A newborn baby's heart is the size of a table tennis ball.

Tight squeeze

The heart sits in the chest, surrounded by the rib cage and between the two lungs, which take up most of the rest of the space in the chest cavity.

Right lung

Spine

Heart

Left lung

Chest cross-section
This scan shows the chest as if it had been sliced through horizontally. The left lung is smaller than the right lung, as it shares space with the heart.

Vital supplies

To keep the heart beating, the cells need a constant supply of fuel and oxygen. This is delivered by the coronary blood supply—the heart's own network of blood vessels, which penetrate the heart's walls to reach the muscle.

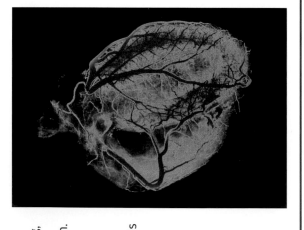

Healthy heart
This colored X-ray of the heart, called an angiogram, shows an intricate network of blood vessels branching off the main arteries.

Heart

The heart is the engine at the center of the body's circulation system. It starts working even before we are born—and from then on, it beats constantly, throughout our lives.

Made from a special kind of muscle not found anywhere else in the body, the hardworking heart contracts and relaxes about 70 times every minute. This rhythmic pumping pushes essential blood out to the body, then fills the heart up again, ready for the next beat.

Mighty muscle

A healthy adult's heart is about the size of a clenched fist. It sits in the thorax (chest), and in most people the tip points toward the left side of the body.

Pulmonary artery
Blood is carried to the lungs by this vessel.

Aorta
The body's main artery carries blood from the heart to the rest of the body.

Superior vena cava
This large vein returns oxygen-poor blood from the upper body to the heart.

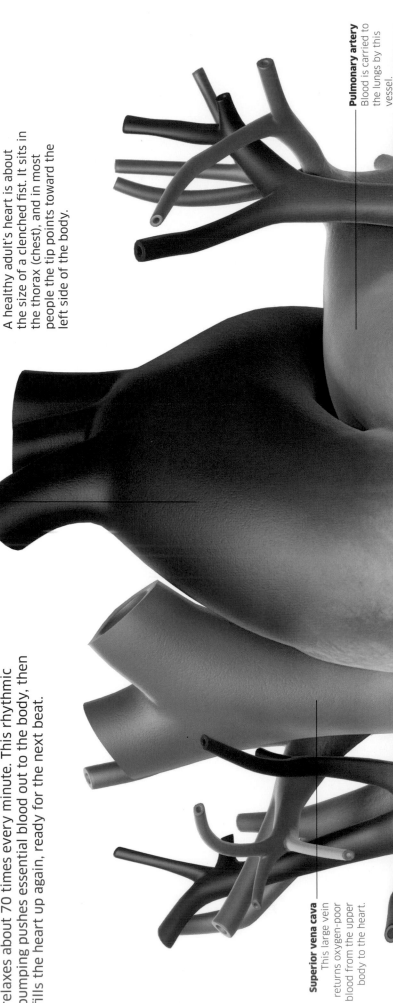

The **"lub-DUP" sound of a heartbeat is made** by different valves in the heart closing.

2.5 billion—the number of times the **heart will beat** in an average lifetime.

105

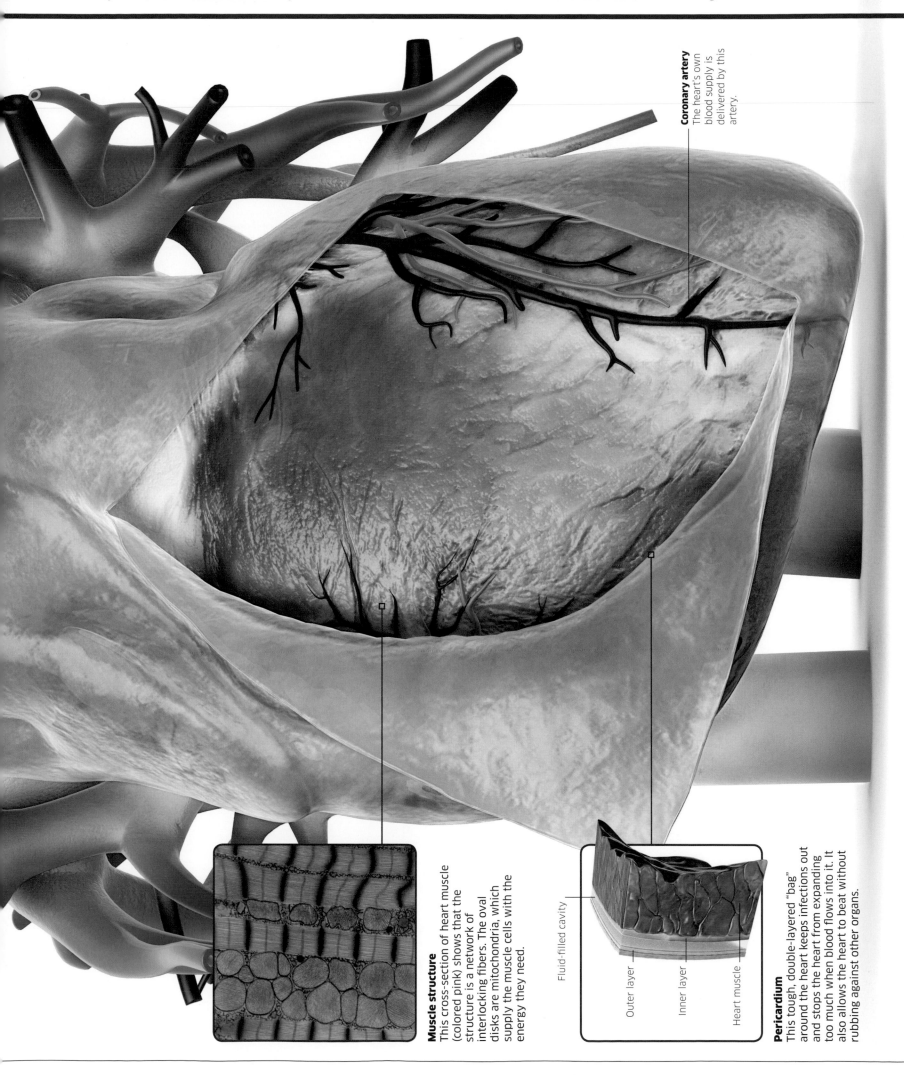

Coronary artery
The heart's own blood supply is delivered by this artery.

Muscle structure
This cross-section of heart muscle (colored pink) shows that the structure is a network of interlocking fibers. The oval disks are mitochondria, which supply the muscle cells with the energy they need.

Fluid-filled cavity

Outer layer

Inner layer

Heart muscle

Pericardium
This tough, double-layered "bag" around the heart keeps infections out and stops the heart from expanding too much when blood flows into it. It also allows the heart to beat without rubbing against other organs.

The heart **pumps blood** through the aorta at **1 mph (1.6 km/h)**.

How the heart works

Although a heartbeat lasts just one second, it has three stages. The rate at which the heart beats is controlled by a pacemaker located in the wall of the right atrium, which sends electrical signals to all parts of the heart.

Key
- Oxygen-rich blood
- Oxygen-poor blood

1 Blood flows into the atria The heart muscle is relaxed and blood enters the upper left and right heart chambers (atria).

- Blood flows in from the upper body
- Blood flows in from the left lung
- Left atrium fills with oxygen-rich blood
- Right atrium fills with blood
- Blood flows in from the lower body

2 From atria to ventricles The two atria contract and squeeze blood into the chambers below them (ventricles).

- Left atrium contracts
- Valve opens
- Ventricle fills with blood
- Right atrium contracts
- Valve opens and right ventricle fills up

3 Blood leaves the heart Last, the ventricles contract and force blood either to the lungs or around the body.

- Blood flows to left lung
- Ventricles contract, pushing blood out
- Blood flows to upper body
- Blood flows to right lung
- Blood flows to lower body

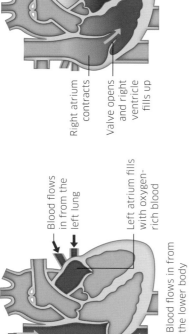

Inside the heart

Each side of the heart has a small upper space, called an atrium, and a larger space below, called a ventricle. During each heartbeat, blood is pumped from atrium to ventricle, then out of the heart. Valves open and close to make sure that the blood only flows in one direction.

Inside the heart

The heart is really two pumps in one, working in a continuous cycle. The right side pumps blood to the lungs, while the left side receives blood back from the lungs, then sends it around the rest of the body.

The heart pumps out about a cup of blood about 70 times a minute, speeding up when necessary to meet body cells' increased demand. Over a lifetime, the heart beats more than 2.5 billion times without resting.

Pulmonary veins
Oxygen-filled blood is carried from the lungs to the heart by these veins.

Pulmonary artery
This major blood vessel delivers oxygen-poor blood to the lungs.

Aorta
The aorta is the body's largest artery.

The average **adult man's heart** weighs around 12 ounces (340 g), about the same as a can of soup.

Water makes up about three-quarters of the weight of a human heart.

107

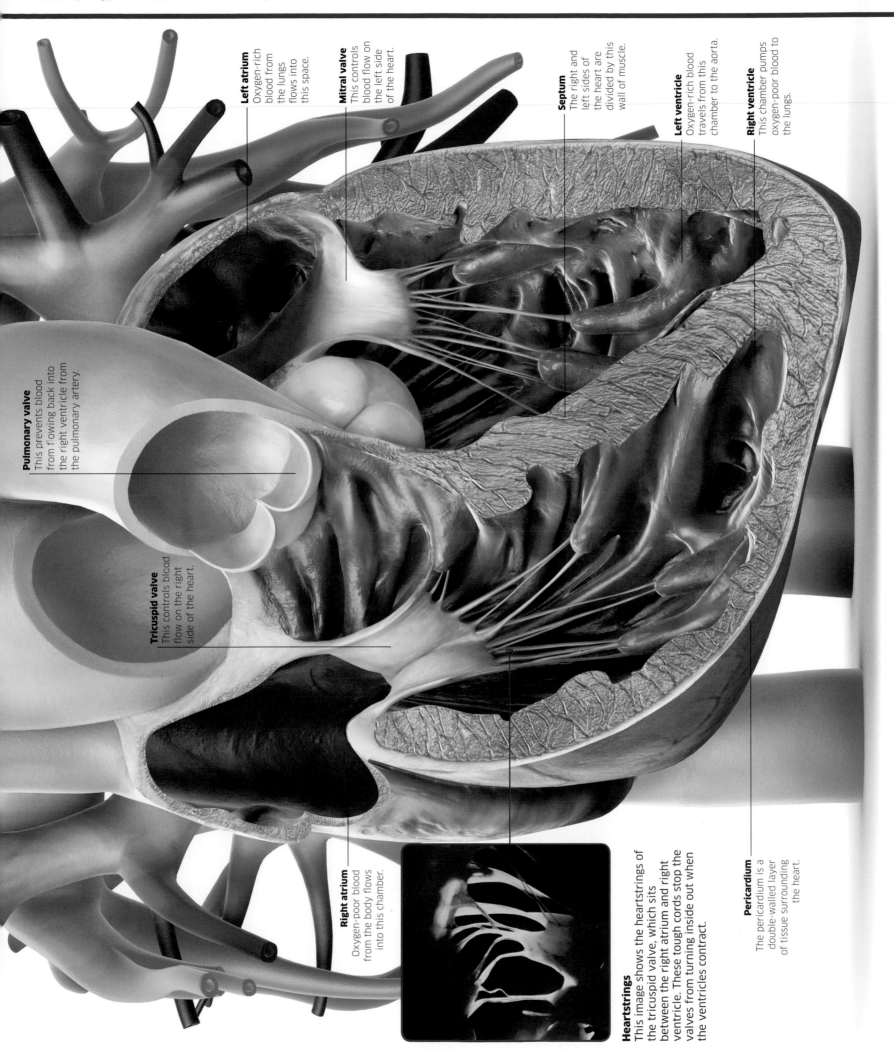

Left atrium
Oxygen-rich blood from the lungs flows into this space.

Mitral valve
This controls blood flow on the left side of the heart.

Septum
The right and left sides of the heart are divided by this wall of muscle.

Left ventricle
Oxygen-rich blood travels from this chamber to the aorta.

Right ventricle
This chamber pumps oxygen-poor blood to the lungs.

Pulmonary valve
This prevents blood from flowing back into the right ventricle from the pulmonary artery.

Tricuspid valve
This controls blood flow on the right side of the heart.

Right atrium
Oxygen-poor blood from the body flows into this chamber.

Heartstrings
This image shows the heartstrings of the tricuspid valve, which sits between the right atrium and right ventricle. These tough cords stop the valves from turning inside out when the ventricles contract.

Pericardium
The pericardium is a double-walled layer of tissue surrounding the heart.

Blood vessels

Pumped by the heart, blood circulates around the human body through millions of blood vessels. These deliver oxygen and other essential substances to the body's cells and tissues.

The three types of blood vessels are arteries, veins, and capillaries. Arteries carry oxygen-rich blood away from the heart. Veins carry oxygen-poor blood back to the heart. These two networks are linked by the smallest blood vessels, capillaries. Oxygen seeps through their thin walls into cells and tissues, while carbon dioxide goes in the other direction, from cells to capillaries.

Elastic layer
These layers allow the artery to stretch and bounce back into shape.

Membrane
A thin, protective covering surrounds the inner layer.

Muscle layer

Elastic layer

Inner layer
The smooth inner lining lets blood flow easily.

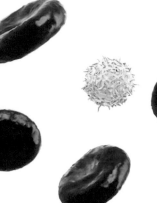

Blood
Blood is made up of three types of cells floating in a yellowish liquid called plasma.

Wall of muscle
Arteries' muscular walls stretch to cope with the high-pressure pulses of blood pumped out by the heart. The muscle contracts to make the artery narrower and reduce blood flow, and relaxes to widen it and allow blood to flow more freely.

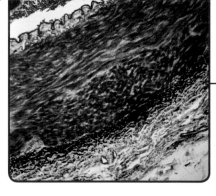

Muscle layer
The layer of muscle is thinner than an artery's.

Valve
Valves in the veins make sure the blood flows one way only.

Membrane

Arteries and veins

The walls of both arteries and veins are made up of three main layers—a tough outer coating, a wall of muscle, and a smooth, inner lining. Arteries have a thicker middle layer of muscle, to control the flow, or pressure, of blood. Pressure needs to be high enough to push blood around the system, but not so strong that it damages delicate capillaries.

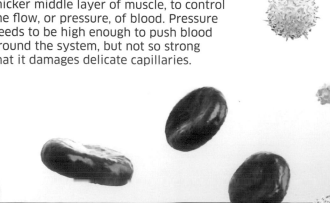

The **biggest arteries and veins** are the width of a thumb, but many capillaries can **only be seen** through a microscope.

98% of the **total length** of the blood vessel network is made up of capillaries.

109

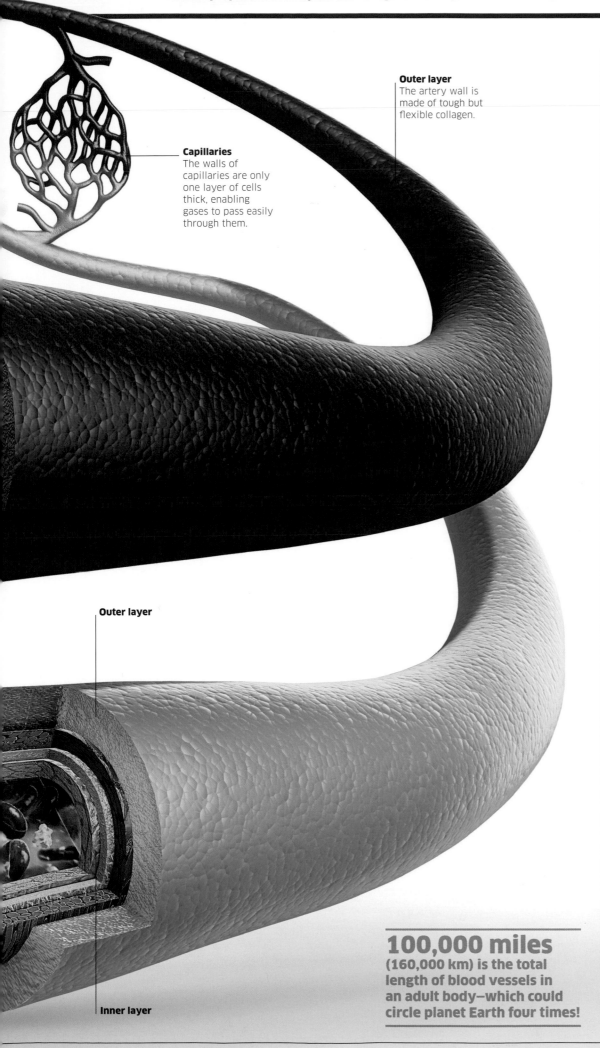

Capillaries
The walls of capillaries are only one layer of cells thick, enabling gases to pass easily through them.

Outer layer
The artery wall is made of tough but flexible collagen.

Outer layer

Inner layer

100,000 miles
(160,000 km) is the total length of blood vessels in an adult body—which could circle planet Earth four times!

Capillary connection

Capillaries connect arteries and veins. The wall of each capillary is formed from an ultra-thin layer of flattened cells. This lets gases and nutrients pass easily through the wall. Some capillaries also have pores, called fenestrations, to make the exchange even quicker.

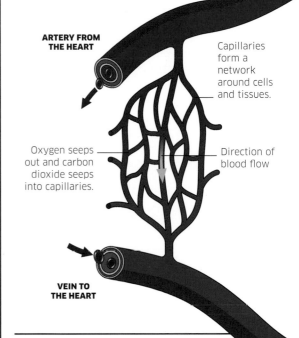

ARTERY FROM THE HEART

Capillaries form a network around cells and tissues.

Oxygen seeps out and carbon dioxide seeps into capillaries.

Direction of blood flow

VEIN TO THE HEART

Vein valves

The long veins in the leg have valves to make sure that blood travels up toward the heart and doesn't fall back down to the feet. When the muscles around the vein contract, they open the valve and push blood upward. When the surrounding muscles relax, the valves close to stop the blood flowing back down.

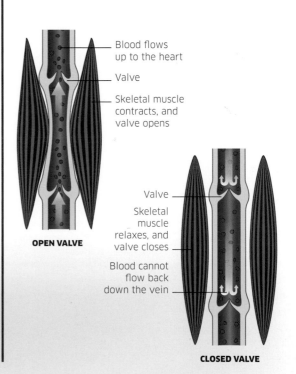

Blood flows up to the heart

Valve

Skeletal muscle contracts, and valve opens

Valve

Skeletal muscle relaxes, and valve closes

Blood cannot flow back down the vein

OPEN VALVE

CLOSED VALVE

BLOOD

Blood circulates endlessly through the human body to keep it alive. This fluid contains trillions of cells and countless chemicals, all floating in watery plasma. Blood is pumped by the heart through a network of blood vessels to deliver nutrients, oxygen, and other essential substances to cells. Blood also transports waste, helps keep the body temperature steady, and fights germs.

⊙ TRANSPORTATION SYSTEM

Blood is constantly moving oxygen, nutrients, proteins, and waste products around the body. Some of these help cells grow and function, others are converted into new substances, and the rest are removed from the body.

Oxygen carrier

Red blood cells contain a protein called hemoglobin. Oxygen that enters the blood in the lungs attaches to this hemoglobin and is later released into the body's tissues. It is hemoglobin that gives blood its red color—and the more oxygen hemoglobin carries, the brighter red it becomes.

Oxygen molecule

Hemoglobin molecule

Oxygen bonded with hemoglobin molecules

Oxygen released into tissue cell

1 When red blood cells pass through the lungs, hemoglobin binds with oxygen.

2 Red blood cells carrying oxygen travel where they are needed in the body.

3 When the red blood cell arrives at its destination, th hemoglobin releases oxygen.

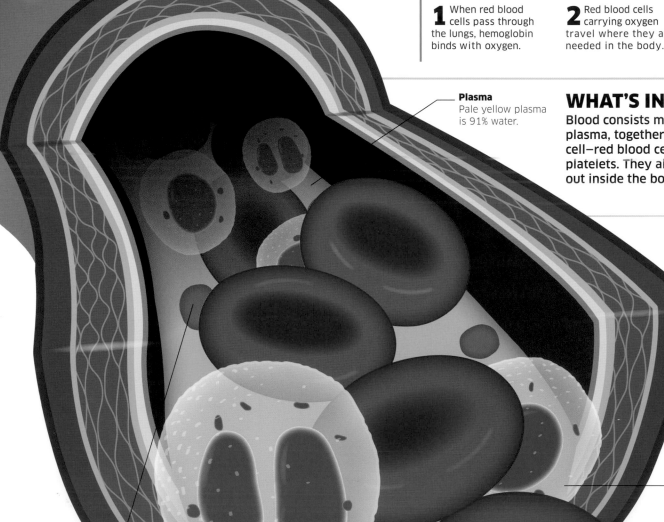

Plasma
Pale yellow plasma is 91% water.

WHAT'S IN BLOOD?

Blood consists mostly of a fluid called plasma, together with three types of blood cell—red blood cells, white blood cells, and platelets. They all have different jobs to carry out inside the body.

Blood breakdown

Plasma is made of water with substances dissolved in it, including salts, nutrients, and hormones. Red blood cells take oxygen to cells and remove carbon dioxide. White blood cells hunt and kill bacteria and viruses, while platelets repair damage by plugging a wound and helping blood to clot (thicken).

White blood cells
These cells are the largest in the blood.

Platelets
Rounded platelets become spiked when blood clots.

Red blood cells
Just under half of blood is made up of red blood cells.

Transportation superhighway

The bloodstream provides an efficient delivery service, delivering essential fuel and oxygen to cells, and at the same time taking away waste and toxins to keep cells and tissues healthy.

Oxygen
Red cells pick up oxygen in the lungs and deliver it to all the cells in the body.

Nutrients
Nutrients enter the blood from the digestive system and are delivered around the whole body.

Waste products
Waste is delivered to the liver for recycling, or to the kidneys to be made into urine.

Hormones
The blood delivers chemical messengers, called hormones, to specific destinations.

Body defenses
White cells are carried to fight germs. Platelets are delivered to wound sites.

Carbon dioxide
Carbon dioxide made by cells is delivered to the lungs to be breathed out of the body.

ONE BLOOD CELL
GOES THROUGH THE
HEART AND
AROUND THE BODY
1,000 TIMES A DAY.

HOW BLOOD CLOTS

After a cut, blood seeps from the wound, triggering an immediate repair process. The blood cells take action immediately. They stop the leak, form a plug, and destroy harmful bacteria. A scab forms, and the clot dissolves when the wound has healed.

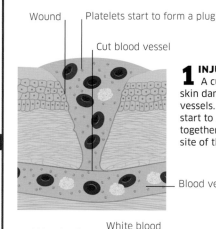

Wound — Platelets start to form a plug
Cut blood vessel
Blood vessel

1 INJURY
A cut in the skin damages blood vessels. Platelets start to group together at the site of the injury.

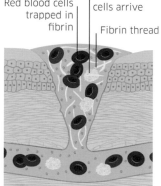

Red blood cells trapped in fibrin — White blood cells arrive
Fibrin thread

2 PLUG
The platelets release chemicals that make fibrin, a sticky threadlike protein. Red cells get stuck in the threads, forming a plug. White blood cells arrive to hunt for germs.

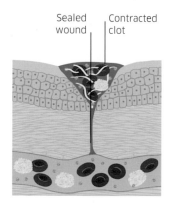

Sealed wound — Contracted clot

3 CLOT
The fibrin threads contract, binding red blood cells and platelets together in a sticky clot, which closes the wound.

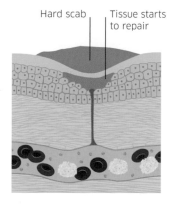

Hard scab — Tissue starts to repair

4 SCAB
The clot near the skin's surface dries out to form a protective scab, which covers the healing wound.

LIFE OF A RED BLOOD CELL

All blood cells are made in red bone marrow. Almost all the bones of young people contain red bone marrow. For adults, it is only found in the skull, ribs, shoulder blades, hips, and the ends of long bones.

Cell cycle

A red blood cell lives for up to 120 days before being swallowed by a type of white blood cell, called a macrophage, in the liver or spleen.

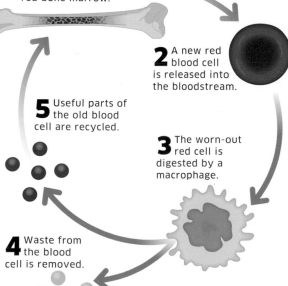

1 New blood cells are made by red bone marrow.

2 A new red blood cell is released into the bloodstream.

3 The worn-out red cell is digested by a macrophage.

4 Waste from the blood cell is removed.

5 Useful parts of the old blood cell are recycled.

BLOOD TYPES

There are four main types of blood—A, B, AB, and O. The type mostly depends on special markers on the surface of red blood cells, called antigens. These help the body to identify blood cells that do not belong to you. Patients who need a blood transfusion must receive the right blood type, or the body will reject the donated blood, making them even more unwell.

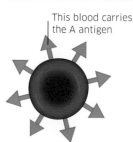

This blood carries the A antigen

Type A
This can be donated to those with A or AB blood types.

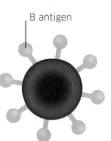

B antigen

Type B
This can be donated to those with type B or AB blood.

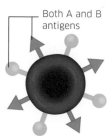

Both A and B antigens

Type AB
This blood can only be donated to other people with the AB blood type.

Type O
These blood cells have no antigens and so can be donated to people of any blood type.

112 chest and back ○ LUNGS

2,900 gal (11,000 liters)—the **amount of air** a typical adult breathes in and out in **one day**.

Lungs

The two lungs take up most of the space in the chest. Their key function is to get oxygen into, and waste gases out of, the bloodstream. That oxygen is used by the body's cells to release energy, a process that produces waste carbon dioxide.

Breathing draws air rich in oxygen into the lungs through the airways, then pushes air containing carbon dioxide in the opposite direction. Lungs are spongy because they are packed with branching, air-filled tubes that get narrower and narrower before ending in tiny air sacs (alveoli). It is here that oxygen is swapped for carbon dioxide.

Inside the lungs

In the main picture, the left lung has been opened up to show its structure. The lungs' system of airways is called the bronchial tree, because it resembles an upside-down tree. The trachea is the trunk, the bronchi are its branches, and the bronchioles are its twigs.

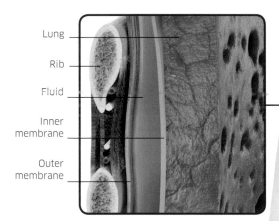

Lung
Rib
Fluid
Inner membrane
Outer membrane

Sliding membranes
Two membranes, called pleurae (one is called a pleura), surround the lungs. A thin layer of fluid between them allows them to slide over one another to ensure the lungs expand and shrink smoothly during breathing.

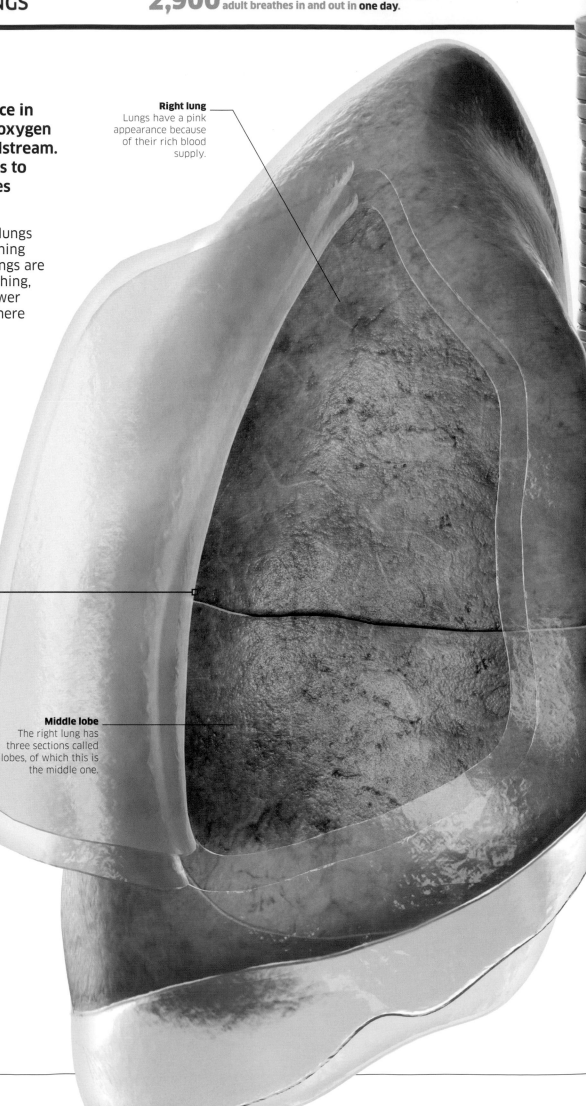

Right lung
Lungs have a pink appearance because of their rich blood supply.

Middle lobe
The right lung has three sections called lobes, of which this is the middle one.

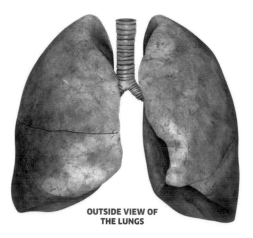

OUTSIDE VIEW OF THE LUNGS

On average, a 10-year-old **breathes in and out** about 20 times every minute.

1,500 miles (2,400 km)—the **total length** of all the lungs' airways (bronchi and bronchioles) put together.

113

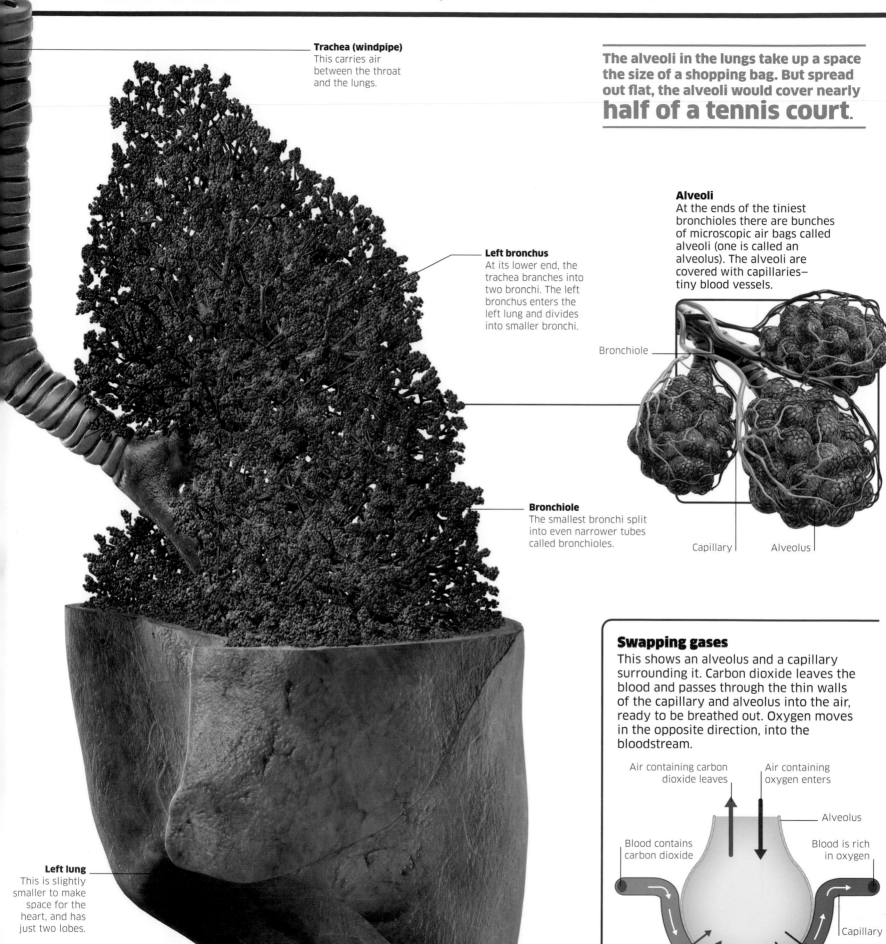

Trachea (windpipe)
This carries air between the throat and the lungs.

Left bronchus
At its lower end, the trachea branches into two bronchi. The left bronchus enters the left lung and divides into smaller bronchi.

Bronchiole
The smallest bronchi split into even narrower tubes called bronchioles.

Left lung
This is slightly smaller to make space for the heart, and has just two lobes.

There are around 300 million alveoli in each lung.

The alveoli in the lungs take up a space the size of a shopping bag. But spread out flat, the alveoli would cover nearly **half of a tennis court.**

Alveoli
At the ends of the tiniest bronchioles there are bunches of microscopic air bags called alveoli (one is called an alveolus). The alveoli are covered with capillaries–tiny blood vessels.

Bronchiole

Capillary

Alveolus

Swapping gases
This shows an alveolus and a capillary surrounding it. Carbon dioxide leaves the blood and passes through the thin walls of the capillary and alveolus into the air, ready to be breathed out. Oxygen moves in the opposite direction, into the bloodstream.

Air containing carbon dioxide leaves

Air containing oxygen enters

Alveolus

Blood contains carbon dioxide

Blood is rich in oxygen

Capillary

Carbon dioxide passes from the blood into the alveolus

Oxygen passes from the alveolus into the blood vessel

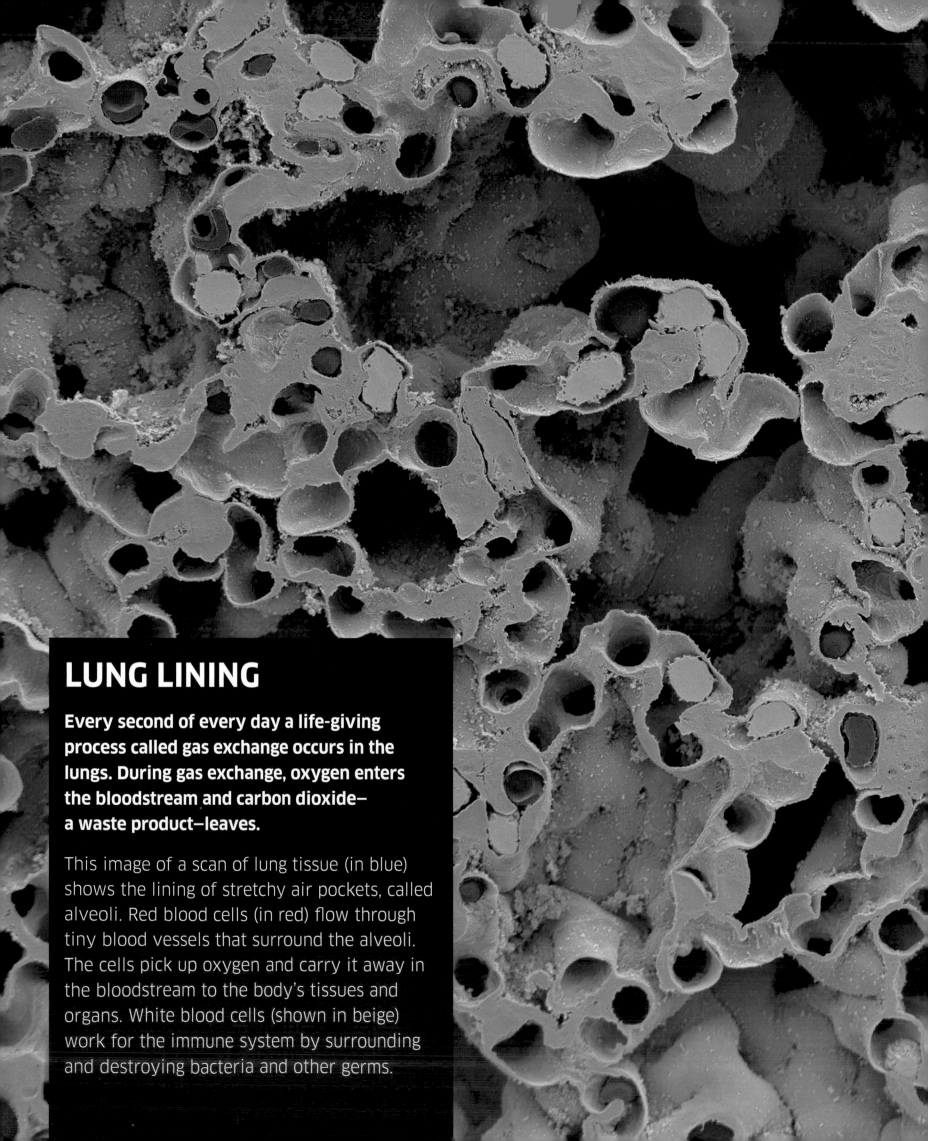

LUNG LINING

Every second of every day a life-giving process called gas exchange occurs in the lungs. During gas exchange, oxygen enters the bloodstream and carbon dioxide—a waste product—leaves.

This image of a scan of lung tissue (in blue) shows the lining of stretchy air pockets, called alveoli. Red blood cells (in red) flow through tiny blood vessels that surround the alveoli. The cells pick up oxygen and carry it away in the bloodstream to the body's tissues and organs. White blood cells (shown in beige) work for the immune system by surrounding and destroying bacteria and other germs.

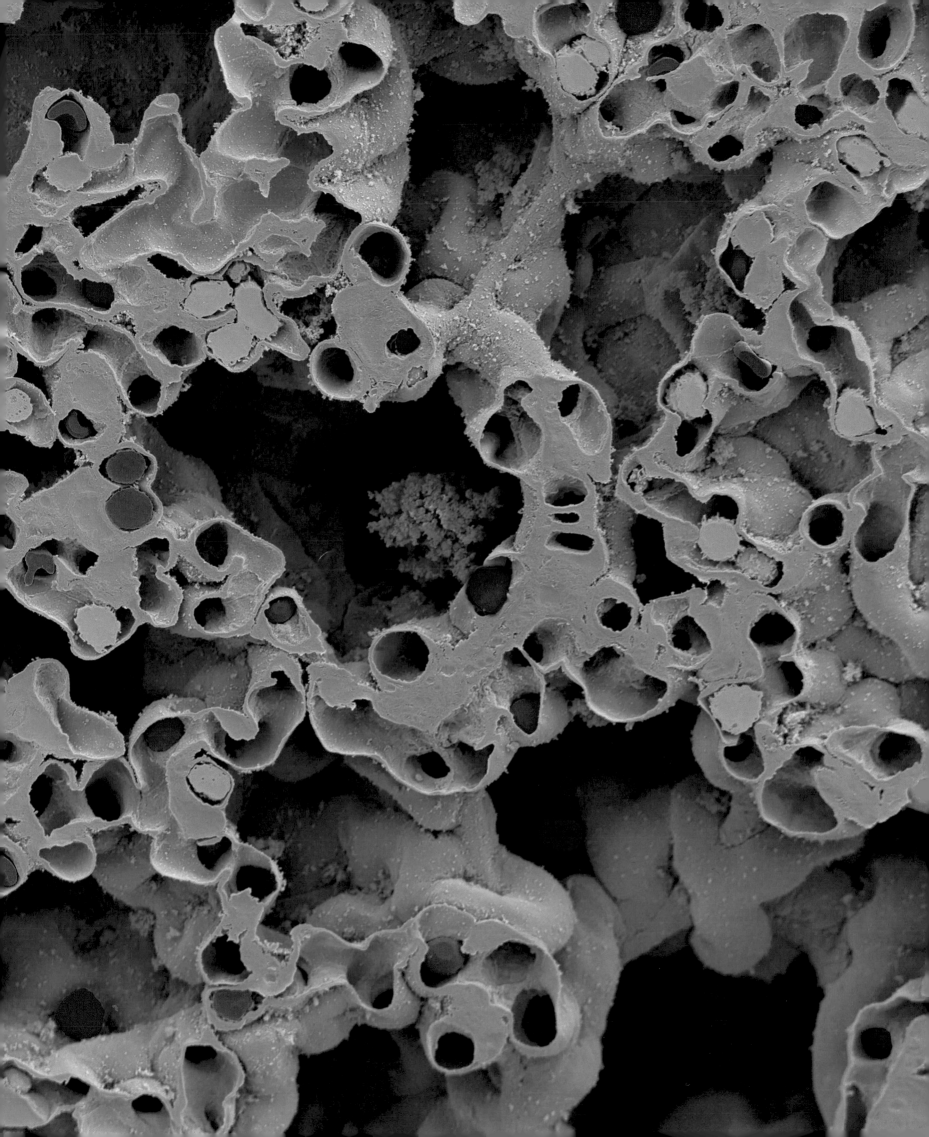

BREATHING AND SPEECH

Humans need to breathe almost constantly in order to provide all the body's cells with the oxygen they need to keep working. We don't need to remember to breathe—the brain makes sure we do it automatically, even when we're asleep. But we can also take control of our breathing, so that we can perform actions such as talking, singing, playing a wind instrument, or just blowing out the candles on a birthday cake. The breath is used for other actions, too, such as sneezing and coughing.

FUELING THE MUSCLES

With each breath we take, oxygen is delivered to the muscle cells to provide the energy that powers movement. The faster the body moves or the harder it works, the more oxygen the cells need. So our breathing speeds up in order to take in, then deliver, more oxygen to where it is needed.

A PERSON WHO LIVES **TO THE AGE OF 80 WILL TAKE ABOUT 700 MILLION** BREATHS IN THEIR LIFETIME.

HOW BREATHING WORKS

When the lungs take a breath in, they expand—but they can't do this on their own. To make them suck in air, the lungs are pulled open by the muscles around them. Then, to breathe out, the muscles relax and the lungs become smaller again, so air is squeezed back out. The muscles used for breathing are the diaphragm, which is below the lungs, and the intercostal muscles, between the ribs.

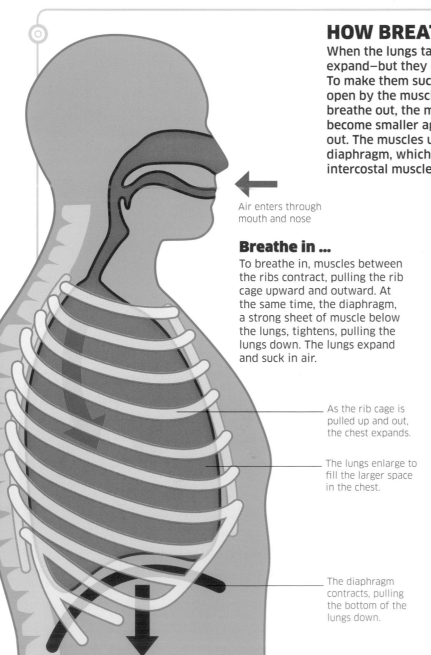

Air enters through mouth and nose

Breathe in ...
To breathe in, muscles between the ribs contract, pulling the rib cage upward and outward. At the same time, the diaphragm, a strong sheet of muscle below the lungs, tightens, pulling the lungs down. The lungs expand and suck in air.

As the rib cage is pulled up and out, the chest expands.

The lungs enlarge to fill the larger space in the chest.

The diaphragm contracts, pulling the bottom of the lungs down.

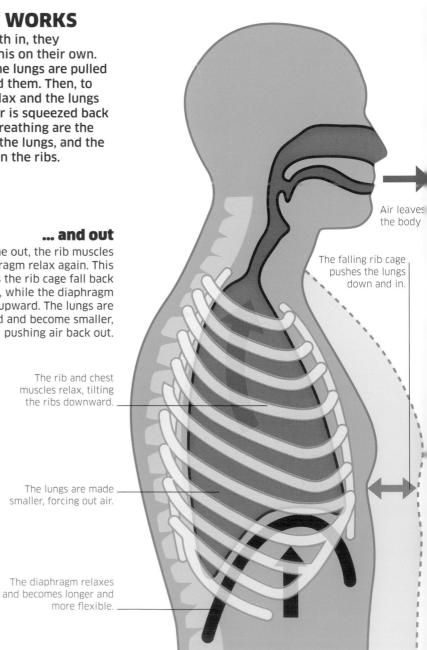

... and out
To breathe out, the rib muscles and diaphragm relax again. This makes the rib cage fall back down, while the diaphragm moves upward. The lungs are squeezed and become smaller, pushing air back out.

Air leaves the body

The falling rib cage pushes the lungs down and in.

The rib and chest muscles relax, tilting the ribs downward.

The lungs are made smaller, forcing out air.

The diaphragm relaxes and becomes longer and more flexible.

Breathing rates

Breathing rate, or speed, depends on a person's age, size, health, and fitness level as well as on what they are doing. This shows a typical adult's breathing rates when they are taking part in different activities.

Reading
15 breaths per minute

Walking
20 breaths per minute

Jogging
40 breaths per minute

Running fast
Up to 70 breaths per minute

Fitness and breathing

When we exercise, we breathe heavily to take in extra oxygen. With regular exercise, the lungs increase their ability to hold air, and our bodies get more efficient at using the oxygen they take in. This means we don't have to breathe as fast to get the same amount of oxygen to the muscles.

Fighting fit

The more physically fit a person is, the easier they will find it to work out in the gym, dance, or run for a bus, without panting or getting out of breath.

UNUSUAL BREATHS

Normal breathing happens in a regular, repeated pattern. Sometimes, though, there's a different kind of breath, such as a cough, sneeze, or hiccup.

Sneezing

When something irritating gets inside the nose, the brain's response is to trigger a sneeze to clear the air passages. After a sharp breath, muscles in the chest and abdomen contract to force the air back out, carrying the intruding particles with it.

Snoring

Sometimes, the breaths we take while asleep can be heard—in fact, the sound can be loud enough to wake the sleeper. Snoring is caused by relaxed tissues vibrating as air passes over them.

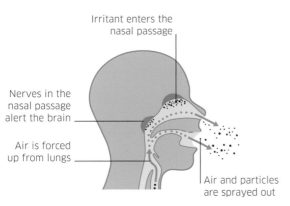

Irritant enters the nasal passage

Nerves in the nasal passage alert the brain

Air is forced up from lungs

Air and particles are sprayed out

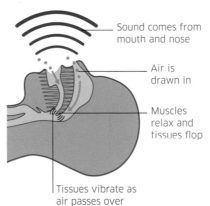

Sound comes from mouth and nose

Air is drawn in

Muscles relax and tissues flop

Tissues vibrate as air passes over

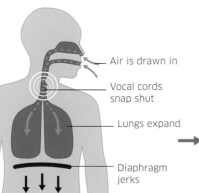

Air is drawn in

Vocal cords snap shut

Lungs expand

Diaphragm jerks

Hiccups

Hiccups happen when nerves around the diaphragm get irritated, for example, by eating quickly. The diaphragm jerks, making the lungs suddenly suck in air. This makes the vocal cords snap shut, making a "hic!" sound.

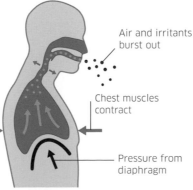

Air and irritants burst out

Chest muscles contract

Pressure from diaphragm

Coughing

Coughing occurs when the body tries to clear something irritating, such as smoke, from the airways. The vocal cords close, so that no air can get through. Then the lungs push air against the cords so they suddenly open, releasing an explosive breath.

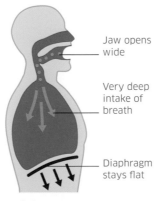

Jaw opens wide

Very deep intake of breath

Diaphragm stays flat

Yawning

A yawn is a deep breath with the mouth wide open, stretching the eardrums and muscles around the throat. Though we often yawn when we're tired, no one knows exactly what yawning is for. It may help to cool the brain, or help to keep you awake and alert.

THE HUMAN VOICE

In addition to supplying the body with oxygen, breathing is also essential for another job: making sounds using the voice. Humans are social beings, so communicating with those around us is very important. We use our voices to deliver information or express our feelings through talking, laughing, or even singing.

How speaking works

As air is breathed out, it passes through the voice box (larynx), below the back of the tongue. Stretched across the larynx are two flexible membranes called the vocal cords. When we want to speak, muscles pull the vocal cords closer together. Air pushes through the small gap, making the cords vibrate to produce a sound. This sound is shaped into a series of words by moving the mouth, lips, and tongue into different positions.

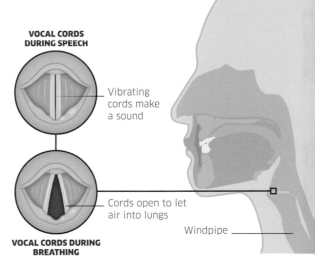

VOCAL CORDS DURING SPEECH

Vibrating cords make a sound

Cords open to let air into lungs

Windpipe

VOCAL CORDS DURING BREATHING

High and low pitch

People's voices have different tones and pitches. Men tend to have deeper voices, as their vocal cords are long and thick, producing a lower sound. Women have higher-pitched voices, and children's are the highest of all, because their vocal cords are much shorter.

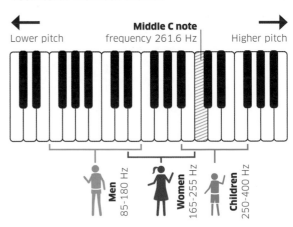

Lower pitch

Middle C note
frequency 261.6 Hz

Higher pitch

Men
85-180 Hz

Women
165-255 Hz

Children
250-400 Hz

Range of the human voice

We measure pitch in hertz (Hz), which describes how fast the vocal cords vibrate per second (frequency).

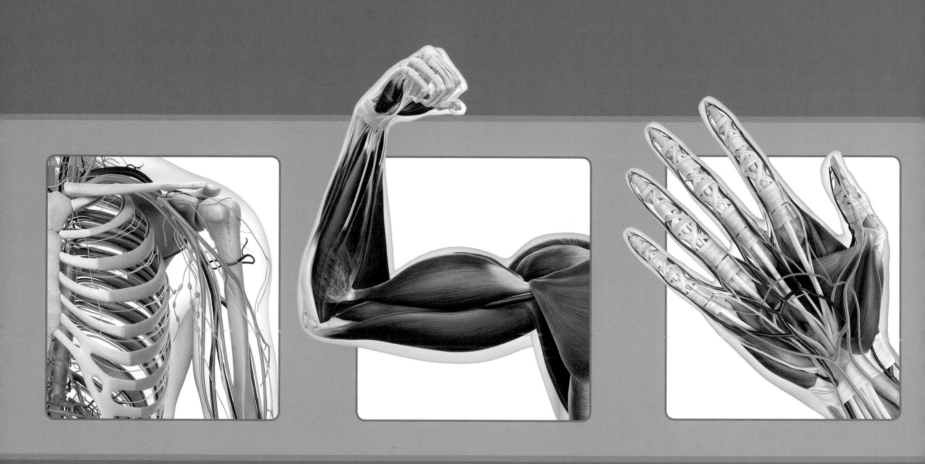

ARMS AND HANDS

The upper limbs are the body's most flexible parts. Shoulder and elbow joints allow the arms to move in all directions. Attached to the arms are our versatile hands. They have countless capabilities, allowing us to touch, lift, throw, and grip. A team of muscles, tendons, and ligaments move and support these limbs.

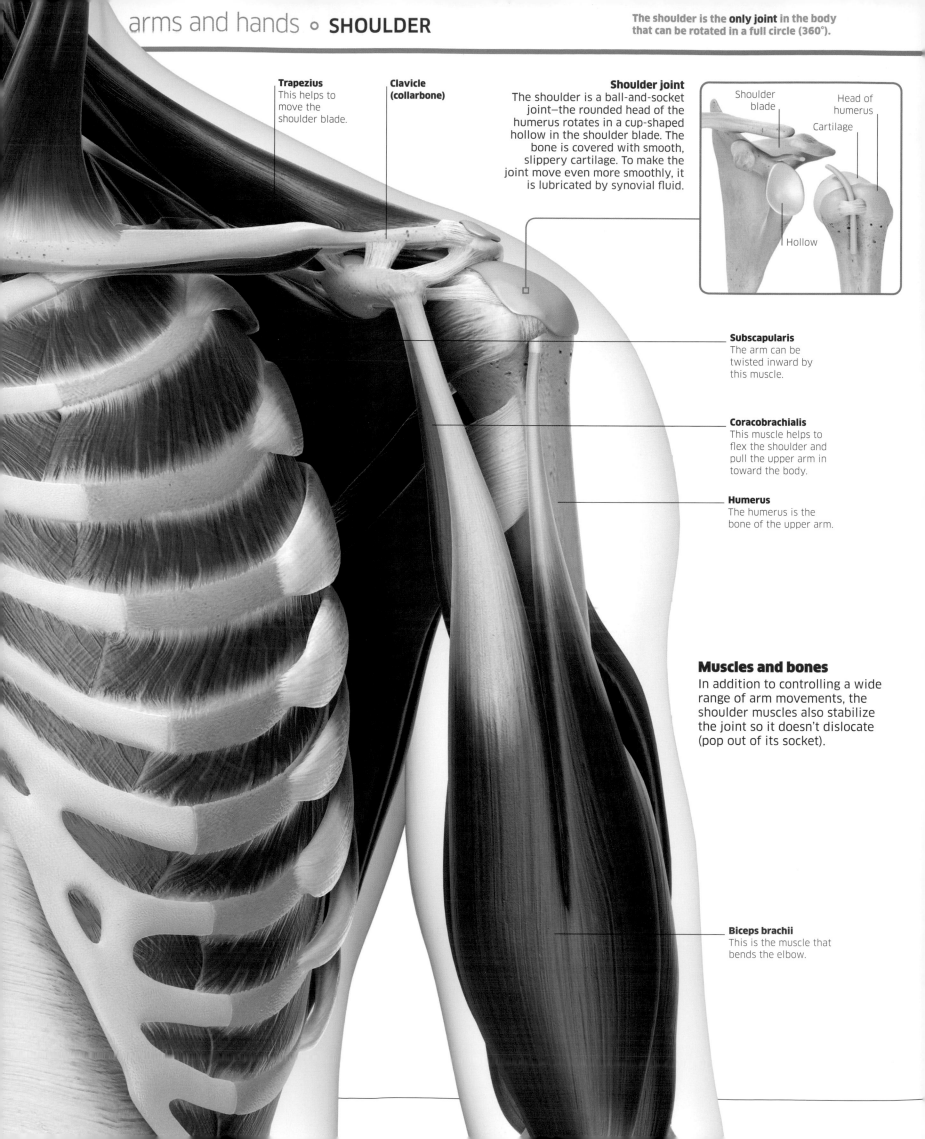

The shoulder is the **only joint** in the body that can be rotated in a full circle (360°).

Trapezius
This helps to move the shoulder blade.

Clavicle (collarbone)

Shoulder joint
The shoulder is a ball-and-socket joint—the rounded head of the humerus rotates in a cup-shaped hollow in the shoulder blade. The bone is covered with smooth, slippery cartilage. To make the joint move even more smoothly, it is lubricated by synovial fluid.

Shoulder blade

Head of humerus

Cartilage

Hollow

Subscapularis
The arm can be twisted inward by this muscle.

Coracobrachialis
This muscle helps to flex the shoulder and pull the upper arm in toward the body.

Humerus
The humerus is the bone of the upper arm.

Muscles and bones
In addition to controlling a wide range of arm movements, the shoulder muscles also stabilize the joint so it doesn't dislocate (pop out of its socket).

Biceps brachii
This is the muscle that bends the elbow.

7 **different muscles** connect the arm bone to the shoulder blade.

105 mph (169 kph) is the **fastest ever recorded throw** of a ball—by a baseball pitcher in 2010.

Shoulder

The shoulder joint—where the upper arm and shoulder blade meet—is the most flexible joint in the body. This mobility, combined with long arms and grasping hands, enables humans to perform a huge range of arm movements.

The bony framework of the shoulder joint is formed by three bones—the shoulder blade (scapula), the collarbone (clavicle), and the top of the upper arm bone (humerus). Deep muscles make the joint stable, while an outer layer of muscles pulls on the bones to move the joint.

Axillary artery
The job of this artery is to supply blood to the shoulder and arm.

Axillary vein
The function of this vein is to carry blood from the arm to the heart.

Lymph node
Lymph nodes trap toxins and germs so they can be eliminated from the body.

Median nerve
The muscles that bend the hands and fingers are controlled by this nerve.

Blood, nerves, and lymph nodes

The shoulder area is rich in lymph nodes, which play a major role in fighting infections. It's also the point at which major blood vessels branch off to supply blood to the arms and hands.

Throwing a ball

This sequence shows the range of muscles, and the amount the shoulder rotates in order to perform a throwing action.

1 **Preparing to throw**
Muscles in the shoulder, back, and arm contract to raise the arm and pull it backward.

2 **Snapping forward**
Just before throwing, the chest and upper arm muscles contract to lift the arm up and forward, rotating the shoulder joint.

3 **Following through**
As the ball is released, chest and side muscles contract to pull the arm down and around the body, rotating the shoulder farther.

Arm and elbow

Walking on two legs has freed our arms up to evolve a huge range of movements. The shoulder joint is the basis for arm flexibility, but the hinged elbow joint provides even more movement.

The three bones that form the elbow joint—the humerus, ulna, and radius—interact with one another so that the forearm forms a hinge with the upper arm, and can also rotate almost 180°. These different kinds of movement are helpful when we eat, for example—the hand can reach out to pick an apple, twist it off its stem, then bring the fruit to the mouth.

Muscles and bones

Most of the muscles that control the wrist and hand are found in the forearm. Muscles that cross the elbow joint either bend or straighten the elbow.

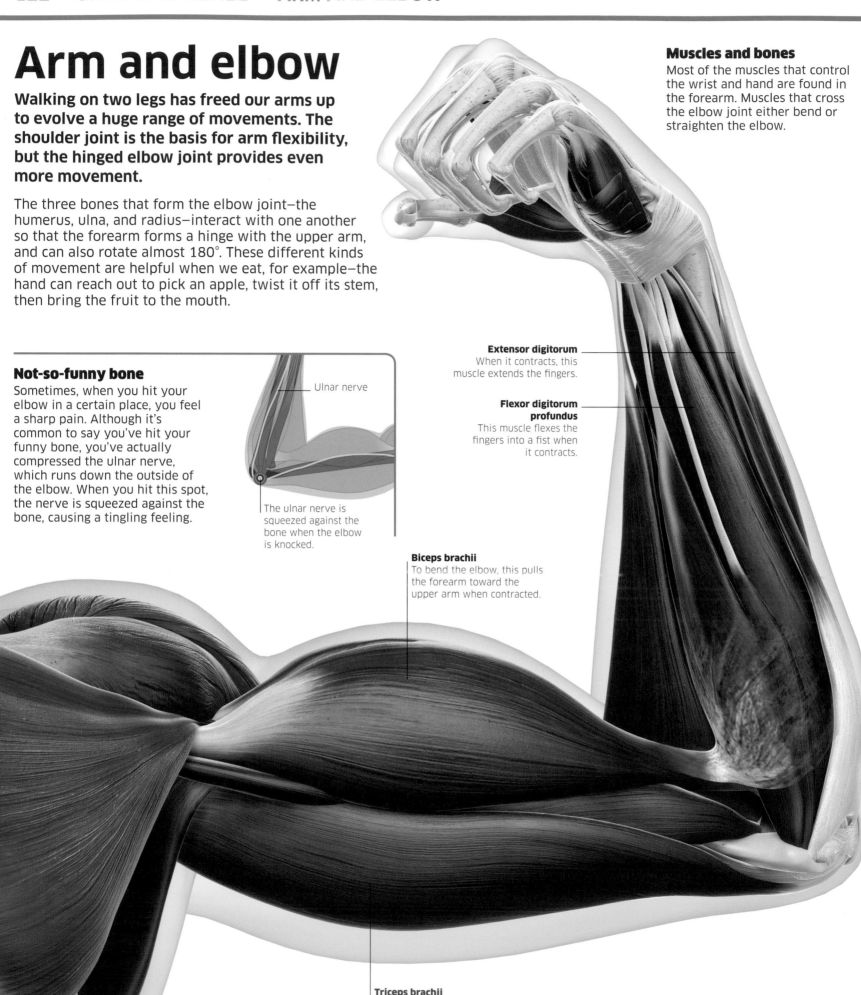

Not-so-funny bone

Sometimes, when you hit your elbow in a certain place, you feel a sharp pain. Although it's common to say you've hit your funny bone, you've actually compressed the ulnar nerve, which runs down the outside of the elbow. When you hit this spot, the nerve is squeezed against the bone, causing a tingling feeling.

Ulnar nerve

The ulnar nerve is squeezed against the bone when the elbow is knocked.

Extensor digitorum
When it contracts, this muscle extends the fingers.

Flexor digitorum profundus
This muscle flexes the fingers into a fist when it contracts.

Biceps brachii
To bend the elbow, this pulls the forearm toward the upper arm when contracted.

Triceps brachii
The elbow straightens when this muscle is contracted.

50% of all **adult bone breakages** happen to one of the arm bones.

The bony lump at the **very tip of the elbow** is called the olecranon (pronounced oh-LEK-ra-non).

123

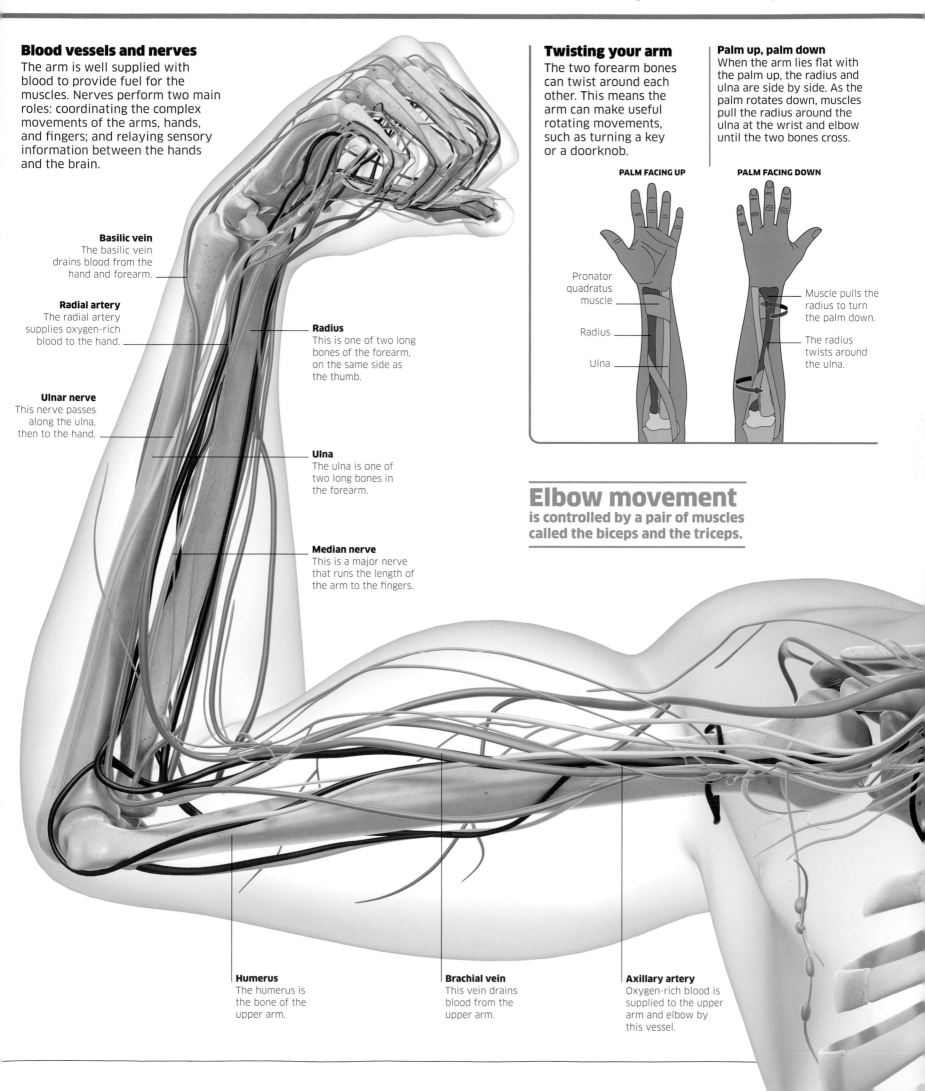

Blood vessels and nerves

The arm is well supplied with blood to provide fuel for the muscles. Nerves perform two main roles: coordinating the complex movements of the arms, hands, and fingers; and relaying sensory information between the hands and the brain.

Basilic vein
The basilic vein drains blood from the hand and forearm.

Radial artery
The radial artery supplies oxygen-rich blood to the hand.

Ulnar nerve
This nerve passes along the ulna, then to the hand.

Radius
This is one of two long bones of the forearm, on the same side as the thumb.

Ulna
The ulna is one of two long bones in the forearm.

Median nerve
This is a major nerve that runs the length of the arm to the fingers.

Twisting your arm

The two forearm bones can twist around each other. This means the arm can make useful rotating movements, such as turning a key or a doorknob.

Palm up, palm down

When the arm lies flat with the palm up, the radius and ulna are side by side. As the palm rotates down, muscles pull the radius around the ulna at the wrist and elbow until the two bones cross.

PALM FACING UP

PALM FACING DOWN

Pronator quadratus muscle

Radius

Ulna

Muscle pulls the radius to turn the palm down.

The radius twists around the ulna.

Elbow movement
is controlled by a pair of muscles called the biceps and the triceps.

Humerus
The humerus is the bone of the upper arm.

Brachial vein
This vein drains blood from the upper arm.

Axillary artery
Oxygen-rich blood is supplied to the upper arm and elbow by this vessel.

Flexible joints

Wherever two or more bones meet, they form a joint. Some of these joints aren't moveable, such as the skull, but most are flexible, allowing some movement between the bones.

Joints give skeletons flexibility for all the different ways we move our bodies—from running and jumping to picking up objects, or sitting down. It is still the muscles that make the movement happen by pulling on the bones, but the kind of movement each joint makes depends on the shape of the ends of the bones that meet.

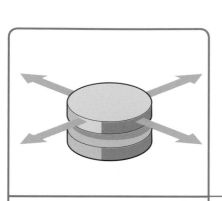

Plane joint
Also called a gliding joint, this is where two flat-ended bones slide against each other. This type of joint is found in the ankles and wrists.

Fixed joint
The different bones of an adult's skull form fixed joints. They are securely fused together and don't allow any movement.

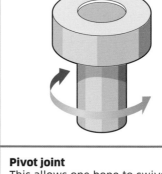

Pivot joint
This allows one bone to swivel around another. In the forearm, the ulna forms a pivot with the radius just below the elbow, allowing the arm to twist palm-up or palm-down.

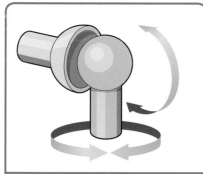

Ball and socket
The ball-shaped head of one bone fits into the cup shape of another bone. This type of joint allows for a wide range of movement and is found in the shoulder and the hip.

Head and neck
A pivot joint at the top of the backbone allows the head to swivel from side to side.

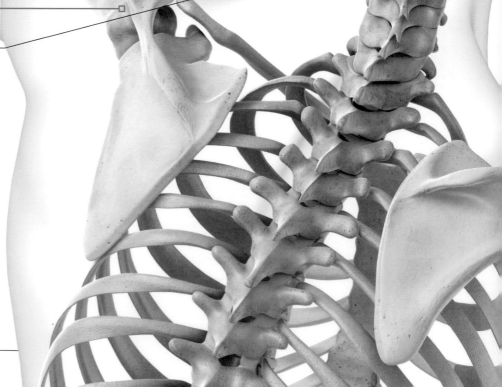

Types of joint

There are six different types of moving joint in the body. Each of them allows a different range of movements. The arms and hands contain examples of all of these types of joint, but they are found in other parts of the body, too.

The only human bone that doesn't have a joint is the **hyoid bone** of the lower jaw.

Cartilage moving against cartilage is **eight times more slippery** than **ice**.

125

Inside a joint

The six types of joint described here are all synovial joints. They allow movement while protecting the bones from damage when they move against each other. Bone ends are covered with smooth, slippery cartilage, which helps reduce friction. The space between the bones is filled with a liquid called synovial fluid. This lubricates the joint and provides a liquid cushion between the bones. Non-synovial joints, such as the sutures of the skull, do not move.

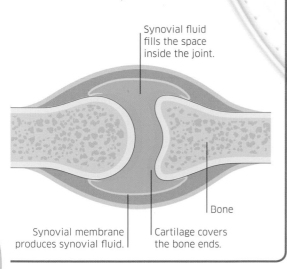

Synovial fluid fills the space inside the joint.

Bone

Synovial membrane produces synovial fluid.

Cartilage covers the bone ends.

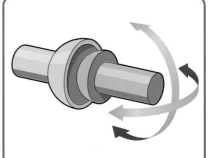

Condyloid joint

This joint is found in the knuckles and toes. An oval, rounded bone fits into an oval, cup-shaped bone. This enables side-to-side and up-and-down movement, so you can spread your fingers apart and move them up and down.

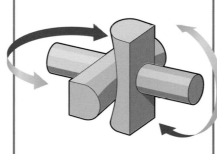

Saddle joint

This is found at the base of the thumb where two U-shaped bones meet, allowing the thumb to rotate in two directions. This enables the thumb to touch each fingertip, as well as sweep across the palm of the hand.

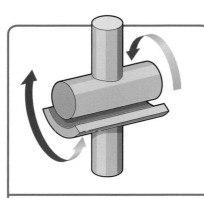

Hinge joint

Just as a door hinge only allows a door to open or close, the hinge joint at the elbow lets the arm bend and straighten. The knee is also a hinge joint.

300 is the approximate number of joints in the body.

MIGHTY MUSCLES

Every movement you make uses muscles. They allow you to smile, walk, lift, and run. Muscles also move blood around the body and food through the digestive system. Some muscles must be ordered by the brain to move, while others work without us even thinking about them.

MUSCLE STRUCTURE

Muscles are packed full of parallel bundles of fibers. These consist of many cells, called myocytes. When they contract, the muscle shortens and creates a pulling action. There are three types of muscle in the body.

Skeletal muscle
This type of muscle pulls on bones to move the skeleton. Skeletal muscle is made of long, cylindrical cells called muscle fibers, each crammed with threads called myofibrils. These contain long protein filaments that slide over each other to make muscles contract.

Blood vessels supply oxygen to muscle fibers.

Bundle of muscle fibers

Myofibril

MUSCLE MOTION

Muscles work by contracting, which means they shorten. As a muscle contracts, it pulls on whatever it is attached to. In general, the larger the muscle, the more pulling power it has. Muscles can pull but not push, which is why they work in pairs, acting in opposite directions. When one muscle pulls, its partner muscle relaxes.

BUILD UP YOUR MUSCLES **BY GETTING A GOOD NIGHT'S REST. DURING** DEEP SLEEP, HORMONES **ARE RELEASED THAT** STIMULATE THE MUSCLES TO GROW AND REPAIR THEMSELVES.

Pulling together

All the skeletal muscles work in pairs. In the upper arm, the biceps and triceps muscles work as a team to bend and straighten the arm. The triceps pulls the forearm down, and the biceps pulls it up again.

Triceps
When the triceps muscle contracts, it straightens the arm at the elbow. The biceps, opposite the triceps, is relaxed.

Muscle attachment
The triceps is attached to the shoulder blade at this point.

Firmly fixed
The biceps is attached to the shoulder blade at these two points.

Biceps

Biceps
When the biceps contracts, it pulls the forearm bones up and bends the arm. The triceps muscle is relaxed.

Triceps

Tendons
Muscles are firmly attached to bones by tendons.

ELBOW STRAIGHTENED

ELBOW BENT

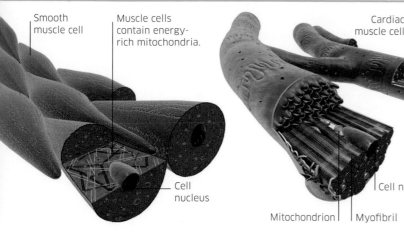

Smooth muscle cell

Muscle cells contain energy-rich mitochondria.

Cell nucleus

Smooth muscle
Arranged in muscular sheets, smooth muscle makes things move along inside the body. For example, it mixes food in the stomach and pushes it through the intestines.

Cardiac muscle cell

Cell nucleus

Mitochondrion | Myofibril

Heart muscle
This type of muscle is found only in the heart, where it is used to pump blood around the body. Heart muscle never gets tired, and it never stops working.

MOVING MESSAGES

Muscles receive their instructions from nerves. Signals from the brain travel down the spinal cord, and then go out to the muscles along nerves. Nerves branch out so they reach each part of the muscle. The signals tell the muscles to contract, and the body moves.

Nerve-muscle junction
Signals from the brain are passed via nerves to muscle fibers. The contact point where they meet is called a nerve-muscle junction.

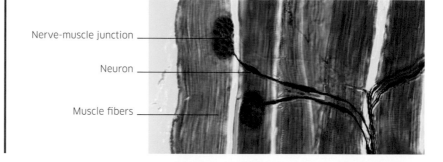

Nerve-muscle junction

Neuron

Muscle fibers

TWITCH TYPES

Muscles are either fast-twitch or slow-twitch. Fast-twitch muscles contract quickly to generate lots of power. Slow-twitch muscles contract slowly and generate less power, but they work for longer without tiring. A healthy body has an equal split of fast- and slow-twitch muscle.

Speedy sprint
Athletes use their fast-twitch muscles for competitive high-speed sprints. These fibers shorten rapidly but tire quickly.

Steady walk
Walkers and climbers use their slow-twitch muscles to cover long distances. These fibers contract gradually but keep going.

HEAT GENERATORS

Working muscles use oxygen to make energy. A by-product of this chemical process is the production of heat. The harder muscles work, the hotter they become. Shivering in cold weather is caused by your muscles twitching, trying to make more heat.

Hot spots
This thermogram image, showing the hottest parts of the body in red, demonstrates how hard this athlete is working his arm and lower leg muscles.

MAINTAINING MUSCLE

Muscles must be kept strong and healthy, so the body can move easily and function properly. Diet and exercise play a major part in building and maintaining muscle.

Muscle food
Protein, such as that found in pulses such as beans and lentils, meat, nuts, and fish, is needed for building and repairing muscle. Carbohydrates such as cereals, bread, and pasta provide energy for muscles to work. A balanced, healthy diet will provide enough protein and carbohydrates for muscles to stay healthy and active.

 FISH
 PULSES
 NUTS
 CEREAL
 BREAD
 PASTA

Resistance training

Some people build bigger muscles by resistance training. Regular exercise of this kind forces muscles to contract repetitively, which builds and strengthens them. It also tears muscle fibers, which then grow back bigger. Weight training, gymnastics, and some kinds of dancing are all forms of resistance training.

Lifting weights causes tiny tears in muscle fibers, which the body repairs.

The repaired muscle fibers are bulkier than before, so muscles grow bigger.

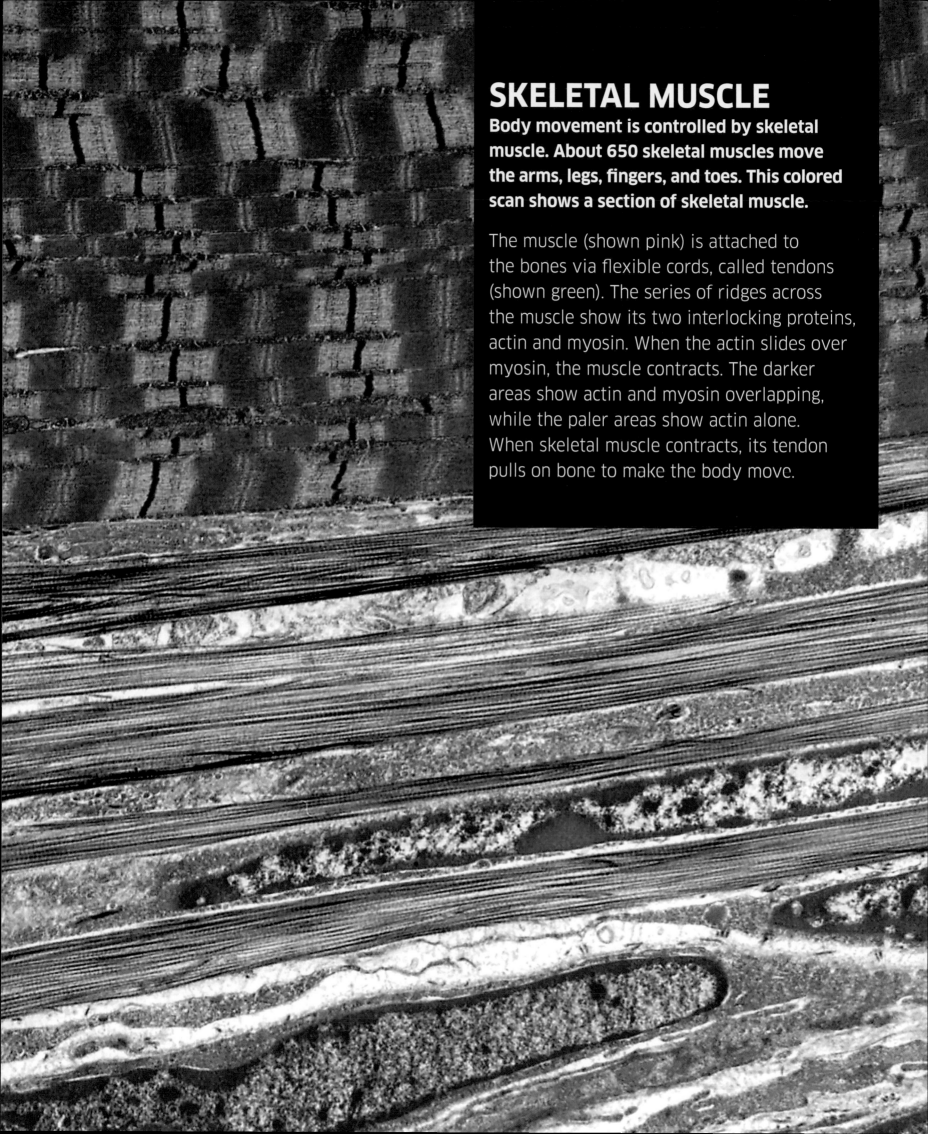

SKELETAL MUSCLE

Body movement is controlled by skeletal muscle. About 650 skeletal muscles move the arms, legs, fingers, and toes. This colored scan shows a section of skeletal muscle.

The muscle (shown pink) is attached to the bones via flexible cords, called tendons (shown green). The series of ridges across the muscle show its two interlocking proteins, actin and myosin. When the actin slides over myosin, the muscle contracts. The darker areas show actin and myosin overlapping, while the paler areas show actin alone. When skeletal muscle contracts, its tendon pulls on bone to make the body move.

130 arms and hands ○ **HAND**

27—the number of bones in a **human hand**.

A quarter of the part of the brain that controls movement is devoted to **hand movements**.

Hand

Because humans walk upright on two feet, it leaves our hands free to take on other tasks. Human hands are incredibly versatile tools, able to perform a huge range of movements.

The hand's adaptability is made possible by the combination of a framework of small, flexible bones, including long finger bones and a highly moveable thumb. This structure is overlaid with an intricate network of muscles and tendons, which move the bones.

Left hand, palm up

The two main arteries of the arm meet in the palm, before branching into smaller blood vessels. Running through the palm are the long tendons that connect to the forearm muscles. These muscles, along with smaller ones in the palm, control the movements of the fingers.

Abductor muscles
These muscles move the thumb toward or away from the palm.

Radial artery

Ulnar artery

Palmar digital nerve of the thumb
This carries sensory information from the side of the thumb.

Fibrous sheath
The flexor tendons are attached to the finger bones by this tissue.

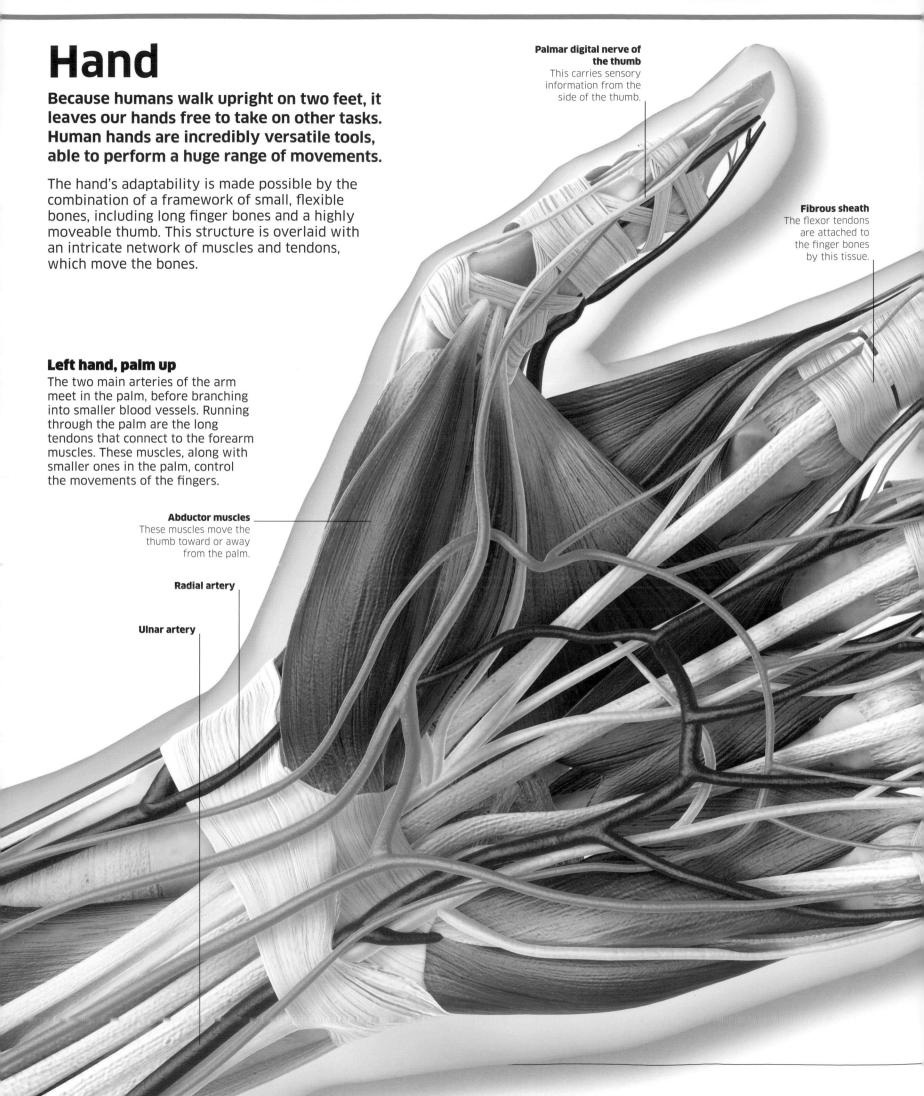

The fingertips contain **more nerve endings** than any other part of our skin.

The fingers contain **no muscles,** just tendons that are moved by muscles in the arm and palm.

131

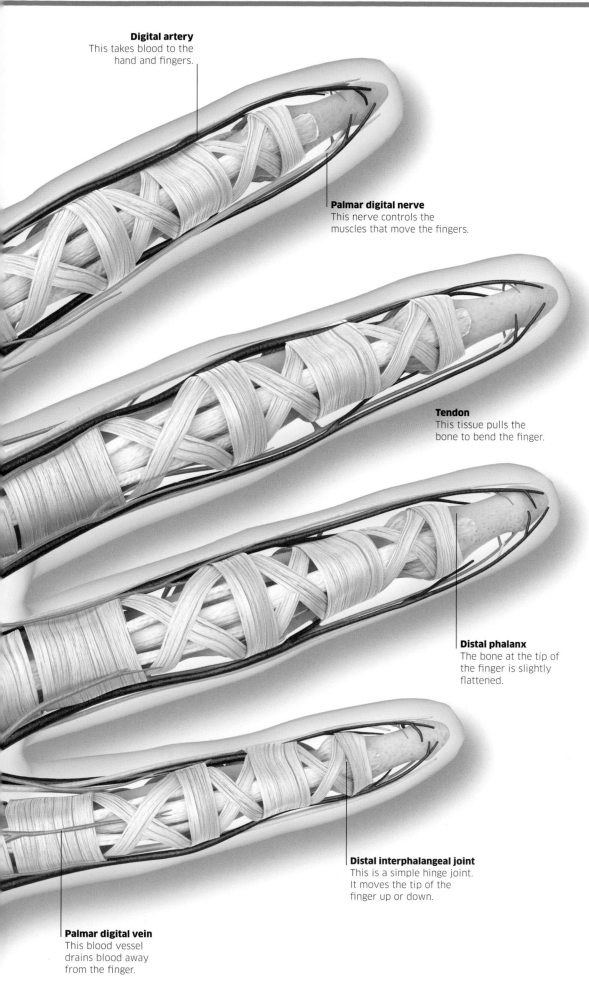

Digital artery
This takes blood to the hand and fingers.

Palmar digital nerve
This nerve controls the muscles that move the fingers.

Tendon
This tissue pulls the bone to bend the finger.

Distal phalanx
The bone at the tip of the finger is slightly flattened.

Distal interphalangeal joint
This is a simple hinge joint. It moves the tip of the finger up or down.

Palmar digital vein
This blood vessel drains blood away from the finger.

Bones

The 27 bones of the hand are made up of 8 small wrist bones (carpals), 5 palm bones (metacarpals), and 14 finger bones (phalanges; one is called a phalanx).

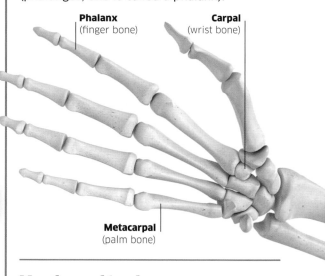

Phalanx
(finger bone)

Carpal
(wrist bone)

Metacarpal
(palm bone)

Muscles and tendons

The fingers are bent and straightened by tendons that extend from the forearm muscles and attach to the finger bones.

Middle finger bends when bone is pulled by tendon

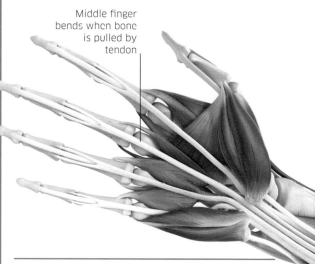

Nerves and blood vessels

Nerves control movement and send signals to the brain from sensors in the skin. Arteries and veins carry blood to and from muscles, tendons, and skin.

Fingertips are rich in nerve endings.

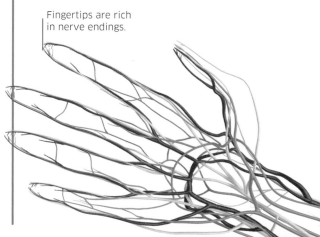

Hands in action

Humans have the ability to move their thumbs to touch—or oppose—each of the fingers on the same hand. This simple ability means that our hands are able to pick up, handle, and grip objects with incredible precision and dexterity.

Opposable thumbs were crucially valuable to early humans, who used them to make tools, throw spears, and pick berries. This advantage over other mammals helped make humans the dominant species on Earth. Modern humans rely on their hands just as much as our ancestors did—for instance, to write, paint, draw, play musical instruments, use tools, and operate technology.

Precision grip
A pen is held carefully in a delicate precision grip.

Metacarpals
Five long metacarpal bones on each hand support the palms.

Hinge joints
These simple joints connect the finger bones together.

Phalanges
Every finger has three phalanges, but the thumb has only two.

Nails
Nails heighten the sense of touch by putting pressure on the fingertips.

Apical tufts
Finger bones have spadelike tips, which support the soft flesh of the fingertips.

Protective pad
A fleshy pad on the end of each thumb helps with grip.

Fingers and thumbs

It is not just the opposable thumb that has transformed the capability of the human hand. The thumb has a thick pad of flesh at the end that helps to hold objects, while the finger bones have wide, flat ends to improve the strength of grip.

Most **apes and monkeys** also have opposable thumbs, but the **human thumb is the most mobile.**

The palm of your hand contains **3,200 sweat glands** per square inch (500 per square centimeter).

133

Researchers have found that the area of the brain that **controls the thumbs** is much more active in people who use touchscreens every day.

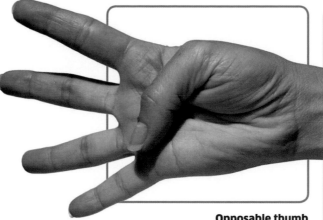

Flexible framework
The multiple joints and bones of the hand provide flexible and versatile movement.

Muscle movements
Many of the hand's intricate movements are produced by muscle tendons that cross the wrist.

Opposable thumb
Thumbs move in the opposite way to fingers, which is why they are called opposable. It is the unique arrangement of bones, joints, and muscles in the thumb and wrist that allows this type of movement.

Carpals
The eight small carpal bones make up the wrist.

Saddle joint
At the base of the thumb, a specialized joint allows the thumb to move in all directions without twisting.

Power and precision
The way we use our hands to grip different things affects the amount of force applied to the object. Hand grips can be described as either power or precision, depending on the position of the hand.

Power grip
A power grip is one in which the fingers curl tightly around an object, forming a cylinder or sphere shape with the hand. This position gives the maximum holding force. Fingers can be close together or spread apart, such as when holding a ball.

CYLINDRICAL GRIP **SPHERICAL GRIP**

Precision grip
A precision grip is one in which the hand pinches an object between the thumb and fingertips. This gives extremely fine control over movements, but only 25 percent of the strength of a power grip.

PRECISION OR PINCH GRIP

Communicating with hands
People use hand gestures every day to communicate. A greeting could be an informal wave hello or good-bye, or a formal handshake. A thumbs up or down can quickly convey good or bad news. Some hand gestures are used so widely that they are recognized across different cultures.

Sign language
The dexterity of human hands has led to the creation of sign language, which allows people with hearing problems to communicate using a recognized range of hand movements.

THANK YOU **SORRY**

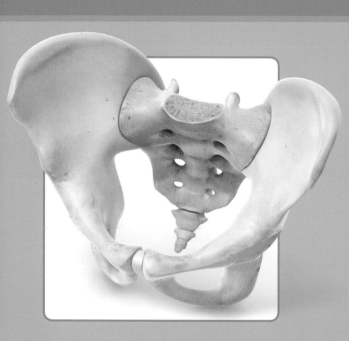

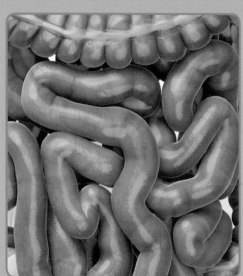

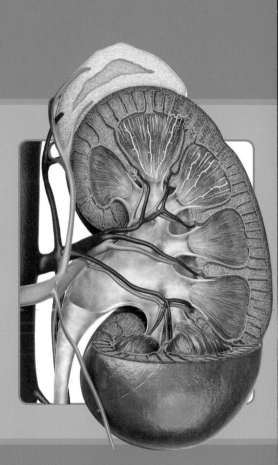

ABDOMEN AND PELVIS

The abdomen contains hardworking organs from many of the body's systems. Most of them help to digest food, clean the blood, or dispose of waste. Supporting them from beneath is a strong framework of bone and muscle called the pelvis.

Inside the abdomen

Many of the body's most important organs lie in the abdomen, the area between the chest and pelvis.

The abdomen contains organs belonging to various body systems, including most of the digestive system, the urinary system, and the reproductive organs. This area is protected by the muscles and other tissues of the abdominal wall. This wall and many of the organs are covered with a slippery membrane called the peritoneum, which allows them to slide over each other.

View from behind

This back view of the body from below shows how many organs and other soft body structures are packed inside the abdominal cavity. Although it looks like a hodgepodge, in fact, each structure has its own place and connection with other structures.

Esophagus
This long tube carries food to the stomach.

Liver
Blood is processed inside the liver.

Kidney
A pair of kidneys filter blood to make urine.

Gallbladder
This small bag stores bile, which helps to digest fat.

Adrenal glands
Two adrenal glands release several hormones, including adrenaline, which helps the body to react under stress.

Stomach
Food is partly digested in the stomach.

Pancreas
This organ helps with digestion and makes hormones to regulate blood sugar levels.

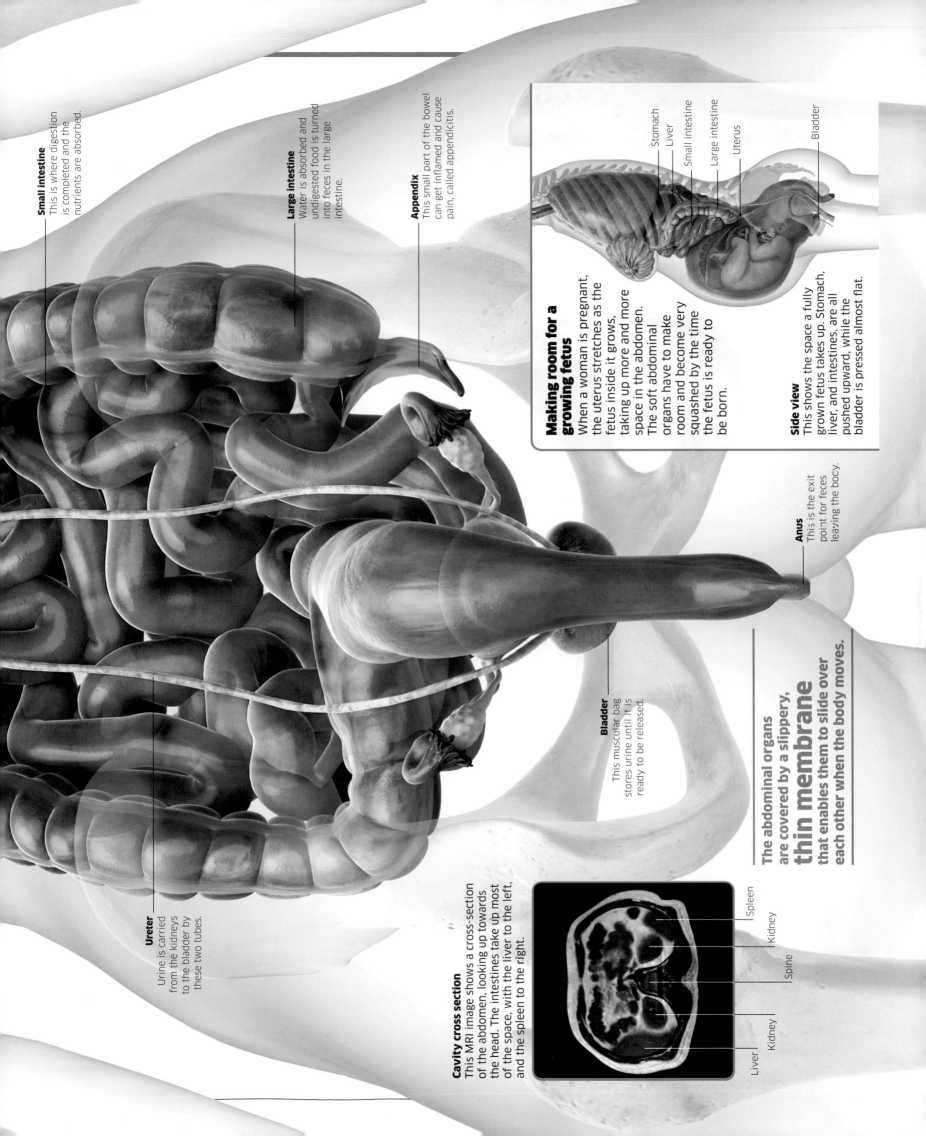

Small intestine
This is where digestion is completed and the nutrients are absorbed.

Large intestine
Water is absorbed and undigested food is turned into feces in the large intestine.

Appendix
This small part of the bowel can get inflamed and cause pain, called appendicitis.

Making room for a growing fetus

When a woman is pregnant, the uterus stretches as the fetus inside it grows, taking up more and more space in the abdomen. The soft abdominal organs have to make room and become very squashed by the time the fetus is ready to be born.

Stomach
Liver
Small intestine
Large intestine
Uterus
Bladder

Side view
This shows the space a fully grown fetus takes up. Stomach, liver, and intestines, are all pushed upward, while the bladder is pressed almost flat.

Anus
This is the exit point for feces leaving the body.

Bladder
This muscular bag stores urine until it is ready to be released.

The abdominal organs are covered by a slippery, **thin membrane** that enables them to slide over each other when the body moves.

Ureter
Urine is carried from the kidneys to the bladder by these two tubes.

Cavity cross section
This MRI image shows a cross-section of the abdomen, looking up towards the head. The intestines take up most of the space, with the liver to the left, and the spleen to the right.

Spleen
Kidney
Spine
Kidney
Liver
Liver

In and out

After the stomach fills, it takes up to four hours for food to be turned into chyme, which is then gradually emptied into the duodenum.

Pyloric sphincter is closed

1 Before a meal
The sight and smell of food triggers the release of gastric juice into the empty, fist-sized stomach.

Food is mixed with gastric juice

2 During a meal
The stomach fills with food and expands like a balloon. Waves of contraction of the stomach wall mix food with gastric juice.

Muscular contractions squeeze chyme

3 After 1–2 hours
Partially digested and churned, the food is turned into chyme, which is pushed toward the pyloric sphincter.

Pyloric sphincter opens

4 After 3–4 hours
The pyloric sphincter opens at intervals and the stomach wall contracts to squirt small amounts of chyme into the duodenum.

Being sick

Vomiting, or throwing up, can happen when toxins (poisons) released by bacteria irritate the stomach's lining. In response, the brain tells the diaphragm and abdominal muscles to contract and squeeze the stomach, forcing its contents upward and out of the mouth to remove the irritation.

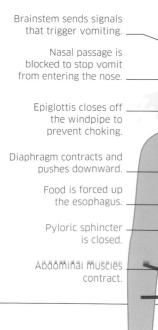

Brainstem sends signals that trigger vomiting.

Nasal passage is blocked to stop vomit from entering the nose.

Epiglottis closes off the windpipe to prevent choking.

Diaphragm contracts and pushes downward.

Food is forced up the esophagus.

Pyloric sphincter is closed.

Abdominal muscles contract.

Stomach

Seconds after swallowing, food enters the stomach, the J-shaped, stretchy bag that links the esophagus to the small intestine. While food is stored in the stomach it is churned into a creamy liquid called chyme. This is released gradually into the small intestine, where digestion is completed.

Two types of digestion happen in the stomach. First, food is doused in acidic gastric juice that contains pepsin, an enzyme that digests proteins. Second, muscles in the stomach's wall create waves of contractions that crush and churn food into mushy chyme.

Inside view

The stomach's wall has three muscle layers that run in different directions. During digestion, these contract in turn to churn food while mixing it with acidic gastric juice. Thick mucus stops gastric juice from damaging the stomach's own delicate lining.

Gastric juice contains hydrochloric acid, which is strong enough to **kill most of the harmful bacteria** that can enter the body in the food we eat.

Pyloric sphincter

Normally closed to keep food in the stomach, this ring of muscle opens slightly once food has been processed (as shown here) to allow a controlled flow of chyme into the duodenum.

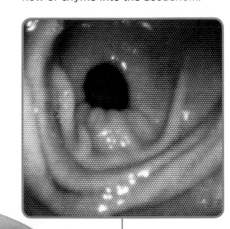

Duodenum
The first part of the small intestine is about 10 in (25 cm) long.

Gastric mucosa
The stomach's inner layer contains gastric glands.

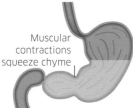
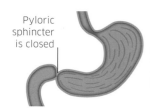
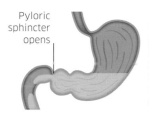

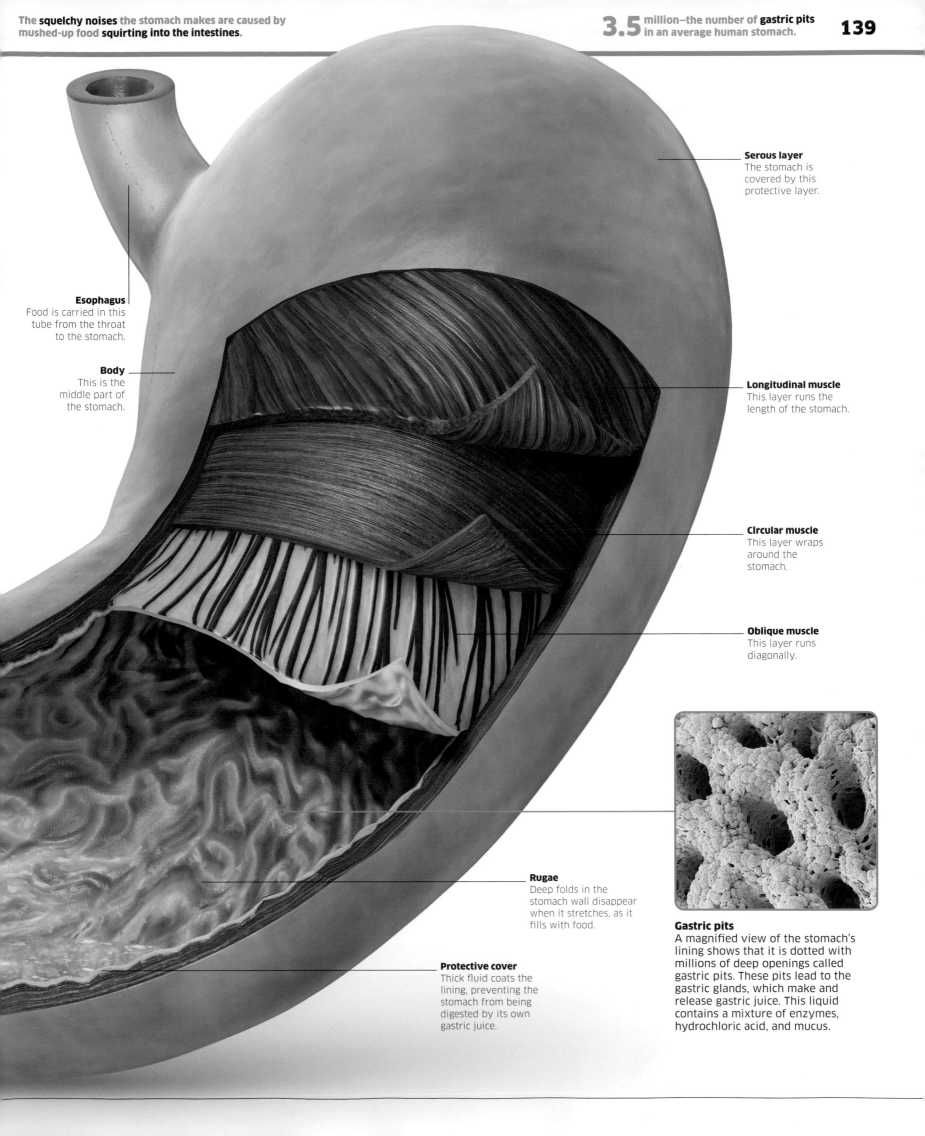

The **squelchy noises** the stomach makes are caused by
mushed-up food squirting into the intestines.

3.5 million—the number of **gastric pits**
in an average human stomach.

139

Serous layer
The stomach is
covered by this
protective layer.

Esophagus
Food is carried in this
tube from the throat
to the stomach.

Body
This is the
middle part of
the stomach.

Longitudinal muscle
This layer runs the
length of the stomach.

Circular muscle
This layer wraps
around the
stomach.

Oblique muscle
This layer runs
diagonally.

Rugae
Deep folds in the
stomach wall disappear
when it stretches, as it
fills with food.

Protective cover
Thick fluid coats the
lining, preventing the
stomach from being
digested by its own
gastric juice.

Gastric pits
A magnified view of the stomach's
lining shows that it is dotted with
millions of deep openings called
gastric pits. These pits lead to the
gastric glands, which make and
release gastric juice. This liquid
contains a mixture of enzymes,
hydrochloric acid, and mucus.

FOOD AND NUTRITION

Nutrition is the food your body needs to grow, move, and keep all its parts working. The body can make some of the substances it needs, but the rest have to come from the food we eat. The digestive system breaks food down into simple chemicals called nutrients that the body can use. Nutrients energize the cells ready for work, provide material for new tissues, and help to repair injuries.

ESSENTIALS FOR LIFE

There are six essential types of nutrient that the body needs to work efficiently. Three of them—carbohydrates, proteins, and fats—have to be broken down by the digestive system into simpler substances that can be absorbed into the bloodstream. Vitamins, minerals, and water can be absorbed directly through the lining of the gut.

Fats
These provide energy and help the brain and nervous system to work efficiently.

Proteins
Proteins help to build cells and repair damage.

Carbohydrates
These provide energy for the body.

Vitamins and minerals
Micronutrients from vitamins and minerals help body parts to work.

Water
Water keeps blood and cells working and helps to flush out waste.

FOOD FOR ENERGY

Everything our body does—breathing, sleeping, running, or just thinking—uses energy. Energy also keeps trillions of body cells working. The food you eat supplies energy that keeps the body going.

Energy levels

Different foods contain varying amounts of energy when broken down inside the body. The energy the body gets from a particular food or drink is measured in calories. The amount of energy a body needs depends on many factors. Teenagers need more energy than adults because they are still growing. Men need to take in more calories than women as they are usually bigger and have more energy-consuming muscle.

Karate kicks
People who participate in sports use up to three times more calories than inactive people.

MALES
FEMALES

APPROXIMATE ENERGY NEEDED PER DAY IN CALORIES

3,000
2,500
2,000
1,500
1,000
500
10

1   7-10   15-18   19-49
AGE IN YEARS

Energy needs
People's individual energy needs vary a huge amount. Very active people use a lot of energy, so they need more calories from their food.

Using energy

Everything we eat contains a certain amount of energy, and everything we do uses energy. Balancing the calories we take in with the activities we do is key to staying healthy.

Fueling activity
A banana contains about 100 calories. Depending on the activity that you do, that amount of energy will fuel you for different lengths of time.

FAST SWIMMING
10 MINUTES

BALLET
15 MINUTES

WALKING
20 MINUTES

CASUAL CYCLING
25 MINUTES

FRISBEE
30 MINUTES

SLEEPING
2 HOURS

A CYCLIST COMPETING IN THE **TOUR DE FRANCE** BURNS ABOUT **5,000 CALORIES** DURING EACH STAGE **OF THE RACE.**

Vitamins and minerals

Vitamins and minerals are essential substances, called micronutrients, that the body needs in small amounts to work at its best.

Versatile vitamins
There are 13 different vitamins, each with a specific role in the body's processes.

Avocados are rich in potassium, which helps control blood pressure.

An avocado also contains other minerals, such as zinc, copper, iron, and magnesium.

Full of minerals
Avocados are an excellent source of minerals, and also contain four different vitamins.

VITAMIN	Body benefits	Good sources
A	Eyesight; growth; sense of taste	Liver, carrots, leafy vegetables, dairy products
B1	Brain and nervous system; muscles; heart	Liver, eggs, meat, nuts, whole grains
B2	Eyesight; skin; hair and nails; growth	Liver, fish, dairy products, leafy vegetables
B3	Brain; blood circulation; skin	Fish, meat, eggs
B5	Hormone production; blood	Eggs, chicken, tomatoes
B6	Brain and nervous system; blood; digestion	Fish, chicken, pork, beans, bananas
B7	Helps break down fat; important for growth	Chicken, meat, eggs
B9	Also called folic acid, it is vital for a baby's development	Leafy vegetables, cereals, meat
B12	Brain and nervous system; blood	Eggs, seafood, meat, dairy products
C	Immune system; keeping cells healthy	Citrus fruit, tomatoes, leafy veg, potatoes
D	Bones; teeth; immune system	Sunlight, oily fish, eggs, dairy products
E	Immune system; skin; muscles	Seed and nut oils, green vegetables, butter, eggs
K	Helping blood to clot	Leafy vegetables, cereals, meat

THE RIGHT BALANCE

A healthy diet means not only eating the essential nutrients, but also getting the proportions right. We don't have to achieve an exact balance with every meal, but a balanced diet overall keeps the body working at its best.

Dietary portions
This chart shows the balanced diet that most doctors currently recommend. Fruit and vegetables, and carbohydrates, make up most of the intake, with smaller amounts of protein, dairy products, and oils.

Water
A good daily intake of water is also essential— about 6-8 glasses is ideal.

Fruit and vegetables should make up at least one-third of our diet.

CARBOHYDRATES

Treats
Very sugary or fatty snacks should only be occasional treats.

FRUIT AND VEGETABLES

Starchy foods such as bread, rice, and pasta should make up about one-third of our diet.

Choose oils and spreads that contain unsaturated fats, such as olive oil.

OILS AND SPREADS

DAIRY

PROTEINS

Good sources of protein are fish, beans and pulses, chicken, and red meat.

Just under 10% of our diet should be made of dairy food such as milk, cheese, and yogurt.

FOOD OR SUPERFOOD?

Most experts agree that no single food is good or bad for our health. Some foods that are especially rich in nutrients are called "superfoods"—but even these should form part of a varied and balanced diet.

Quinoa
Pronounced "keen-wa," this South American grain is very high in protein and contains all the amino acids the body needs.

Blueberries
Some studies suggest that eating this fruit improves blood circulation and boosts mental function.

Beets
Research has shown that this vegetable can help lower blood pressure and improve exercise performance.

EXPERTS RECOMMEND
EATING AT LEAST FIVE
HELPINGS OF FRUIT
AND VEGETABLES
A DAY TO BE HEALTHY.

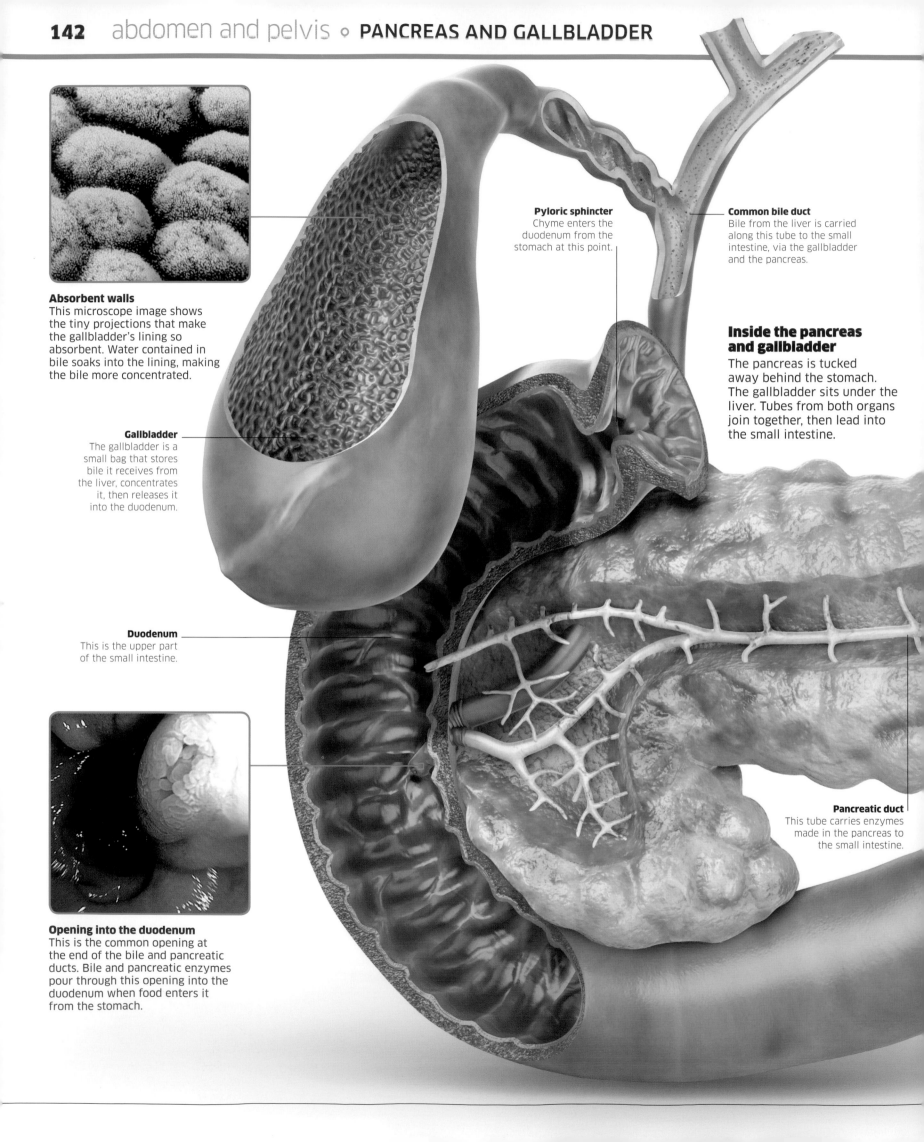

Absorbent walls
This microscope image shows the tiny projections that make the gallbladder's lining so absorbent. Water contained in bile soaks into the lining, making the bile more concentrated.

Pyloric sphincter
Chyme enters the duodenum from the stomach at this point.

Common bile duct
Bile from the liver is carried along this tube to the small intestine, via the gallbladder and the pancreas.

Inside the pancreas and gallbladder
The pancreas is tucked away behind the stomach. The gallbladder sits under the liver. Tubes from both organs join together, then lead into the small intestine.

Gallbladder
The gallbladder is a small bag that stores bile it receives from the liver, concentrates it, then releases it into the duodenum.

Duodenum
This is the upper part of the small intestine.

Pancreatic duct
This tube carries enzymes made in the pancreas to the small intestine.

Opening into the duodenum
This is the common opening at the end of the bile and pancreatic ducts. Bile and pancreatic enzymes pour through this opening into the duodenum when food enters it from the stomach.

An adult's **gallbladder** is about the size of a small pear. The **pancreas** is as big as a banana.

1.7 fluid ounces (50 ml)—the capacity of an adult's **gallbladder** (about three tablespoons).

143

Inside the pancreas
The pancreas contains about one million islets of Langerhans, flowerlike clusters of cells that release the hormones which help the body to store or use glucose. The islets are surrounded by cells that make digestive enzymes.

Islet of Langerhans contains hormone-producing cells

Outer parts of the cluster contain digestive-enzyme-producing cells

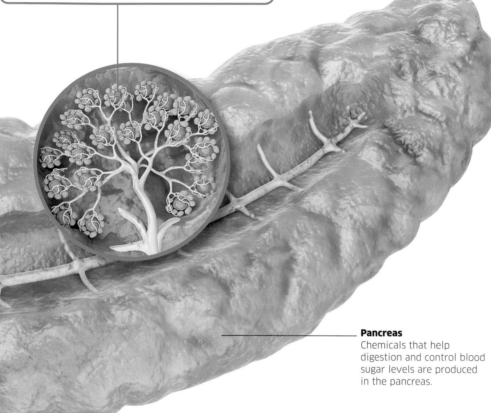

Pancreas
Chemicals that help digestion and control blood sugar levels are produced in the pancreas.

Pancreas and gallbladder

The pancreas and gallbladder play key roles in the next stage of food digestion, which takes place when food arrives in the small intestine from the stomach. Without them, the small intestine could not work properly.

The pancreas and gallbladder release different substances into the small intestine. The pancreas releases pancreatic juice, which is full of enzymes—chemicals that break food into smaller parts, so they can be absorbed into the blood. It also produces hormones that control the amount of sugar in the blood. The gallbladder stores, processes, and releases bile, a liquid that helps the body to digest fat.

Breaking down food
Bile and digestive enzymes work together in the small intestine to digest food. Different enzymes target specific types of foods, dividing them into simpler ingredients so they can easily be absorbed by the body.

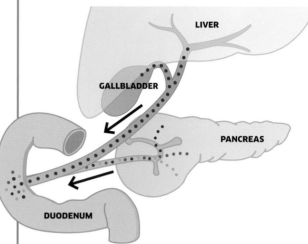

LIVER

GALLBLADDER

PANCREAS

DUODENUM

Key

● **BILE**　　　breaks down fats
● **LIPASE**　　helps to digest fats
● **AMYLASE**　helps to digest sugars
● **PROTEASE**　helps to digest proteins

The route to the duodenum
This shows the route of bile and the digestive enzymes protease, lipase, and amylase as they make their way to the duodenum.

Important insulin
The pancreas produces insulin—the vital hormone that allows glucose in the bloodstream to enter the body's cells and be used as energy. Type-1 diabetes is a condition that causes the pancreas to stop making insulin. Cells are starved of the glucose they need, while blood glucose rises to dangerous levels and causes health problems. To keep healthy, diabetics must inject artificial insulin into their bodies daily.

Daily dose
Many diabetics use a small pump, implanted under the skin, which releases measured doses of insulin at regular intervals.

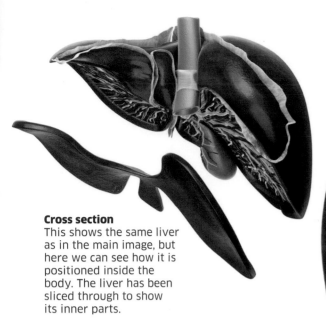

Cross section
This shows the same liver as in the main image, but here we can see how it is positioned inside the body. The liver has been sliced through to show its inner parts.

The liver makes the chemicals that cause clotting—the **blood thickening** process that stops the bleeding after you cut yourself.

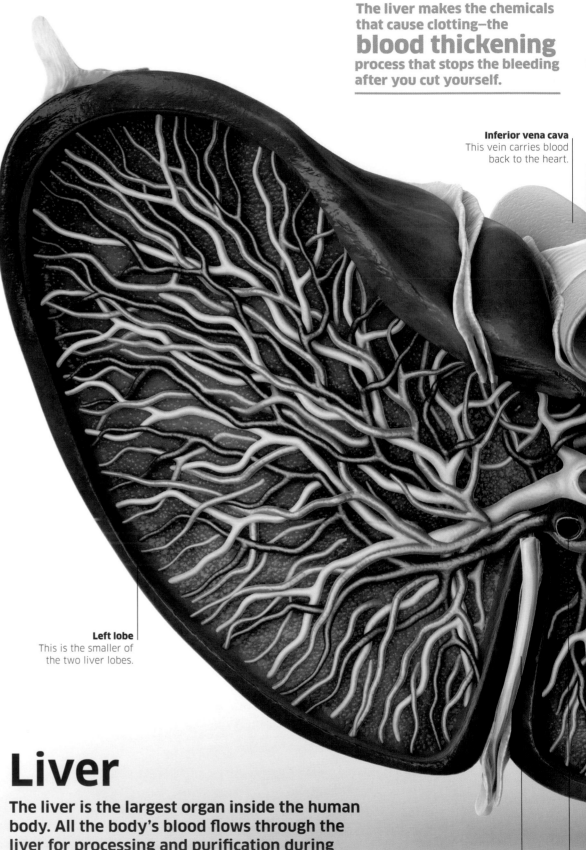

Inferior vena cava
This vein carries blood back to the heart.

Left lobe
This is the smaller of the two liver lobes.

Ligament
This connective tissue lies between the two main lobes.

Hepatic artery
Oxygen-rich blood is supplied to the liver by this artery.

Liver list

The liver performs hundreds of essential processing, manufacturing, and recycling tasks in the body.

Breaking down
The liver breaks down substances into parts the body can use or get rid of, such as:
• chemicals from food
• medicines
• germs entering in food

Recycling
It also breaks up dead blood cells so their ingredients can be used again.

Building up
Nutrients are used to make new substances that the body needs, such as:
• proteins for building body parts
• chemicals to heal injuries
• bile, which helps to digest fat

Storage
Useful body substances are stored, then released when necessary, such as:
• glucose for energy
• minerals, such as iron and copper
• vitamins A, D, K, and B12

Heating
The liver even gives out heat to help warm the body.

Liver

The liver is the largest organ inside the human body. All the body's blood flows through the liver for processing and purification during this vital stage of the digestive system.

The liver has many different roles, but one of the most important is controlling the chemical makeup of the blood to keep body conditions stable. Nutrient-rich blood from the small intestine flows directly into the liver, which makes these nutrients more useful for the body and removes harmful chemicals. The liver also makes bile, a fluid used by the small intestine to help digest fats.

15% of the **body's blood is** inside the liver at any time.

The liver **filters blood** at a rate of 3 pints (1.4 liters) every minute.

1 million—the approximate number of blood-filtering **lobules** inside a liver.

145

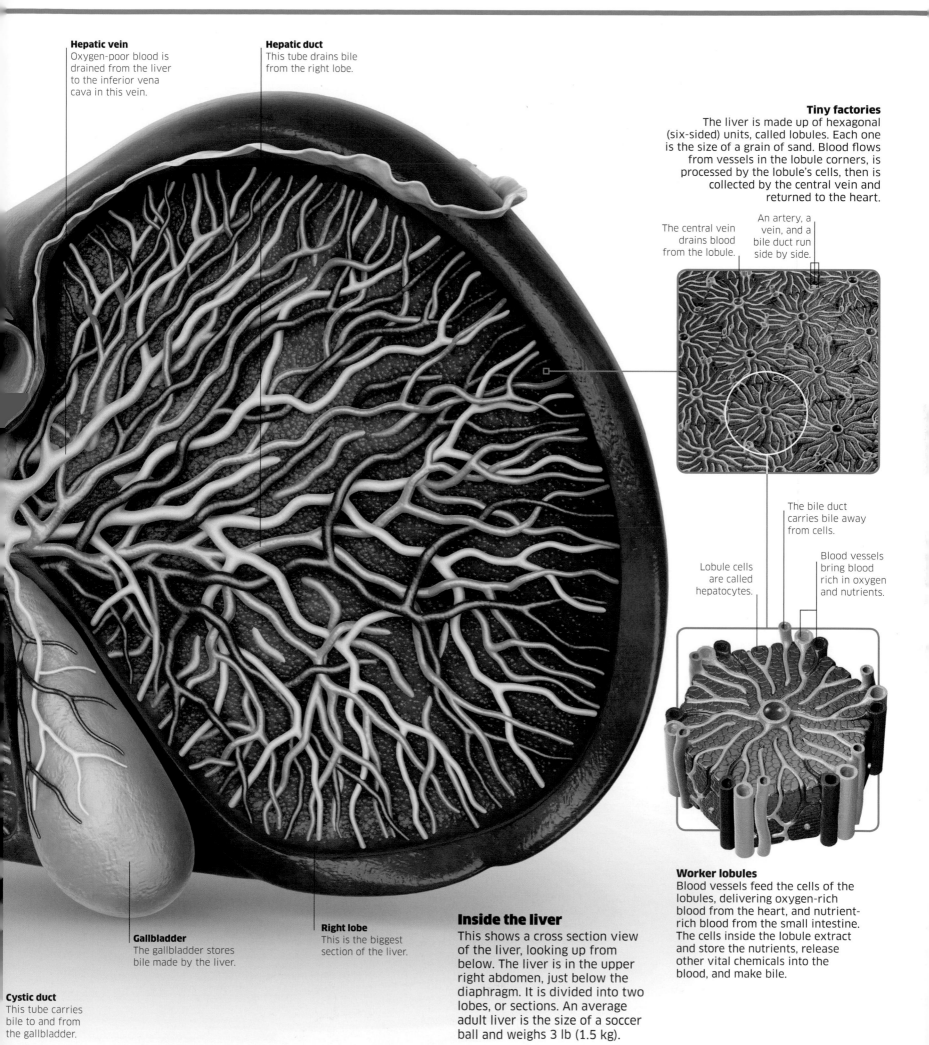

Hepatic vein
Oxygen-poor blood is drained from the liver to the inferior vena cava in this vein.

Hepatic duct
This tube drains bile from the right lobe.

Tiny factories
The liver is made up of hexagonal (six-sided) units, called lobules. Each one is the size of a grain of sand. Blood flows from vessels in the lobule corners, is processed by the lobule's cells, then is collected by the central vein and returned to the heart.

The central vein drains blood from the lobule.

An artery, a vein, and a bile duct run side by side.

The bile duct carries bile away from cells.

Lobule cells are called hepatocytes.

Blood vessels bring blood rich in oxygen and nutrients.

Gallbladder
The gallbladder stores bile made by the liver.

Right lobe
This is the biggest section of the liver.

Inside the liver
This shows a cross section view of the liver, looking up from below. The liver is in the upper right abdomen, just below the diaphragm. It is divided into two lobes, or sections. An average adult liver is the size of a soccer ball and weighs 3 lb (1.5 kg).

Worker lobules
Blood vessels feed the cells of the lobules, delivering oxygen-rich blood from the heart, and nutrient-rich blood from the small intestine. The cells inside the lobule extract and store the nutrients, release other vital chemicals into the blood, and make bile.

Cystic duct
This tube carries bile to and from the gallbladder.

146 abdomen and pelvis ○ **SMALL INTESTINE**

5 hours—roughly how long it takes **food to pass through** the small intestine.

Small intestine

The small intestine is the longest part of the digestive system. It's where most of the digestive process takes place, releasing the nutrients in food so that they can be used to fuel the body's cells.

By the time food reaches the small intestine, the stomach has turned it into a liquid called chyme. This chyme is squirted into the duodenum, the first part of the small intestine, along with bile from the gallbladder and enzymes from the pancreas, which break the chyme down even more. Finally, when most of the food has been broken down into simple nutrients, these pass through the walls of the small intestine and into the bloodstream. The remaining food progresses to the next stage—the large intestine.

If you stretched out the small intestine, it would be longer than four adults lying **head to toe.**

Bundled up

The small intestine is at the front of the lower abdomen, surrounded by the large intestine and other organs. Although it's very long—more than 20 ft (6 m)—the small intestine fits into this space because it is bundled up in a series of loops and coils.

Jejunum
This is the middle section of the small intestine, where most of the digestion and absorption of food takes place.

Duodenum
The first part of the small intestine is where bile and enzymes are added to the chyme to help break it down.

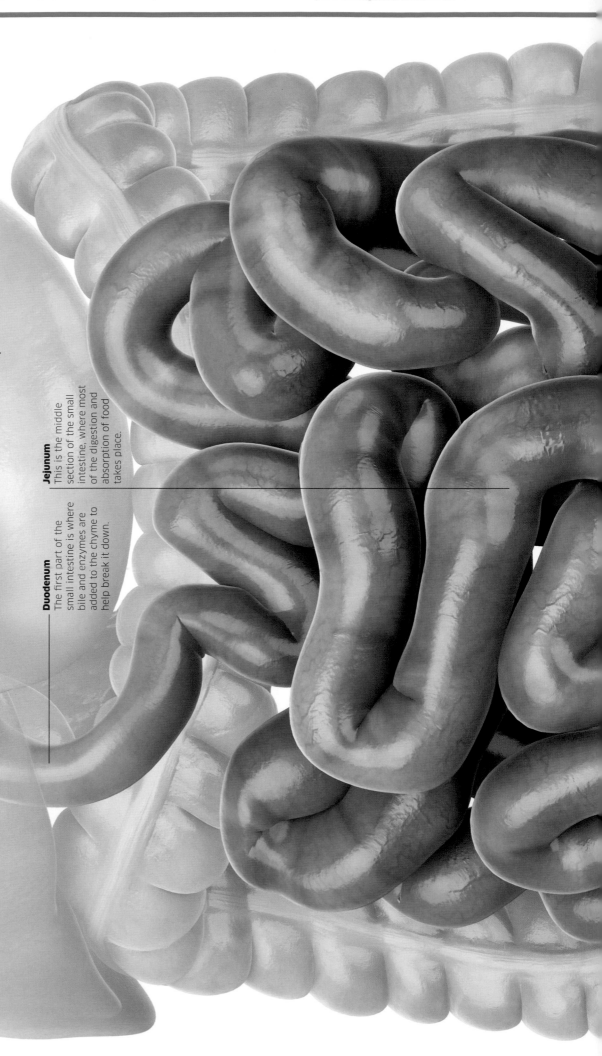

The word villus comes from a **Latin word** meaning "shaggy hair."

If the small intestine were **flattened out**, its area would be about **320 sq ft (30 sq m)—bigger than 10 double beds put together.**

147

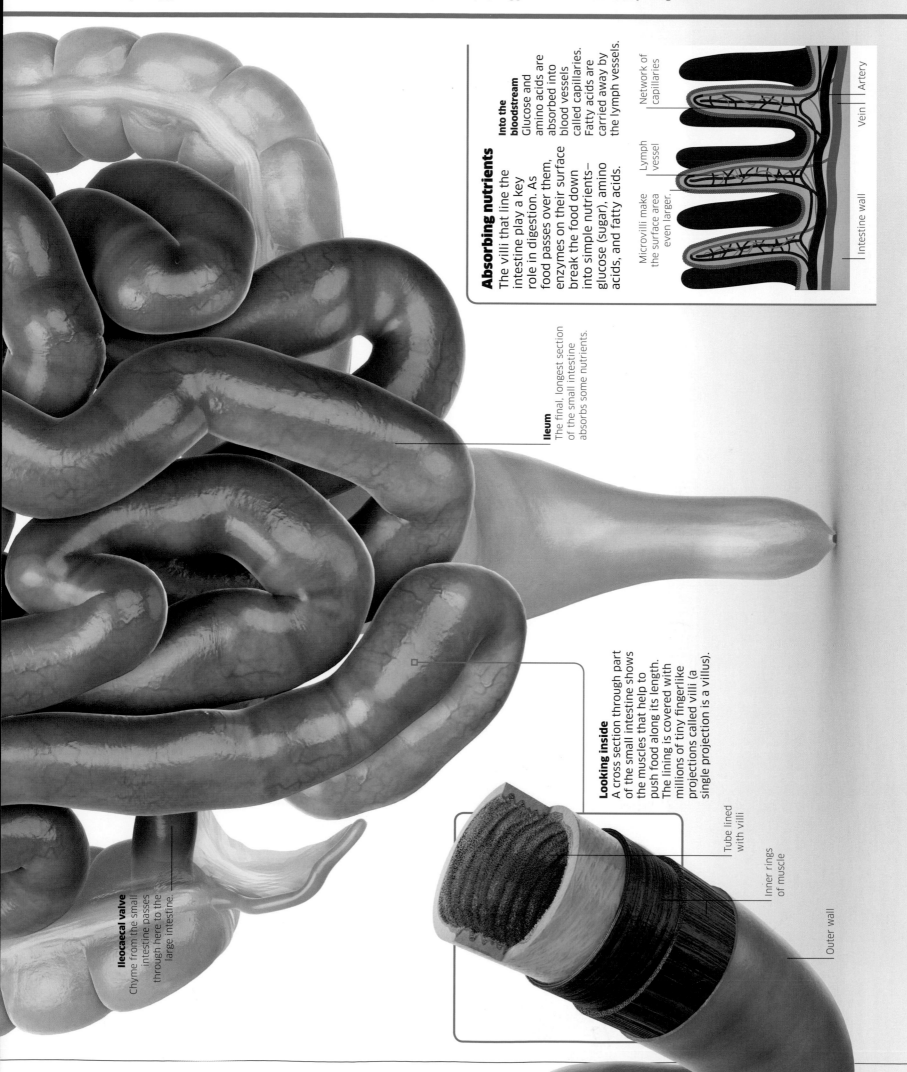

Absorbing nutrients

The villi that line the intestine play a key role in digestion. As food passes over them, enzymes on their surface break the food down into simple nutrients— glucose (sugar), amino acids, and fatty acids.

Into the bloodstream
Glucose and amino acids are absorbed into blood vessels called capillaries. Fatty acids are carried away by the lymph vessels.

Network of capillaries

Artery

Vein

Lymph vessel

Microvilli make the surface area even larger.

Intestine wall

Ileum
The final, longest section of the small intestine absorbs some nutrients.

Looking inside
A cross section through part of the small intestine shows the muscles that help to push food along its length. The lining is covered with millions of tiny fingerlike projections called villi (a single projection is a villus).

Tube lined with villi

Inner rings of muscle

Outer wall

Ileocaecal valve
Chyme from the small intestine passes through here to the large intestine.

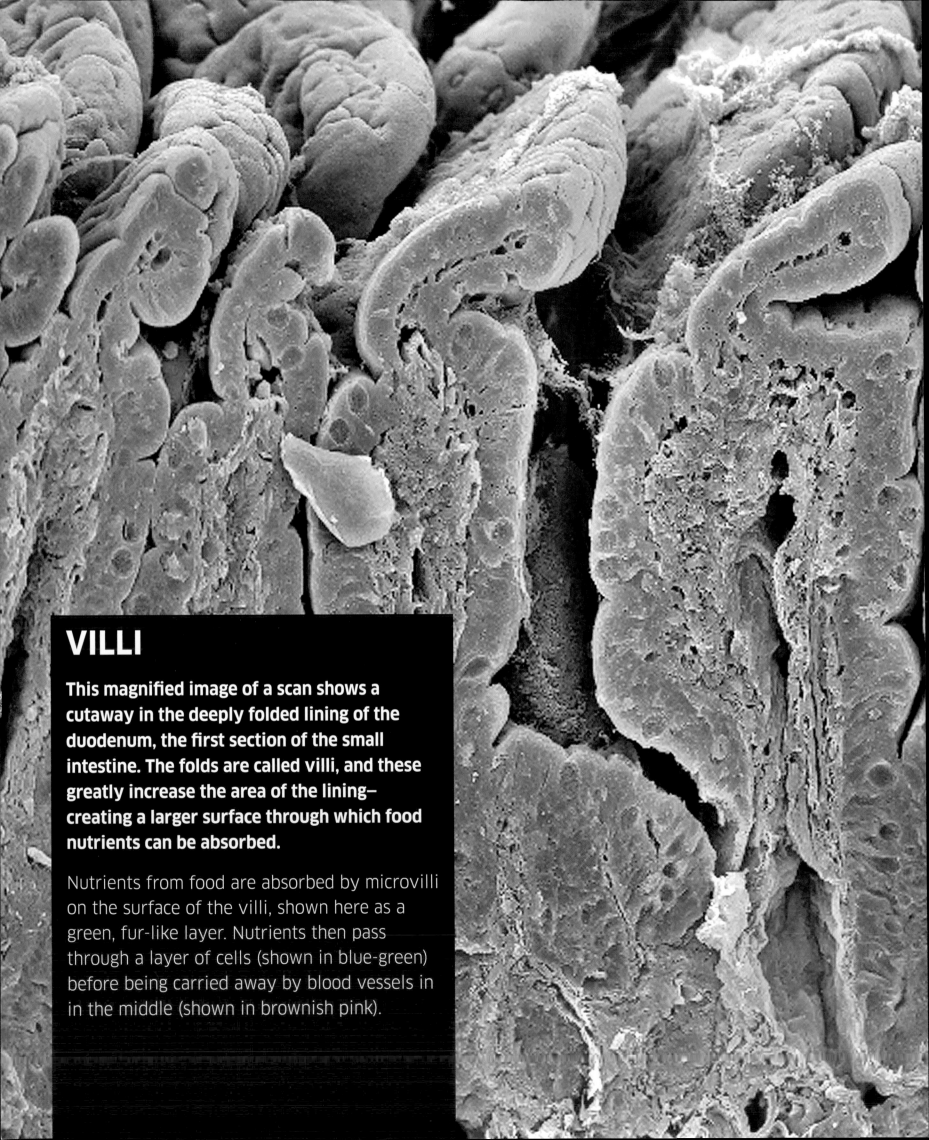

VILLI

This magnified image of a scan shows a cutaway in the deeply folded lining of the duodenum, the first section of the small intestine. The folds are called villi, and these greatly increase the area of the lining–creating a larger surface through which food nutrients can be absorbed.

Nutrients from food are absorbed by microvilli on the surface of the villi, shown here as a green, fur-like layer. Nutrients then pass through a layer of cells (shown in blue-green) before being carried away by blood vessels in in the middle (shown in brownish pink).

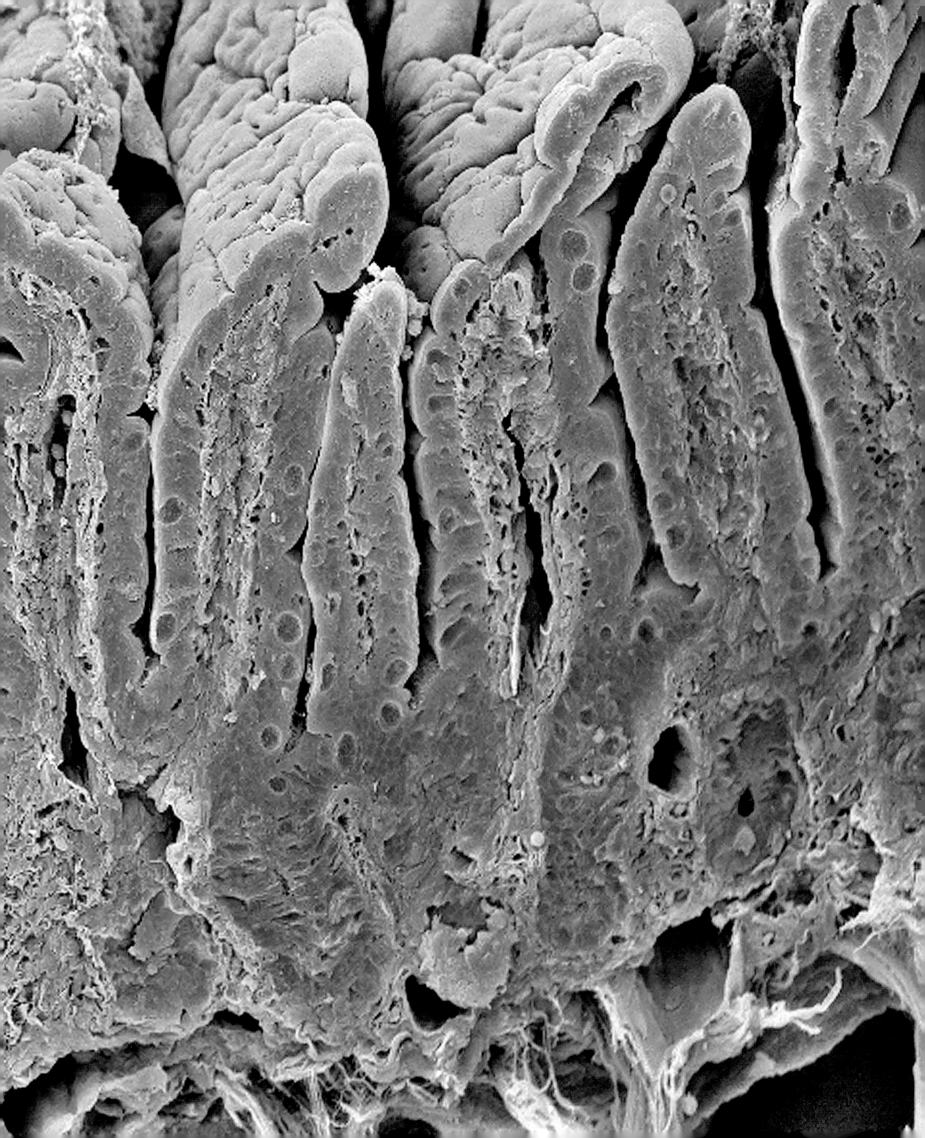

Large intestine

The large intestine is the final stage of the digestive system. It's where most of the water, and the last few nutrients, are taken from the chyme that enters from the small intestine. It then moves unusable waste out of the body.

Most nutrients have been taken from the food before it gets to the large intestine—but there is still vital work for it to do. Here, trillions of bacteria help to break the remaining food down into valuable nutrients. The large intestine is wider than the small intestine, but it's not nearly as long.

Bacteria in the large intestine produce a number of **different vitamins,** especially vitamin K and biotin, a B vitamin.

Up, across, and down

The large intestine is a wide tube that goes around the small intestine. The tube goes up, across the abdomen, then down again. It has a lumpy appearance because of the way the muscles in its wall contract.

Transverse colon
Passing just below the stomach, this is the middle part of the large intestine.

Descending colon
This section passes down the left side of the abdomen.

Gut bacteria

Trillions of bacteria live in the large intestine. Most are either harmless, or actively help to complete digestion by processing the remaining nutrients that could not be digested by enzymes. However, some microorganisms that enter the digestive system can cause illness.

BIFIDOBACTERIA

Ascending colon
On the right side of the abdomen, this section of the intestine rises from the cecum.

700—the number of different types of **bacteria** in the large intestine.

4½ lb (2 kg)—the total **weight** of all the bacteria that live in the intestines.

151

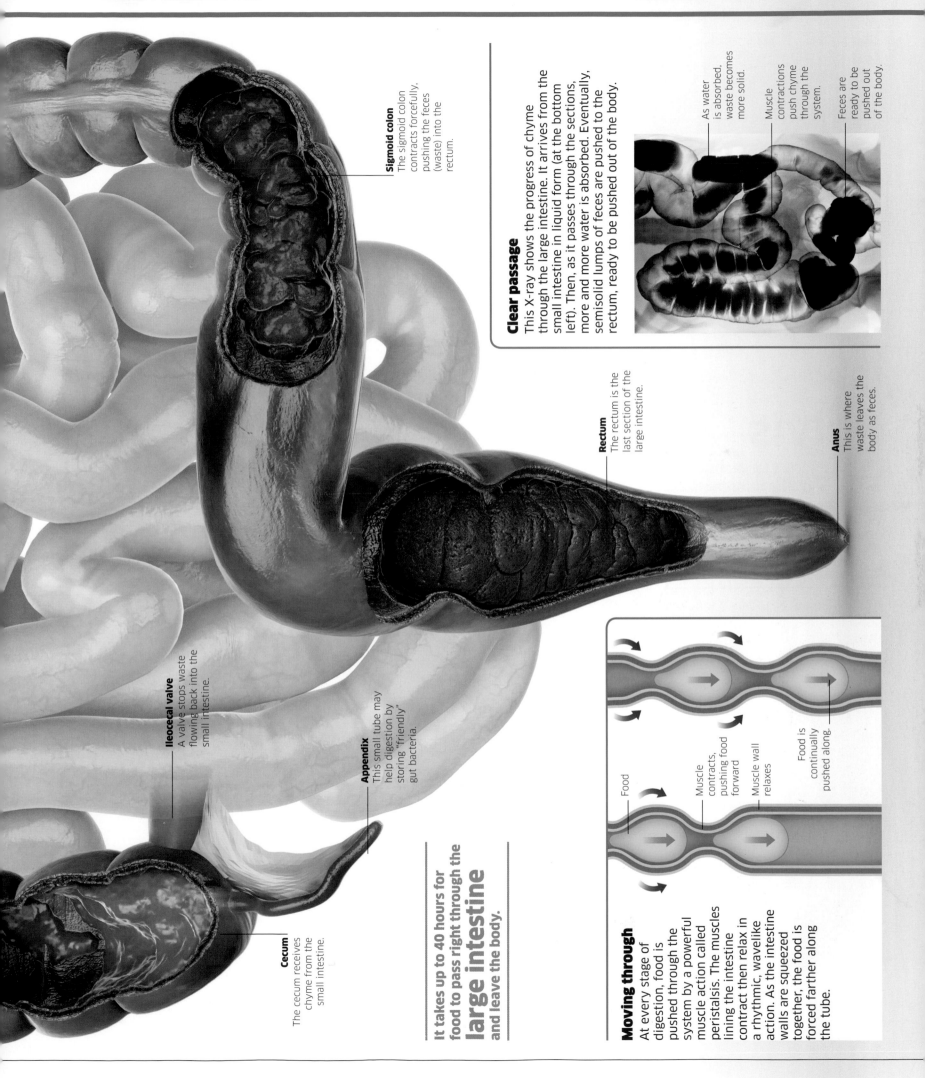

Sigmoid colon
The sigmoid colon contracts forcefully, pushing the feces (waste) into the rectum.

Clear passage
This X-ray shows the progress of chyme through the large intestine. It arrives from the small intestine in liquid form (at the bottom left). Then, as it passes through the sections, more and more water is absorbed. Eventually, semisolid lumps of feces are pushed to the rectum, ready to be pushed out of the body.

As water is absorbed, waste becomes more solid.

Muscle contractions push chyme through the system.

Feces are ready to be pushed out of the body.

Rectum
The rectum is the last section of the large intestine.

Anus
This is where waste leaves the body as feces.

Ileocecal valve
A valve stops waste flowing back into the small intestine.

Appendix
This small tube may help digestion by storing "friendly" gut bacteria.

It takes up to 40 hours for food to pass right through the
large intestine
and leave the body.

Cecum
The cecum receives chyme from the small intestine.

Moving through
At every stage of digestion, food is pushed through the system by a powerful muscle action called peristalsis. The muscles lining the intestine contract then relax in a rhythmic, wavelike action. As the intestine walls are squeezed together, the food is forced farther along the tube.

Food

Muscle contracts, pushing food forward

Muscle wall relaxes

Food is continually pushed along.

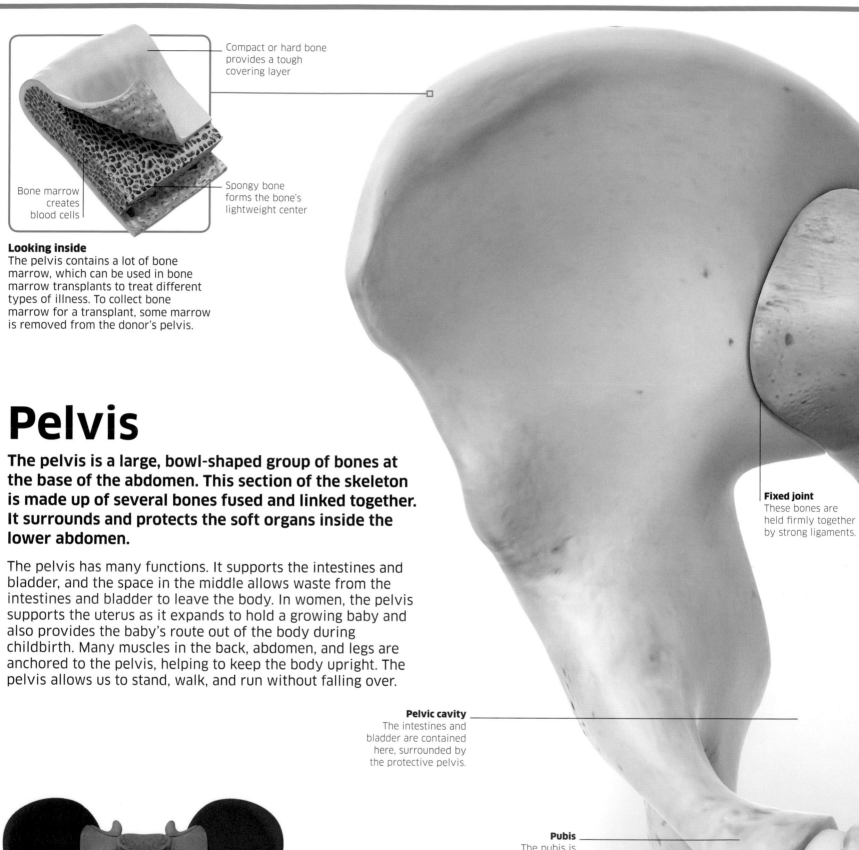

Compact or hard bone provides a tough covering layer

Bone marrow creates blood cells

Spongy bone forms the bone's lightweight center

Looking inside
The pelvis contains a lot of bone marrow, which can be used in bone marrow transplants to treat different types of illness. To collect bone marrow for a transplant, some marrow is removed from the donor's pelvis.

Pelvis

The pelvis is a large, bowl-shaped group of bones at the base of the abdomen. This section of the skeleton is made up of several bones fused and linked together. It surrounds and protects the soft organs inside the lower abdomen.

The pelvis has many functions. It supports the intestines and bladder, and the space in the middle allows waste from the intestines and bladder to leave the body. In women, the pelvis supports the uterus as it expands to hold a growing baby and also provides the baby's route out of the body during childbirth. Many muscles in the back, abdomen, and legs are anchored to the pelvis, helping to keep the body upright. The pelvis allows us to stand, walk, and run without falling over.

Fixed joint
These bones are held firmly together by strong ligaments.

Pelvic cavity
The intestines and bladder are contained here, surrounded by the protective pelvis.

Pubis
The pubis is one of the two smallest bones in the pelvis.

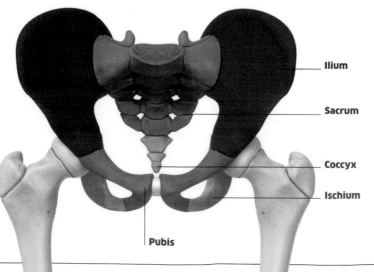

Ilium

Sacrum

Coccyx

Ischium

Pubis

Child's pelvis
At birth, a baby's pelvic bones are still each in three parts—the ilium, ischium, and pubis. During childhood, these slowly fuse together. This image shows the pelvis of a four-year-old child, with the different bones colored so we can see them more easily.

Pubic symphysis
This strong cartilage joint connects the two pubis bones together.

23 —the age when all the bones in the **pelvis are fully fused**.

An **elephant's pelvis** is the **size of an armchair**!

Organs don't fall through the pelvis because there is a layer of strong muscles, called **the pelvic floor**, beneath.

153

Pelvic girdle

The pelvis is made up of two hip bones, one on each side. Each hip bone has three parts—the ilium, ischium, and pubis. They connect to the sacrum—the lower part of the spine—to form a ringlike shape, called the pelvic girdle.

Sacrum
At the base of the spine, this triangular-shaped bone connects the two hip bones.

Ilium
The largest bone in the pelvis is the ilium, or hip bone. One on each side connects the muscles used to stand and walk.

Spine
The spine, or backbone, is a column of bones that runs from the pelvis to the neck.

Holes
Small holes in the bones are for nerves and blood vessels.

Coccyx
Below the sacrum is the coccyx, or tailbone—all that remains of the tail of our distant ancestors.

Hip joint
The ball-shaped top of the thigh bone sits in this hollow, creating the ball-and-socket hip joint.

Ischium
The lowest bone in the pelvis, the ischium carries all the weight when the body is sitting down.

Male and female

The male pelvis is usually tall and narrow, while the female's is wider, with a larger space in the middle, called the pelvic inlet, to allow babies to pass through in childbirth.

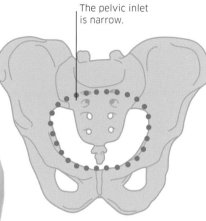

The pelvic inlet is narrow.

MALE PELVIS

The pelvic inlet is much wider, for a baby to go through.

FEMALE PELVIS

Standing up

From four-legged ape-like creatures, we evolved into humans that walk on two legs. As a result, the human pelvis became shorter, rounder, and more upright, so the abdomen could be supported on top of the legs.

Upright pelvis for walking

Pelvis tilted forward for semi-upright movement

GORILLA

HUMAN

Kidneys

Your two kidneys filter and clean the blood by removing toxic chemicals. Like the heart, the kidneys are at work every second of every day, producing a continuous flow of clean blood.

As blood circulates, it picks up waste substances produced by the body's cells. These would poison you if they were not removed from the body. The kidneys extract the toxins and excess water from the blood and process them to make urine. In addition to cleaning the blood, the kidneys also release hormones, stimulate red blood cell production, and keep the body's water content balanced. They release more urine if you have drunk a lot and less if you are dehydrated.

Adrenal gland

Renal artery
This artery carries blood into the kidney to be filtered.

Renal vein
Cleaned blood is carried from the kidney by the renal vein.

Multipurpose organs
The two kidneys sit high in the back of the abdomen. Each one is about the size of a fist, shaped like a bean, and surrounded by a protective layer of tissue.

The average pair of kidneys produces
93,000 pints
(44,000 liters) of urine in a lifetime—that's 550 bathtubs full!

Outer casing
The kidneys and adrenal glands are wrapped in a layer of fat and strong outer tissue.

The amount of **blood that flows** through the kidneys in a lifetime could fill **18 Olympic swimming pools.**

It takes **just under an hour** for the kidneys to clean all the blood in your body.

155

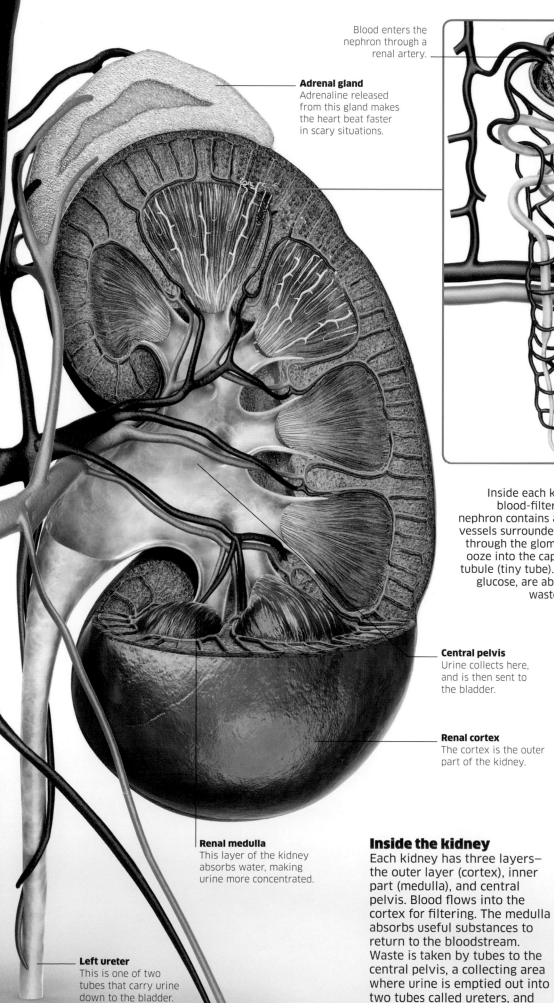

Blood enters the nephron through a renal artery.

Adrenal gland
Adrenaline released from this gland makes the heart beat faster in scary situations.

Blood is filtered as it passes through the glomerulus.

Waste passes from the glomerulus into the coiled tubule.

The collecting duct delivers waste to the hollow pelvis of the kidney.

Cleaned blood is sent back to the heart via the renal vein.

Capillaries absorb water and nutrients back into the blood.

Nephrons
Inside each kidney are around a million tiny blood-filtering units called nephrons. Each nephron contains a glomerulus, a bundle of blood vessels surrounded by a capsule. As blood passes through the glomerulus, waste and excess water ooze into the capsule and are carried away by a tubule (tiny tube). Any useful substances, such as glucose, are absorbed by capillaries, while the waste is carried away to form urine.

Central pelvis
Urine collects here, and is then sent to the bladder.

Renal cortex
The cortex is the outer part of the kidney.

Renal medulla
This layer of the kidney absorbs water, making urine more concentrated.

Left ureter
This is one of two tubes that carry urine down to the bladder.

Inside the kidney
Each kidney has three layers—the outer layer (cortex), inner part (medulla), and central pelvis. Blood flows into the cortex for filtering. The medulla absorbs useful substances to return to the bloodstream. Waste is taken by tubes to the central pelvis, a collecting area where urine is emptied out into two tubes called ureters, and then passes to the bladder.

Clean machine
If the kidneys become damaged or diseased, a dialysis machine can be used to filter the blood instead. This large machine takes up to four times longer than kidneys to clean the body's blood—which shows what an efficient unit the kidneys are.

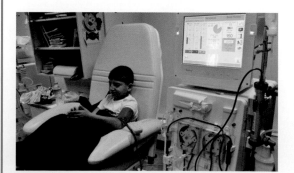

Dialysis
The dialysis machine acts as an artificial set of kidneys. Blood flows from the body to the machine, toxic waste and excess fluid are removed, and the cleaned blood is returned.

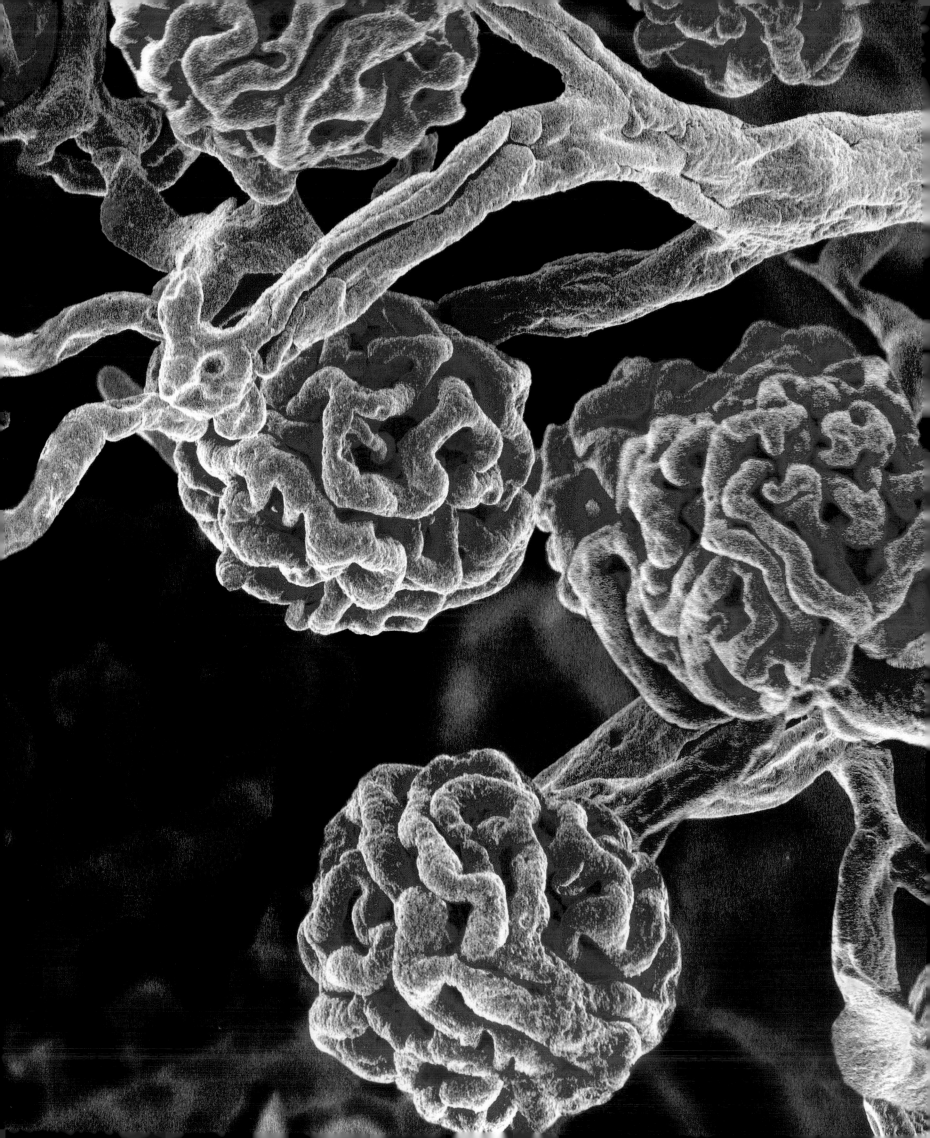

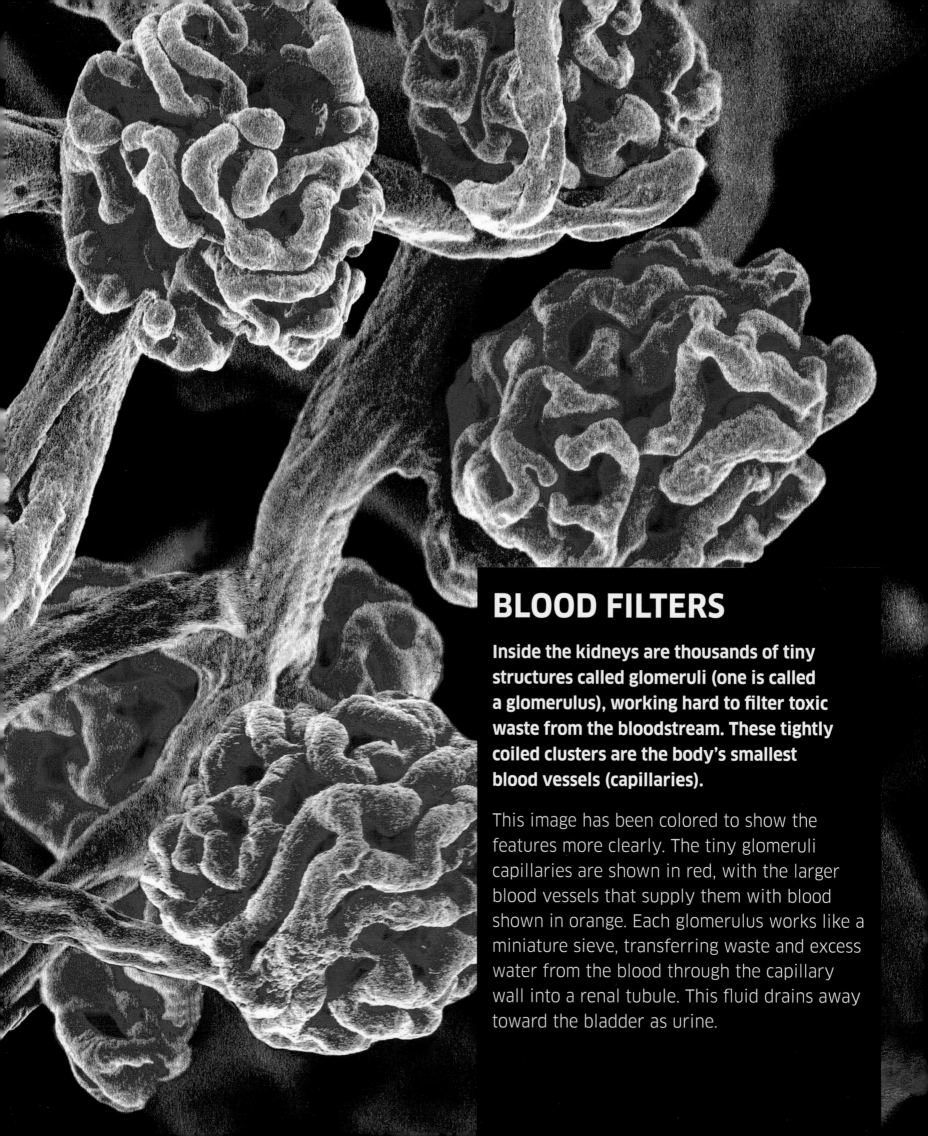

BLOOD FILTERS

Inside the kidneys are thousands of tiny structures called glomeruli (one is called a glomerulus), working hard to filter toxic waste from the bloodstream. These tightly coiled clusters are the body's smallest blood vessels (capillaries).

This image has been colored to show the features more clearly. The tiny glomeruli capillaries are shown in red, with the larger blood vessels that supply them with blood shown in orange. Each glomerulus works like a miniature sieve, transferring waste and excess water from the blood through the capillary wall into a renal tubule. This fluid drains away toward the bladder as urine.

WATER FOR LIFE

The body needs water to stay alive. Every cell, tissue, and organ relies on a regular water supply to function properly. Water makes up more than half of the body. It is found inside cells, as well as in blood and other fluids, such as lymph, tears, saliva, sweat, and urine. The brain constantly monitors water levels inside the body so it can make sure it maintains the correct balance.

WATER LEVELS

The amount of water in a person depends on their age, gender, and weight. The more water-rich muscles they have, the higher their water content. As we grow older, muscles shrink and water levels drop.

Bodies of water

A newborn baby is almost three-quarters water—and the proportion of water in the body drops gradually from then on. Men contain more water than women, as they usually have more water-containing muscle.

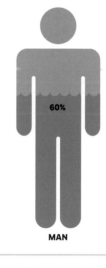

74%

NEWBORN BABY

60%

MAN

50%

WOMAN

40%

ELDERLY PERSON

Body chemistry

Water is an essential ingredient of body cells. The millions of chemical reactions that power life take place in the water contained in the body's cells. Different body tissues contain varying amounts of water, depending on their function. Muscle contains three times more water than bone.

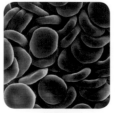

BLOOD 83% WATER

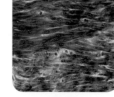

MUSCLE 75% WATER

FAT 25% WATER

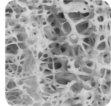

BONE 22% WATER

AN AVERAGE HUMAN **CAN SURVIVE FOR AROUND 100 HOURS** WITHOUT DRINKING WATER.

IN AND OUT

The body needs the right amount of water inside it. We constantly lose water, so we eat and drink to replace it and maintain the correct balance.

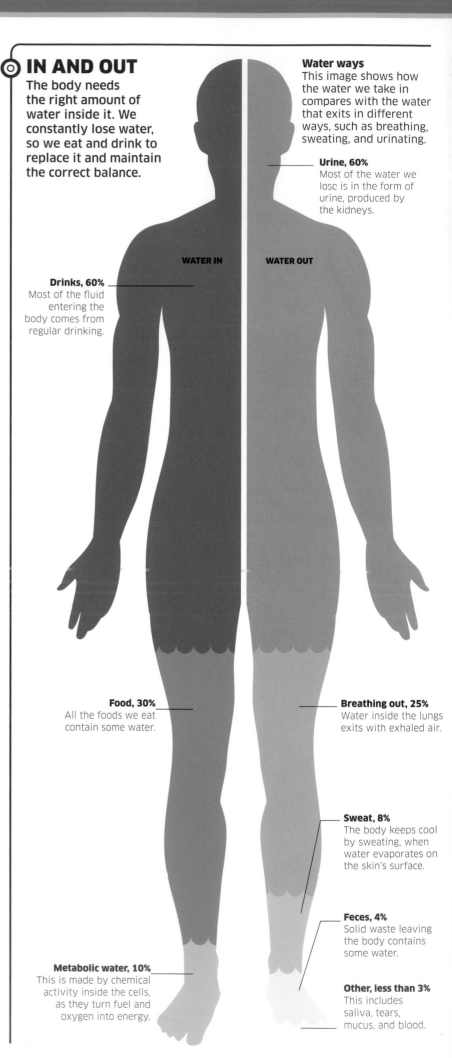

Water ways
This image shows how the water we take in compares with the water that exits in different ways, such as breathing, sweating, and urinating.

Urine, 60%
Most of the water we lose is in the form of urine, produced by the kidneys.

WATER IN   **WATER OUT**

Drinks, 60%
Most of the fluid entering the body comes from regular drinking.

Food, 30%
All the foods we eat contain some water.

Breathing out, 25%
Water inside the lungs exits with exhaled air.

Sweat, 8%
The body keeps cool by sweating, when water evaporates on the skin's surface.

Feces, 4%
Solid waste leaving the body contains some water.

Metabolic water, 10%
This is made by chemical activity inside the cells, as they turn fuel and oxygen into energy.

Other, less than 3%
This includes saliva, tears, mucus, and blood.

WORKING WATER

Water does many different jobs. It helps provide a transportation system around the body. It also regulates body temperature and lubricates parts so they work better.

Blood
Blood is mostly water, so it flows easily through blood vessels.

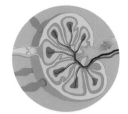

Lymph
Watery lymph flows around the body, recycling chemicals and fighting germs.

Saliva
Saliva moistens foods to help with eating and also kills germs in the mouth.

Sweat
Sweat is released through skin pores to help cool the body down.

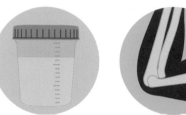

Urine
Urine is a mix of excess water and chemicals from the blood.

Joints
Many moving joints have a lubricating layer of liquid, called synovial fluid.

Tissue fluids
Body tissues contain water, with lean tissue holding more than fatty tissue.

Cell cytoplasm
Cells need water for the chemical reactions that take place inside them.

URINE TEST

Urine can provide valuable clues about health. Dark urine is a sign that a person is dehydrated and needs to drink more. Tests can also detect pregnancy, some infections, hormone changes, and diabetes.

Urine sample
To test urine, a testing strip is dipped into a sample. The colored bands react to different chemicals in the urine, revealing any abnormalities.

What is in urine?

Urine is 94 percent water. The rest is made up of dissolved substances the body has no use for. They include sodium, which is excess salt, and urea, the waste produced by the liver.

WATER MAKES UP 94% OF URINE

Urea, 3.5%
Sodium, 1%
Other substances, 1.5%

WATER BALANCE

The hypothalamus in the brain is responsible for monitoring water levels. If it detects too little or too much water, it responds by telling the pituitary gland to release hormones that communicate with the kidneys and other organs.

Too little water

A shortage of water in the body is called dehydration. The body needs to take in more water and also to conserve the water already inside it.

- **Low water alert**
  The pituitary gland releases a hormone into the bloodstream.

- **Feeling thirsty**
  The hormone triggers an urge to drink.

- **Dry mouth**
  The mouth feels dry, as water is sent to areas that need it more.

- **Kidneys**
  The kidneys receive instructions to remove less water from the blood, so the body produces less urine.

A HUMAN DRINKS AN **AVERAGE OF 158,500 PINTS (75,000 LITERS)** OF WATER IN A LIFETIME.

Too much water

Too much water in the body is called overhydration. This condition is rare, but can be caused by illness or by drinking a large amount very quickly. Cells become too waterlogged to work and the blood pressure becomes too high.

- **High water alert**
  The hypothalamus orders blood vessels to widen, which reduces blood pressure.

- **Kidneys**
  The kidneys are ordered to extract more water from the blood, making more urine.

SALTWATER

The water inside our bodies is salty—in fact, it is as salty as seawater. Salt, or sodium, helps maintain the body's water balance—the amount of salt dissolved in the blood tells the hypothalamus how much water the kidneys should release as urine, and how much to keep. Alongside potassium, salt also plays an essential role in helping nerve cells make signals.

Salt sizes
Salt makes up about 0.4 percent of our body weight. A child's body contains the equivalent of 28 teaspoons of salt, while an adult's body has 40 teaspoons.

Female reproduction

From her teenage years to about her mid-fifties, the role of a woman's reproductive organs is, in combination with a man's sex cells (sperm), to create new human life—a baby.

A woman's main reproductive organs are her ovaries and uterus. The two ovaries are where eggs are stored, then released at regular intervals. If an egg is fertilized by male sperm, the job of the uterus is to nurture and protect the egg as it develops—first into an embryo, then a fetus, which grows into a baby, ready to be born.

Inside the reproductive system

This cross section shows a side view of the female reproductive organs. The uterus is in the middle of the lower abdomen, between the bladder and the rectum. The two ovaries are on either side of the uterus, connected to it by the fallopian tubes.

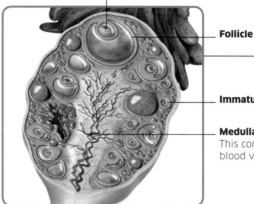

Ripe egg
This egg is mature and ready for release.

Follicle

Immature egg

Medulla
This contains blood vessels.

Inside an ovary

The ovaries contain many thousands of immature eggs, each enclosed in a baglike follicle. Every month, hormones trigger a process where one of the eggs starts to outgrow the others. When it is mature, the egg is released from the ovary.

Preparing for pregnancy

Every month or so, a woman's body goes through the process of preparing for a possible pregnancy. This sequence is called the menstrual cycle.

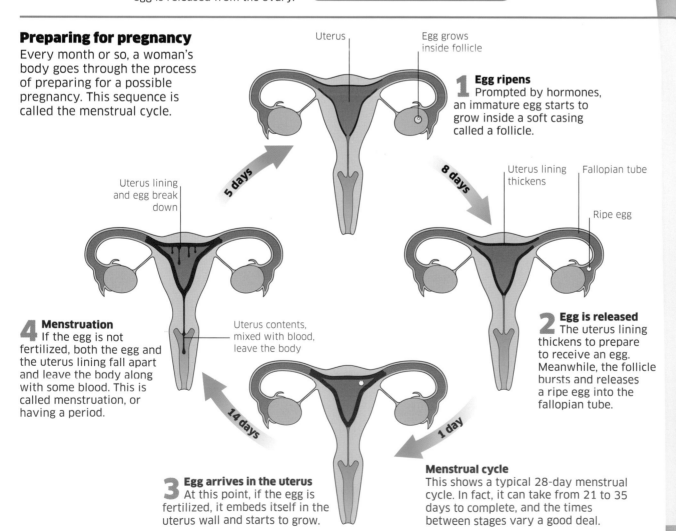

Uterus

Egg grows inside follicle

1 Egg ripens
Prompted by hormones, an immature egg starts to grow inside a soft casing called a follicle.

5 days

8 days

Uterus lining thickens

Fallopian tube

Ripe egg

Uterus lining and egg break down

2 Egg is released
The uterus lining thickens to prepare to receive an egg. Meanwhile, the follicle bursts and releases a ripe egg into the fallopian tube.

4 Menstruation
If the egg is not fertilized, both the egg and the uterus lining fall apart and leave the body along with some blood. This is called menstruation, or having a period.

Uterus contents, mixed with blood, leave the body

14 days

1 day

3 Egg arrives in the uterus
At this point, if the egg is fertilized, it embeds itself in the uterus wall and starts to grow.

Menstrual cycle
This shows a typical 28-day menstrual cycle. In fact, it can take from 21 to 35 days to complete, and the times between stages vary a good deal.

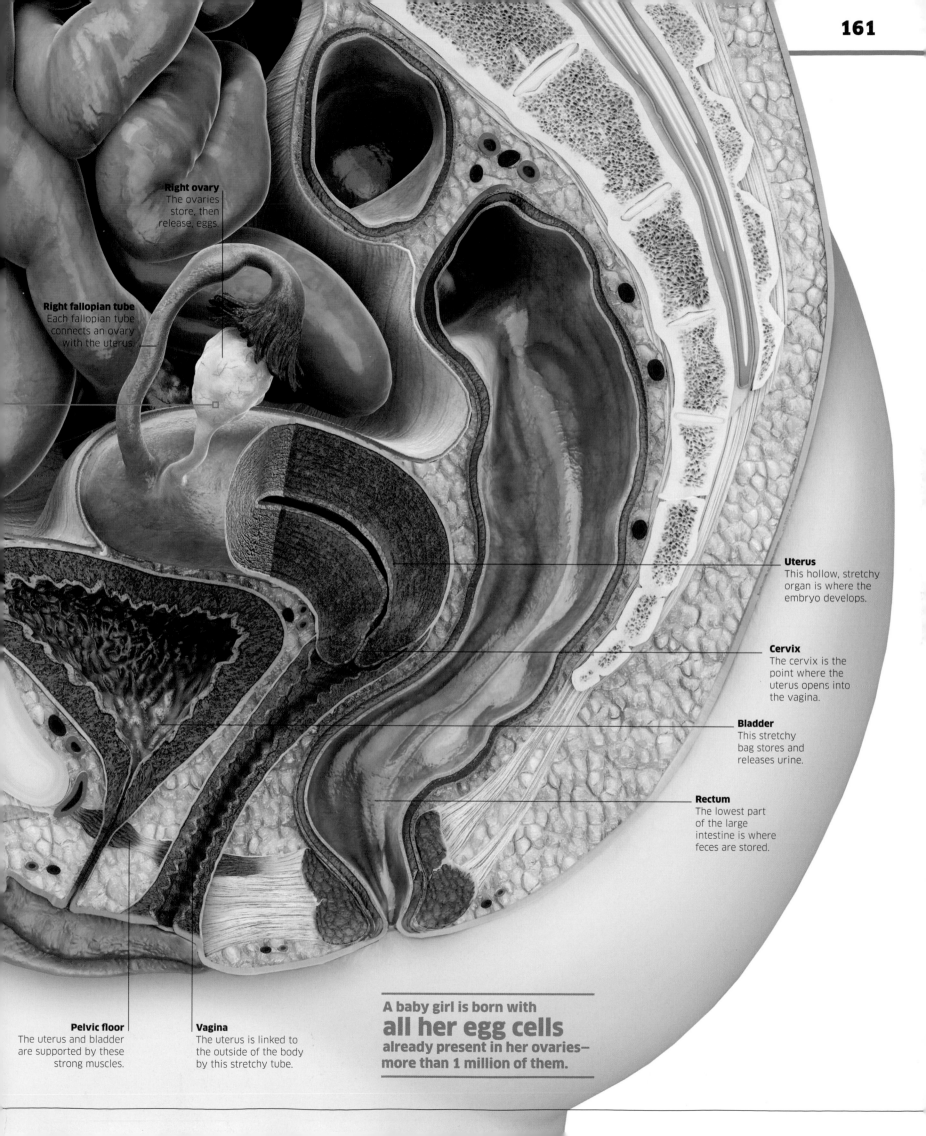

Right ovary
The ovaries store, then release, eggs.

Right fallopian tube
Each fallopian tube connects an ovary with the uterus.

Uterus
This hollow, stretchy organ is where the embryo develops.

Cervix
The cervix is the point where the uterus opens into the vagina.

Bladder
This stretchy bag stores and releases urine.

Rectum
The lowest part of the large intestine is where feces are stored.

Pelvic floor
The uterus and bladder are supported by these strong muscles.

Vagina
The uterus is linked to the outside of the body by this stretchy tube.

A baby girl is born with
all her egg cells
already present in her ovaries—
more than 1 million of them.

Inside the reproductive system

The testes and penis, which are outside the body, are connected by a series of internal tubes and glands. The whole male reproductive system is adapted to produce, mature, and transport sperm to where they can fertilize a female egg.

A man's testes make about
100 million
sperm every day.

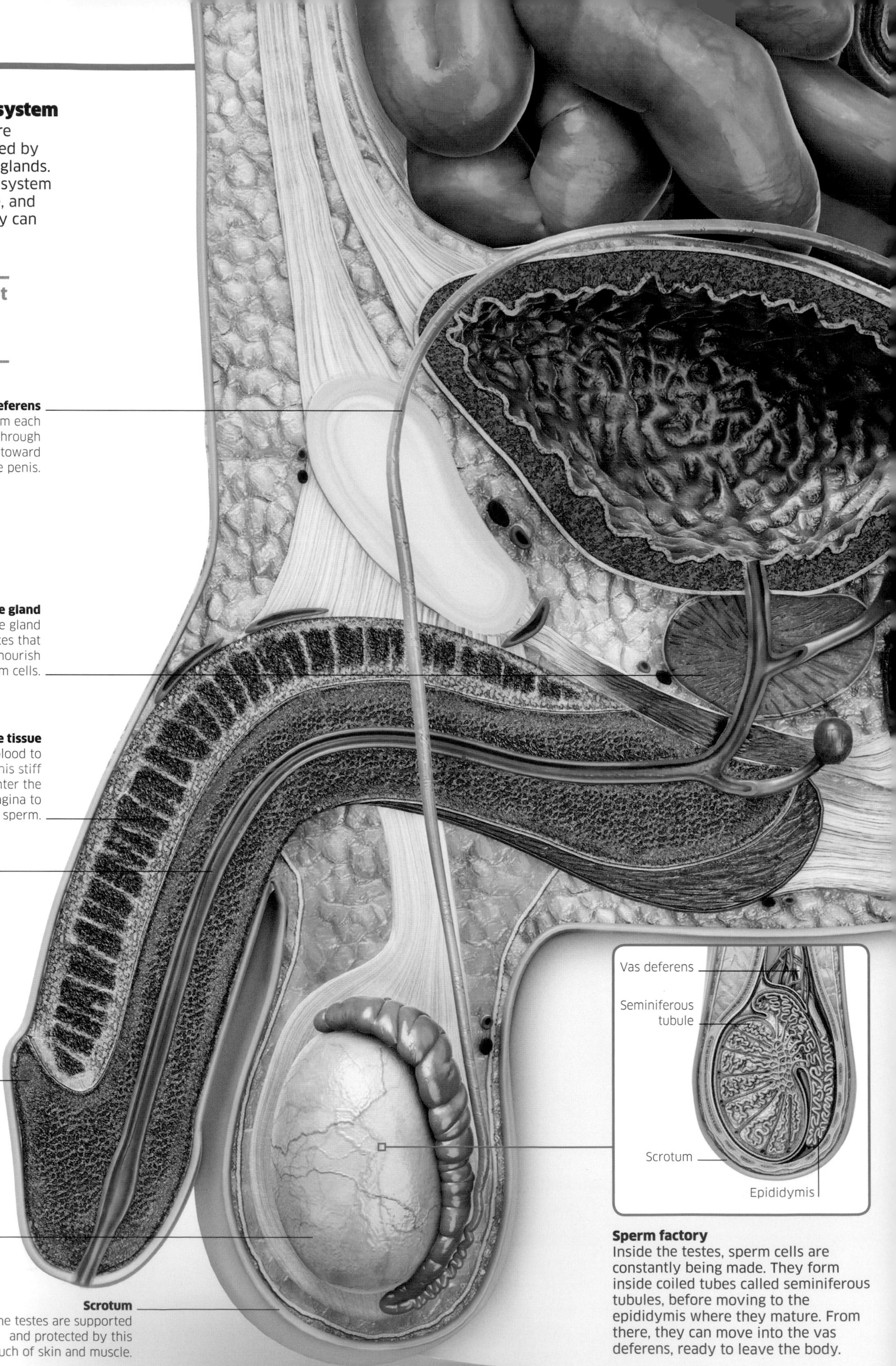

Vas deferens
Sperm from each testis pass through this tube toward the penis.

Prostate gland
The prostate gland adds substances that protect and nourish the sperm cells.

Erectile tissue
This fills with blood to make the penis stiff enough to enter the woman's vagina to deliver sperm.

Urethra
Sperm-carrying semen leaves the body through this tube.

Penis
The penis transfers sperm into a woman's vagina.

Testis
Also called testicles, the two testes make and release sperm cells.

Scrotum
The testes are supported and protected by this pouch of skin and muscle.

Vas deferens

Seminiferous tubule

Scrotum

Epididymis

Sperm factory
Inside the testes, sperm cells are constantly being made. They form inside coiled tubes called seminiferous tubules, before moving to the epididymis where they mature. From there, they can move into the vas deferens, ready to leave the body.

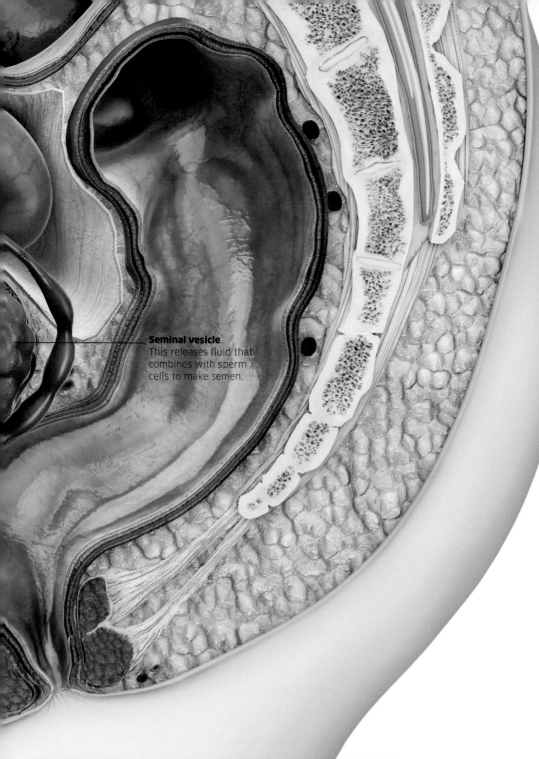

Sperm cells

Sperm cells are among the tiniest human cells, but the nucleus carries half the genetic instructions for creating a new life. Sperm are well adapted to produce enough energy for the long swim to the female egg.

Nucleus

The midpiece is packed with energy-producing mitochondria.

The tail's whiplike action propels the sperm forward.

Seminal vesicle
This releases fluid that combines with sperm cells to make semen.

Male reproduction

The male reproductive organs' role in creating new life is to make sperm (sex cells). The sperm swim to a female egg, where one of them joins with it to create a fertilized egg that will grow into a baby.

A man's main reproductive organs are the testes and penis. The two testes are where sperm are made and stored. Each testis is connected to a tube, which carries the sperm to the penis. On the way, the sperm mix with other substances to make a liquid called semen. During the act of sexual intercourse, the penis becomes stiff and is inserted into a woman's vagina, where it releases the sperm-containing semen.

Fertilization race

To join with an egg, sperm cells must complete the 8–12 in (20–30 cm) journey from the woman's vagina, via the uterus, to the egg in her fallopian tube. This is the equivalent of a 6-mile (10-km) swim for a human. Millions of sperm begin the journey, but just a few survive to reach the egg—and only one will fertilize it.

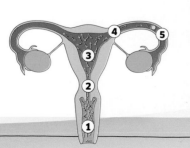

0 HOURS				**UP TO 72 HOURS**
① **Vagina** 250 million sperm	② **Cervix** 70 million sperm	③ **Uterus** 100,000 sperm	④ **Fallopian tube** A few thousand sperm	⑤ **Egg** Fewer than 50 sperm
The race begins The vagina is an acidic environment for the sperm. Millions don't make it beyond this stage.	**Through the gap** The surviving sperm swim through the entrance to the uterus, which is slightly open.	**The race gets tough** Many sperm fail to get through the cervix's protective mucus. The successful ones now face attack from immune system cells in the uterus.	**The last effort** Uterus muscles contract to push the sperm toward the fallopian tubes. Half of them swim toward the correct tube, where the egg is.	**Fertilization** A handful of sperm arrive at the egg. Only one succeeds in burrowing through the egg's outer layer to fertilize it.

Sperm — Egg

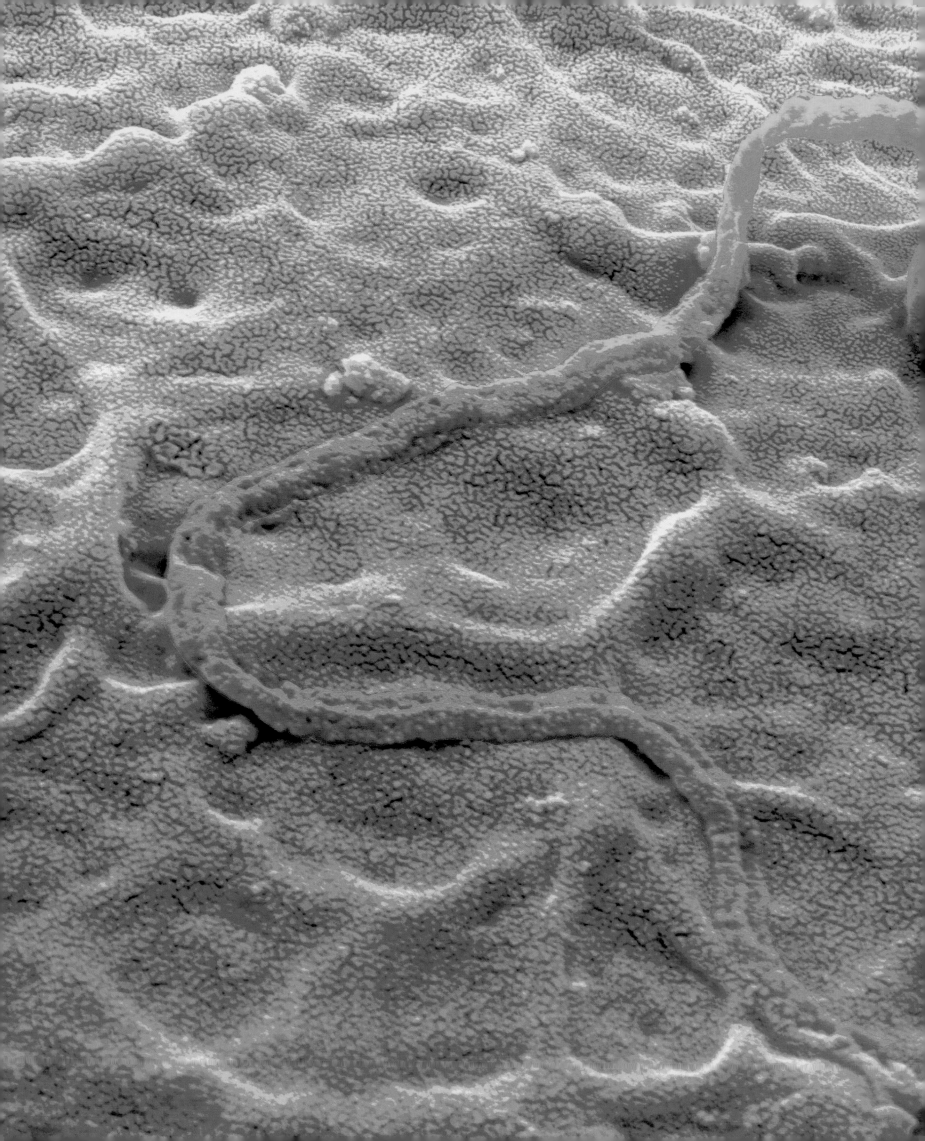

SPERM AND EGG

Each sperm cell (colored orange in this image) has a head made up of genetic material and a tail that enables speedy swimming. Up to 300 million sperm can be released at one time, and they compete to be first to fertilize the female egg (shown in blue).

Inside a woman's fallopian tube, her egg is surrounded by sperm, but only one will gain entry to the egg. As the winning sperm pushes through the outer case of the egg, a chemical reaction shuts out all the other sperm. The successful sperm then fuses with the nucleus of the egg, and fertilization is complete. An embryo is formed, which will eventually develop into a baby.

The growing fetus

Once a sperm cell and an egg cell join, the fertilized egg begins to grow inside the woman's uterus. During pregnancy the female body becomes a complete support system for the unborn baby.

It takes almost nine months for the fertilized egg to become a fully formed baby. Throughout this time, the uterus provides protection and warmth. As the baby develops, the uterus stretches until it is larger than any other organ in the body. The growing fetus shows in the pregnant woman's "bump" at the front of her abdomen.

A fetus begins its development as a single cell—and nine months later, the newborn baby's body consists of about 3 trillion cells.

Villi
The placenta is packed with tiny fingerlike growths. They absorb oxygen and nutrients from the mother's blood, ready to pass to the fetus.

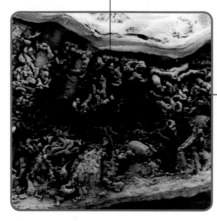

Placenta
The placenta, which is attached to the lining of the uterus, is the fetus's life-support system. It supplies the baby with oxygen and fuel, and also takes waste away, via the umbilical cord.

Amniotic fluid
The amniotic fluid is a mixture of water and nutrients that helps the fetus to grow and cushions it from knocks and jolts.

Uterus
The stretchy uterus expands as the fetus grows inside it.

Skin
A white substance called vernix gives the skin a waterproof coating.

Stages of growth
For the first eight weeks of pregnancy the developing baby is called an embryo. After eight weeks it is known as a fetus. The fetus develops quickly, doubling in weight every five weeks and changing shape as more body parts grow.

Week 5
The embryo is the size of an apple seed. It already has buds from which the arms and legs will grow.

Week 10
The fetus is the size of an olive. All the major organs have grown, new limbs are moving, and its heartbeat is three times faster than that of an adult.

Week 20
The fetus is as long as a banana. It has a big head, a growing brain, and fingers and toes. When the eyes first open, at about week 26, they will be able to detect light and dark.

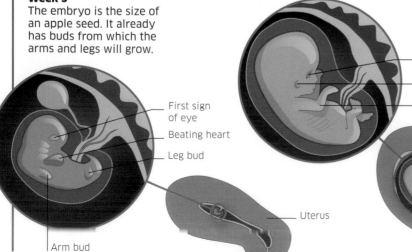

First sign of eye
Beating heart
Leg bud
Arm bud
Uterus

Eye
Ear
Arm

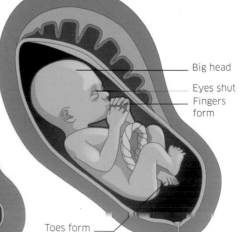

Big head
Eyes shut
Fingers form

Toes form

Full-term fetus
After about 40 weeks, the fetus is fully developed and weighs about 7 lb 12 oz (3.5 kg). It fits tightly inside the uterus, surrounded by a liquid called amniotic fluid. There is little room to move, so it keeps a curled-up position with its limbs bent.

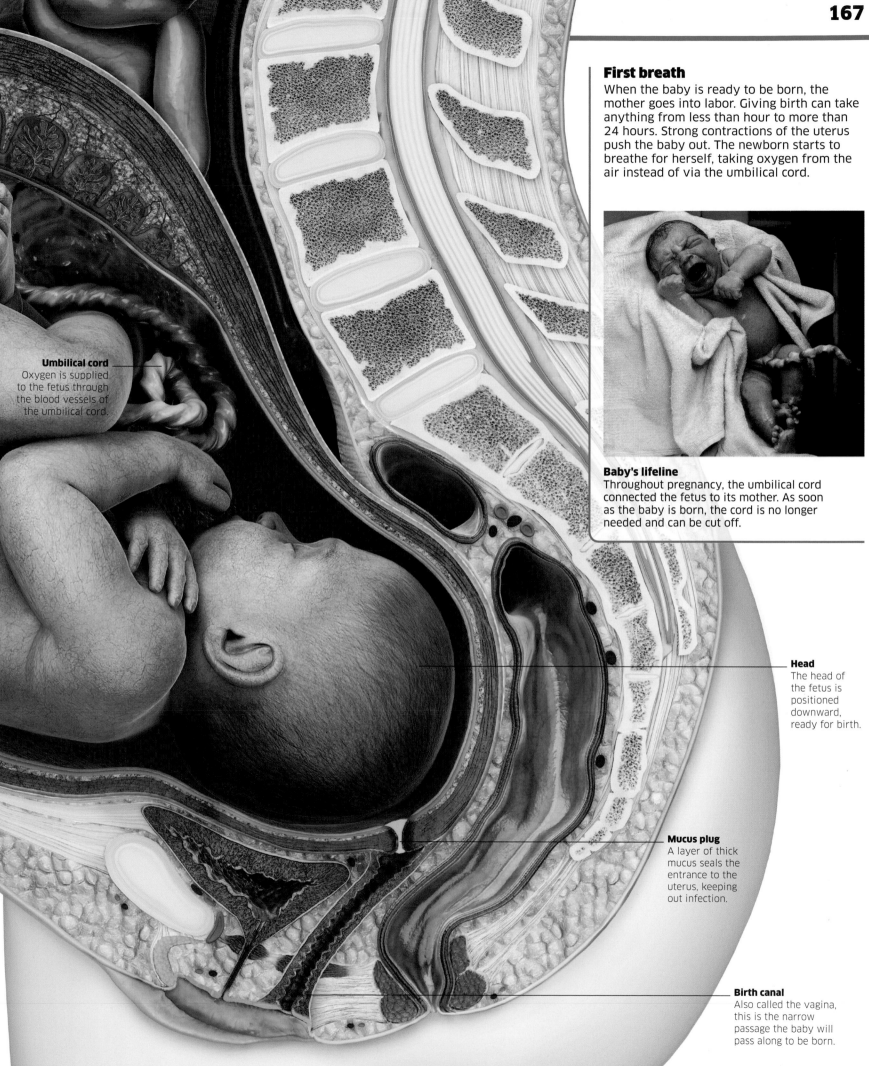

First breath

When the baby is ready to be born, the mother goes into labor. Giving birth can take anything from less than hour to more than 24 hours. Strong contractions of the uterus push the baby out. The newborn starts to breathe for herself, taking oxygen from the air instead of via the umbilical cord.

Baby's lifeline
Throughout pregnancy, the umbilical cord connected the fetus to its mother. As soon as the baby is born, the cord is no longer needed and can be cut off.

Umbilical cord
Oxygen is supplied to the fetus through the blood vessels of the umbilical cord.

Head
The head of the fetus is positioned downward, ready for birth.

Mucus plug
A layer of thick mucus seals the entrance to the uterus, keeping out infection.

Birth canal
Also called the vagina, this is the narrow passage the baby will pass along to be born.

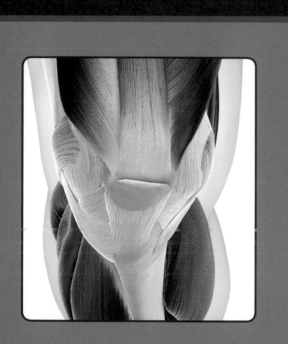

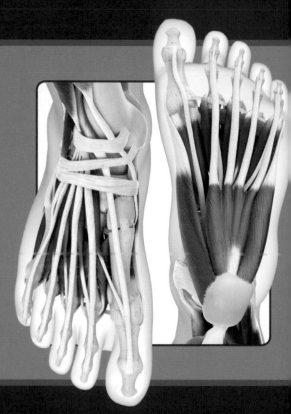

LEGS AND FEET

Our lower limbs are strong, flexible, and powerful. As we move, the bones, joints, and muscles work together to drive our bodies forward. Our feet form a secure base, carry our body weight, and push against the ground to help us walk.

The **gluteus maximus** or buttock muscle is the **biggest muscle** in the human body.

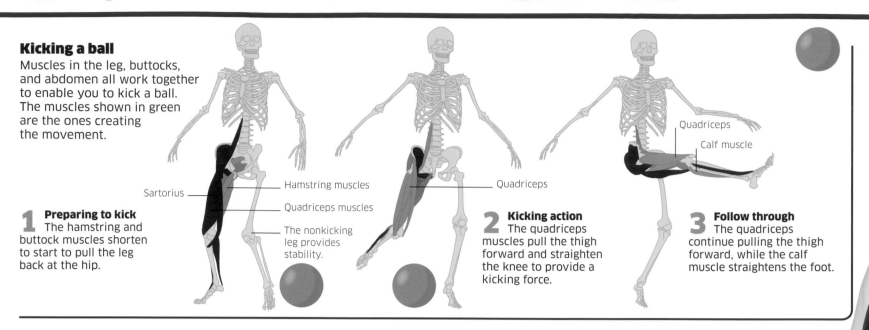

Kicking a ball

Muscles in the leg, buttocks, and abdomen all work together to enable you to kick a ball. The muscles shown in green are the ones creating the movement.

Sartorius

Hamstring muscles

Quadriceps muscles

The nonkicking leg provides stability.

Quadriceps

Quadriceps

Calf muscle

1 Preparing to kick
The hamstring and buttock muscles shorten to start to pull the leg back at the hip.

2 Kicking action
The quadriceps muscles pull the thigh forward and straighten the knee to provide a kicking force.

3 Follow through
The quadriceps continue pulling the thigh forward, while the calf muscle straightens the foot.

Hip and thigh

Unlike most mammals, humans walk upright on two legs. The joints, muscles, and bones of the hip and thigh have to support the downward push of your body as you walk, run, or jump, so they need to be very strong and stable.

The hip and thigh are connected at the hip joint. This joint has to be able to move in a wide range of directions, while staying firm and strong so you don't fall over. When we perform movements such as kicking a ball or dancing, the body is often balanced on just one leg at a time. This means that each side has to be able to hold up the whole body.

Inside the hip and thigh

The femur, or thighbone, connects to the lower part of the pelvis. Surrounding these bones are some of the body's most powerful muscles, which work both to control movement and to pull the body upright.

Gluteus maximus (buttock muscle)
The gluteus maximus is a powerful muscle that helps extend the thigh.

Adductor magnus
The thigh is pulled inward by this muscle.

Semimembranosus
This muscle bends the knee and extends the hip.

Gracilis
The hip is pulled inward by this muscle.

Swinging hips

The mobile hip joint enables the legs to move in three main ways: from side to side, up and down, and rotating, both inward and outward.

Adduction and abduction
This is the sideways movement toward and away from the midline of the body.

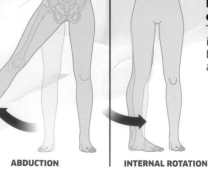

ADDUCTION

ABDUCTION

INTERNAL ROTATION

Internal and external rotation
The leg is turned in toward the body, or outward away from it.

EXTERNAL ROTATION

EXTENSION

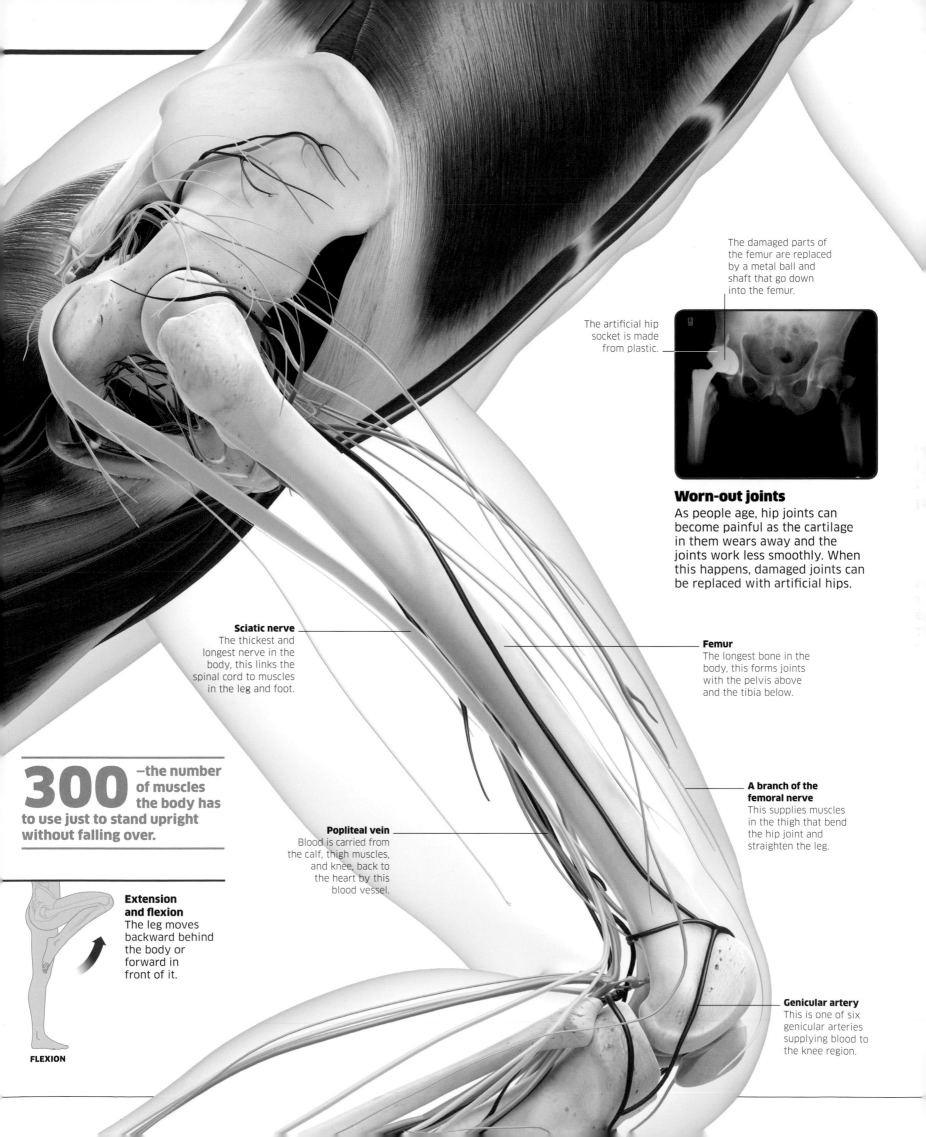

The damaged parts of the femur are replaced by a metal ball and shaft that go down into the femur.

The artificial hip socket is made from plastic.

Worn-out joints
As people age, hip joints can become painful as the cartilage in them wears away and the joints work less smoothly. When this happens, damaged joints can be replaced with artificial hips.

Sciatic nerve
The thickest and longest nerve in the body, this links the spinal cord to muscles in the leg and foot.

Femur
The longest bone in the body, this forms joints with the pelvis above and the tibia below.

300 —the number of muscles the body has to use just to stand upright without falling over.

A branch of the femoral nerve
This supplies muscles in the thigh that bend the hip joint and straighten the leg.

Popliteal vein
Blood is carried from the calf, thigh muscles, and knee, back to the heart by this blood vessel.

Extension and flexion
The leg moves backward behind the body or forward in front of it.

FLEXION

Genicular artery
This is one of six genicular arteries supplying blood to the knee region.

Inside a bone

The bones in a human body are strong to support our mass, but light enough for us to move around easily. They are also slightly flexible, so they are less likely to snap if they are knocked or jarred. Their remarkable structure is what gives bones these different qualities.

A bone's outer layer is made of hard, heavy, compact bone. Within this is a layer of spongy bone–tiny struts of hard bone with spaces in between. This honeycomb structure makes bones light but strong. Like tooth enamel, bone is made of calcium minerals, which make it hard. But unlike enamel, it also contains a stretchy substance called collagen, which gives flexibility.

Longest bone
The femur, or thighbone, is the longest and heaviest bone in the body. The femur is tremendously strong, to withstand the massive forces exerted on it during walking, running, or jumping.

Periosteum
The bone's outer skin contains nerves and blood vessels.

Shaft
The strong, slim shaft can bend slightly to withstand pressure without breaking.

Long bone
Each end of a long bone widens into a broad head, which consists mostly of spongy bone.

Blood vessels
These vessels run through the center of each osteon.

Osteocyte
These cells produce minerals that keep the surrounding bone healthy.

Compact bone
This outermost layer of dense, heavy bone is made up of closely packed, cylinder-shaped units called osteons. Each osteon consists of tubes of strong bone tissue, arranged like the rings of wood in a tree trunk. The osteons also contain blood vessels and cells called osteocytes, which help maintain the health of the bone.

Human bone is five times stronger than a steel bar of the same weight.

15% of an adult's mass is taken up by their bones.

Spongy bone
This honeycomblike bone has spaces in it, like a sponge—but it's firm, not squishy.

Blood vessels
These supply energy-giving oxygen and nutrients.

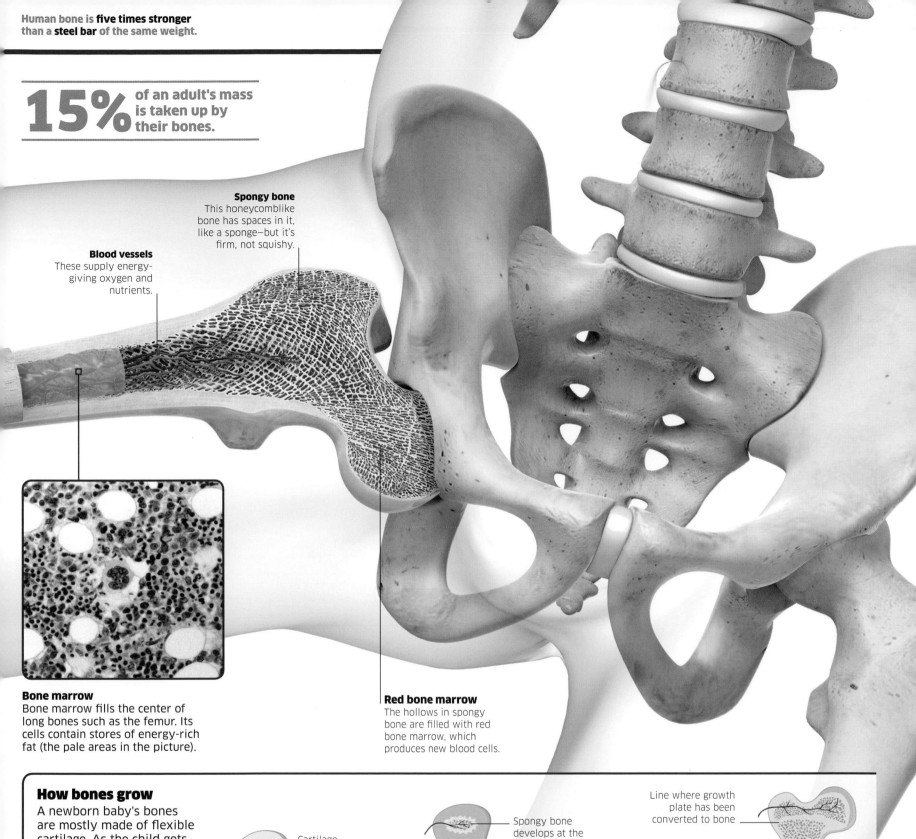

Bone marrow
Bone marrow fills the center of long bones such as the femur. Its cells contain stores of energy-rich fat (the pale areas in the picture).

Red bone marrow
The hollows in spongy bone are filled with red bone marrow, which produces new blood cells.

How bones grow

A newborn baby's bones are mostly made of flexible cartilage. As the child gets older, this cartilage is gradually replaced by bone tissue, the bones grow longer, and the child gets taller. Long bones, such as the femur, have sections near each end called growth plates, where new cartilage is made. This cartilage hardens into new bone.

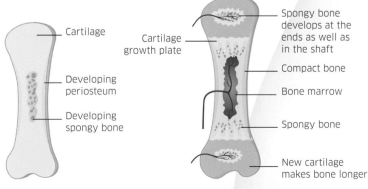

Cartilage

Developing periosteum

Developing spongy bone

Newborn baby
Spongy bone first starts to form in the shaft, in the middle of the bone.

Cartilage growth plate

Spongy bone develops at the ends as well as in the shaft

Compact bone

Bone marrow

Spongy bone

New cartilage makes bone longer

Nine-year-old child
The bone shaft has hardened into bone. Growth plates at each end produce new cartilage, making the bone longer.

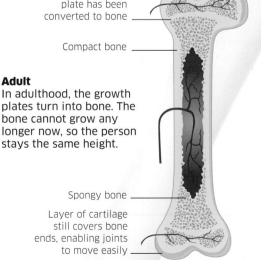

Line where growth plate has been converted to bone

Compact bone

Adult
In adulthood, the growth plates turn into bone. The bone cannot grow any longer now, so the person stays the same height.

Spongy bone

Layer of cartilage still covers bone ends, enabling joints to move easily

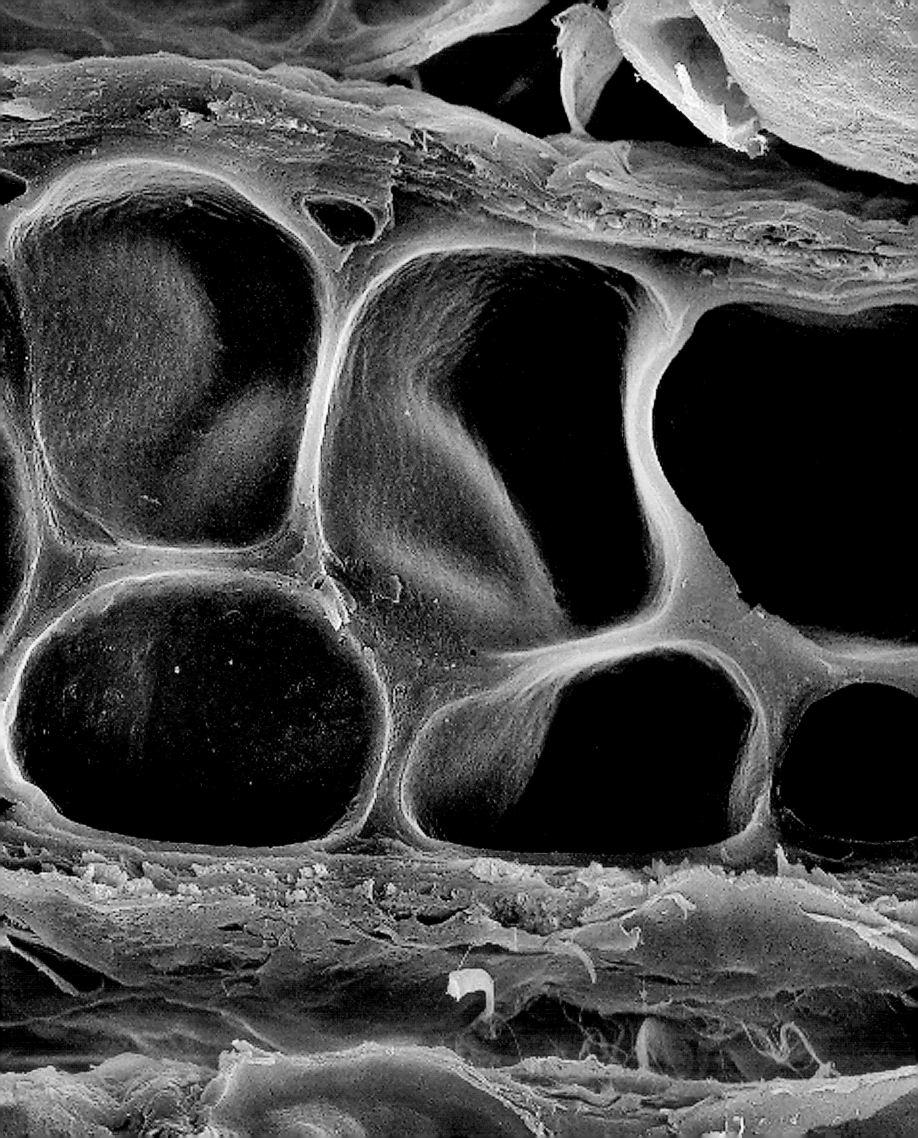

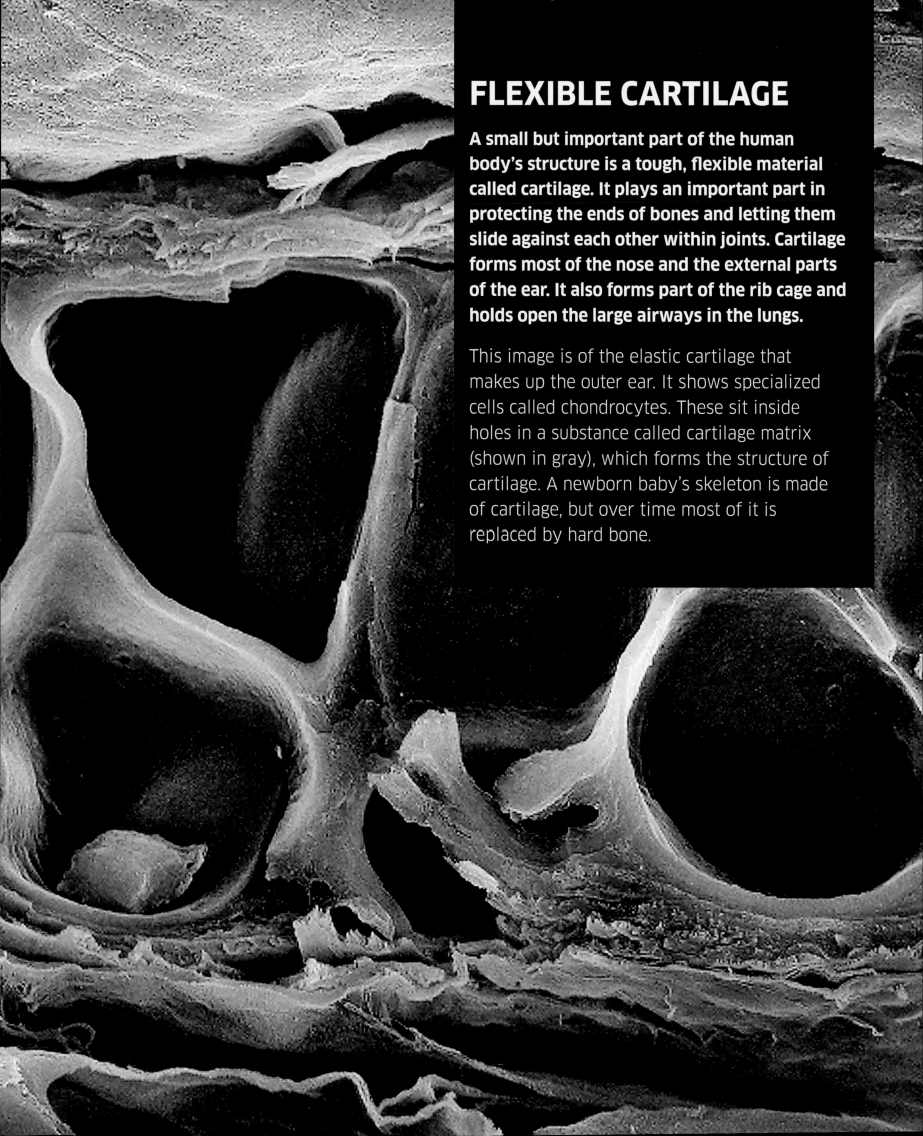

FLEXIBLE CARTILAGE

A small but important part of the human body's structure is a tough, flexible material called cartilage. It plays an important part in protecting the ends of bones and letting them slide against each other within joints. Cartilage forms most of the nose and the external parts of the ear. It also forms part of the rib cage and holds open the large airways in the lungs.

This image is of the elastic cartilage that makes up the outer ear. It shows specialized cells called chondrocytes. These sit inside holes in a substance called cartilage matrix (shown in gray), which forms the structure of cartilage. A newborn baby's skeleton is made of cartilage, but over time most of it is replaced by hard bone.

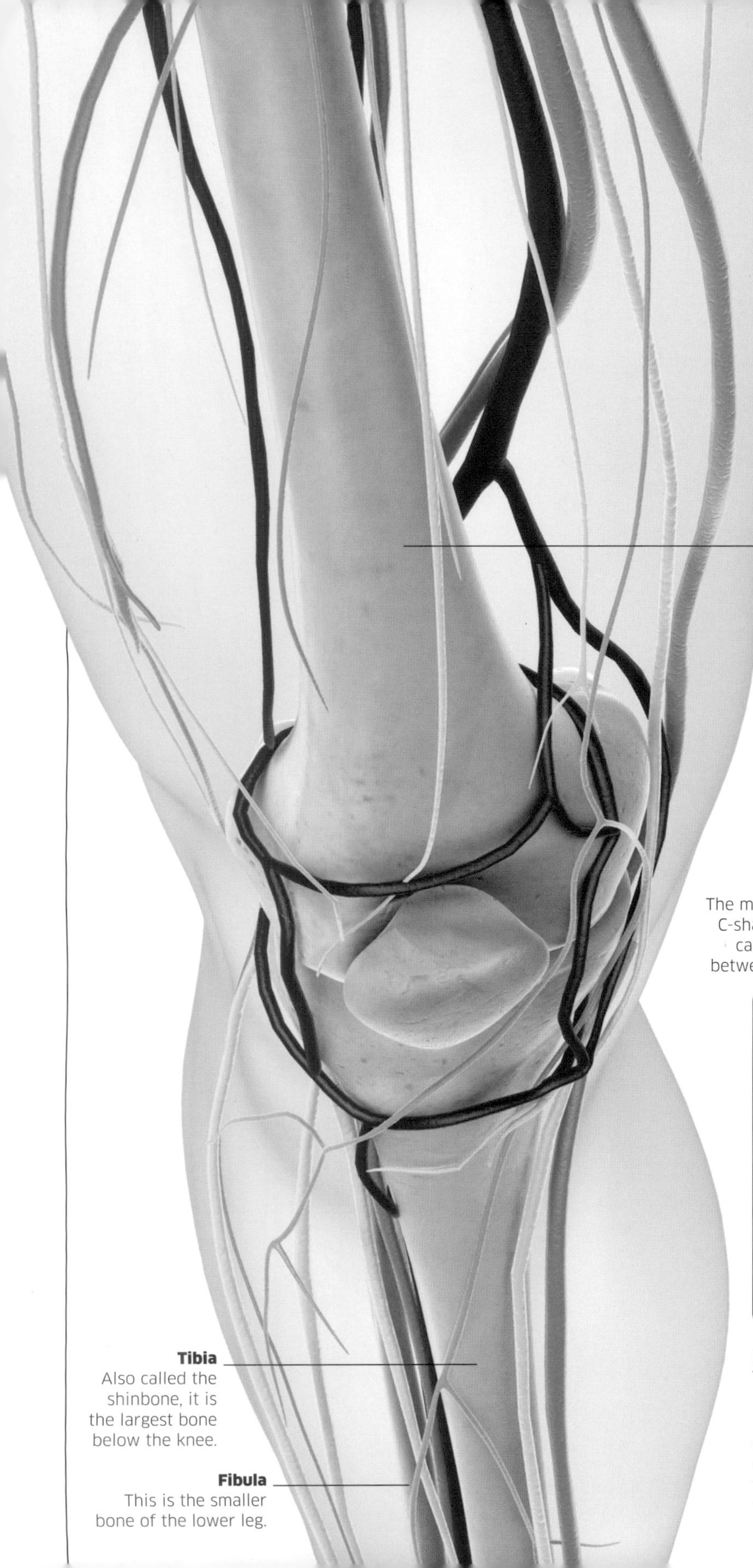
Femur (thighbone)
Tibia
Also called the shinbone, it is the largest bone below the knee.
Fibula
This is the smaller bone of the lower leg.

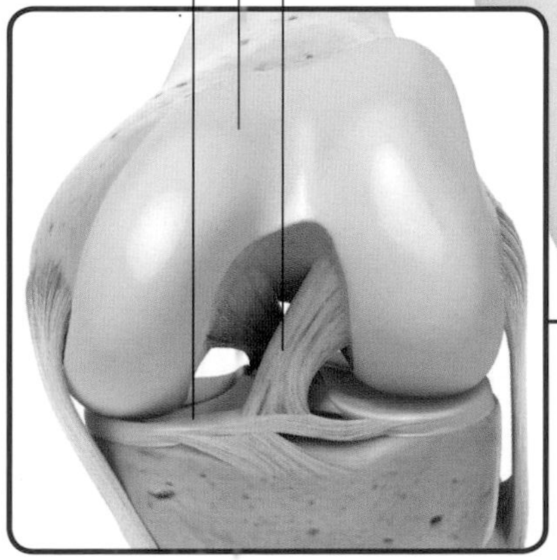
Articular cartilage
Meniscus
The menisci are two C-shaped layers of cartilage that sit between the bones.
Ligament
Ligaments run down each side of and inside the knee.

Inside the knee
The hinged knee joint is held in place by strong ligaments both outside and inside the joint. A layer of cartilage called the meniscus sits between the ends of the two bones. This cushions the impact on the bones when we walk, preventing wear and tear.

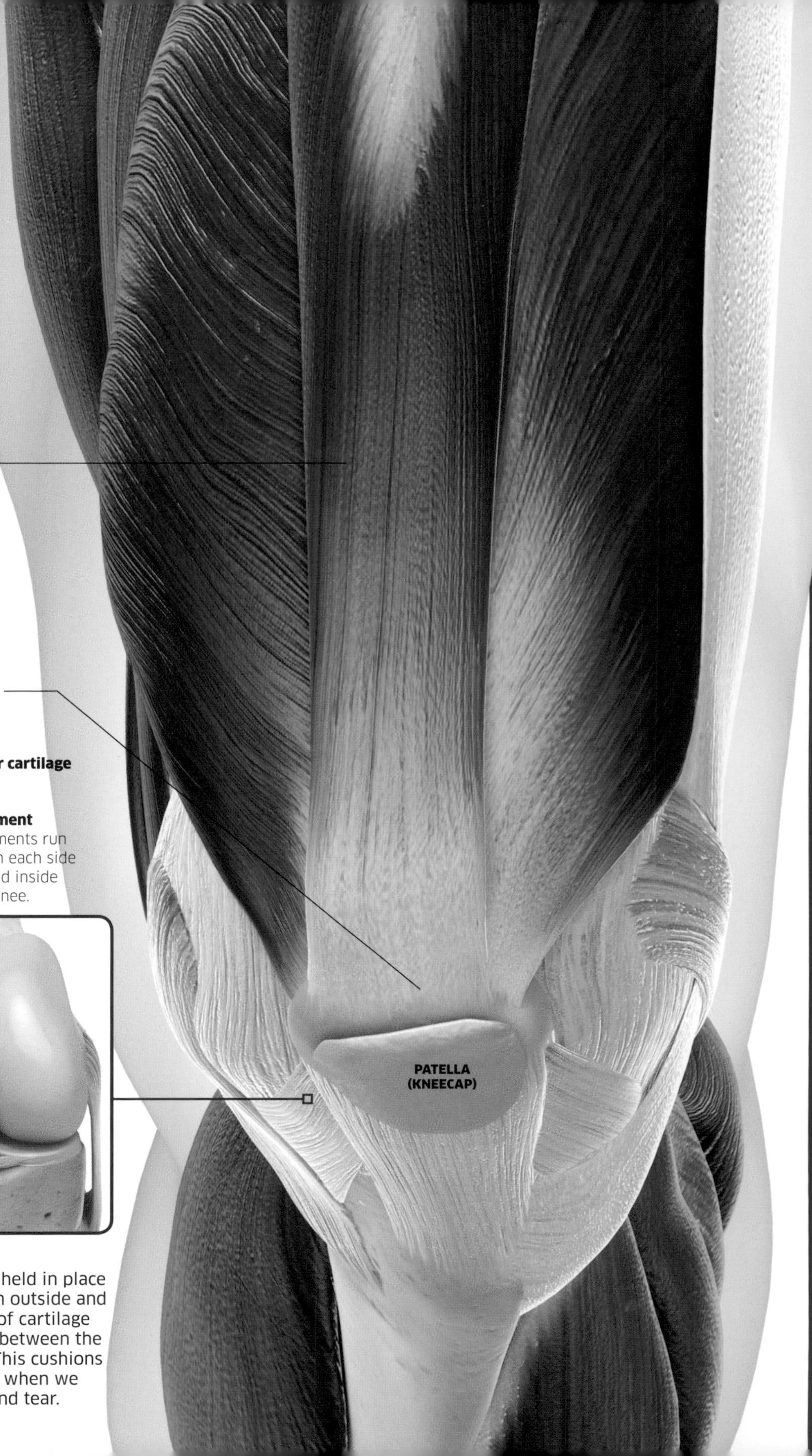
Rectus femoris
This is one of four main muscles that straighten the knee.
Quadriceps femoris tendon
A strong tendon attaches the upper leg muscles to the knee bone.
PATELLA (KNEECAP)

When we land after **jumping**, the knees have to withstand the impact, which can be **12 times more** than the body's weight.

155° is the **angle a typical knee** can flex (bend), enabling us to kneel and squat.

A child's kneecaps do not **harden into bone** until he or she is about three years old.

177

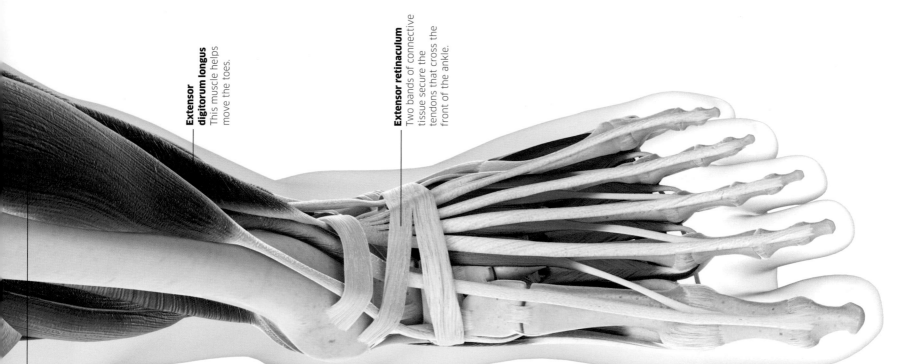

Extensor digitorum longus
This muscle helps move the toes.

Extensor retinaculum
Two bands of connective tissue secure the tendons that cross the front of the ankle.

Tibialis anterior
The foot is bent upward by this muscle.

Great saphenous vein
Blood is carried away from the lower leg and foot by this vein.

Muscles

The lower leg muscles work to bend and straighten the ankle, foot, and toes. They help a person to stand, walk, run, and jump.

Broken bones

Although the lower leg bones are strong, they are among the most often broken bones. Breaks are especially common in people who play sports. The bone heals after a few months, although it may take several years for it to get back to its normal shape.

1 Immediately after injury
Blood fills the area around the break and forms a clot. The surrounding tissue is swollen and painful.

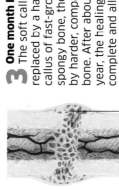

Clot forms

2 After a few days
Cartilage tissue starts to replace the clot. It forms a swelling called a callus, which joins the bone ends and gives some strength back.

Soft callus made of cartilage

New bone tissue

3 One month later
The soft callus is replaced by a hard callus of fast-growing spongy bone, then later by harder, compact bone. After about a year, the healing is complete and all swelling has gone.

A hard callus of spongy bone is gradually replaced by compact bone.

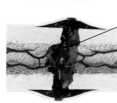

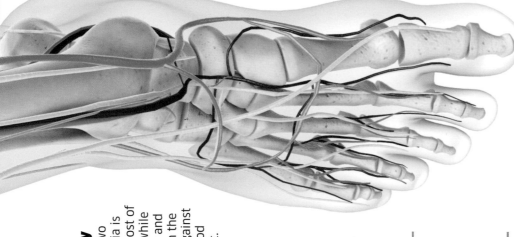

Bones, nerves, and blood supply

The lower leg has two main bones. The tibia is thicker and bears most of the body's weight, while the fibula is smaller and thinner. The veins in the legs have to fight against gravity to carry blood back up to the heart.

The tibia is the second longest bone in the human body, after the femur.

Knee and lower leg

The leg bones are the strongest in the body. They support our full weight and withstand the impact of walking and running. The knee joint, which connects the thighbones and shinbones, is one of the body's largest joints.

Besides providing a hinge between the lower and upper leg bones, the knee has an extra bone, the kneecap. This protects the joint and helps to anchor the knee's tendons, giving the leg muscles more leverage and pulling power.

Ankle and foot

The ankles and feet must carry the weight of the rest of the body. They work together like a spring, pushing off from the ground during running or jumping, and acting as shock absorbers for landing.

Feet are complex body parts. Including the ankle joint, each foot has more than 100 bones, muscles, and ligaments. Whether standing, walking, climbing, or running, the feet can adopt different positions to help the body stay balanced. Feet also have thick skin and toenails to cushion and protect them.

150 million–the number of steps your feet are likely to take in a lifetime.

Feet first
Each foot consists of 26 bones— 14 toe bones, called phalanges, five long bones in the middle, called metatarsals, and seven bones, called tarsals, forming the heel and ankle.

Key

- ■ Phalanges
- ■ Metatarsals
- ■ Tarsals

Bones and nerves
The bones in the foot create a roughly triangular shape, which helps to make it more stable. The arrangement is similar to the hands, but the feet are less flexible because toes are much shorter than fingers. A bundle of nerves provides the ankle and foot with sensation, and the nerves also let the muscles know when to contract.

Superficial fibular nerve
This nerve carries signals from sensors in the feet to the brain.

Anterior tibial artery
This artery carries blood to the front of the lower leg and the top of the foot.

Fibula
Paired with the tibia, this is the thinner leg bone.

Tibia
This is the largest bone in the lower leg.

Ankle bone
These hard bumps on either side of the ankle are the ends of the tibia and fibula bones in the leg.

Talus
The upper tarsal, or talus, forms the ankle joint with the leg bones.

Lateral cuneiform bone
This wedgelike bone is in the center of the foot.

Cuboid
This outer foot bone connects the heel with the fourth and fifth toes.

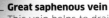

Great saphenous vein
This vein helps to drain blood from the foot.

Phalange
The toe bones are phalanges—the big toe has two, while the others have three.

Calf muscles
Strong, stretchy muscles form the back of the lower leg.

Calf muscle

Achilles tendon

TAKING A FOOTSTEP

Tendon
Attached to the bones, tendons bend and straighten the toes to help the foot grip and balance.

Spring in your step
The feet operate as levers worked by the calf muscle, which is attached to the heel by the strong, slightly stretchy Achilles tendon. In a step or jump, the tendon stretches as your foot hits the ground, then releases energy like a spring as your foot pushes off again.

Calcaneus
Also called the heel bone, it takes the body's weight during walking and running.

Abductor hallucis
This muscle helps to bend the big toe.

Blade runners
Carbon fiber prosthetic blades work like lower legs and feet. Their powerful springs help athletes reach high speeds.

Dorsal interosseus
This is one of four strong muscles between the central bones of the feet.

Natural arch
For most people, tough ligaments pull the foot bones into a natural arched shape, which gives them extra springiness, strength, and stability. Footprints made by bare feet show a gap where the arched part does not touch the ground.

Ball of foot
The ball is a padded section between the toes and the arch.

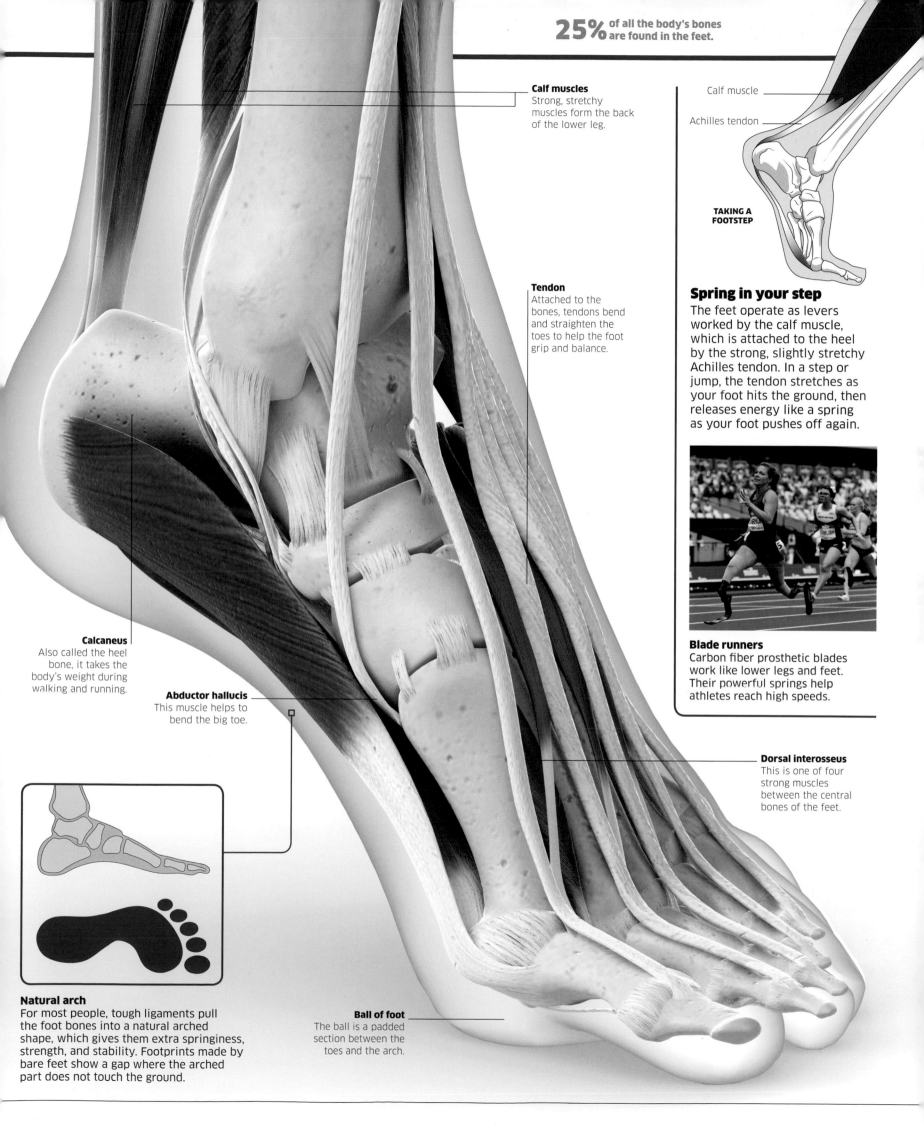

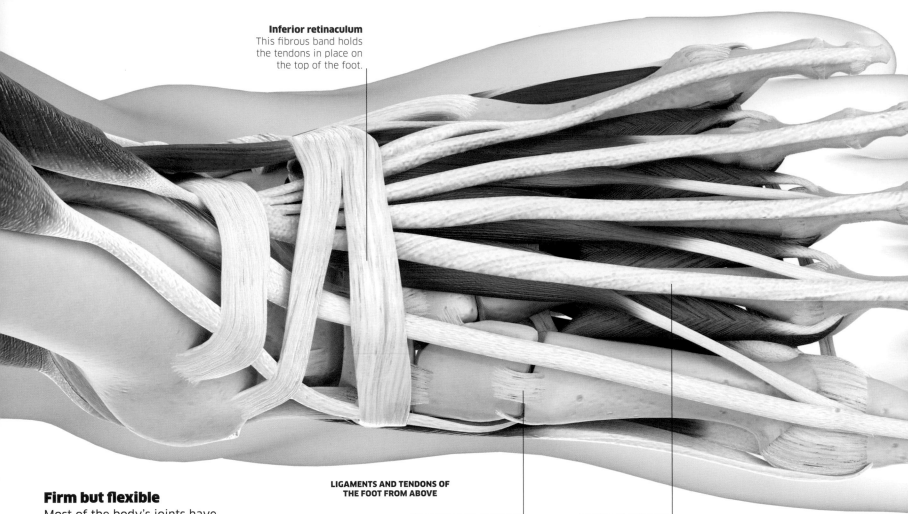

Inferior retinaculum
This fibrous band holds the tendons in place on the top of the foot.

LIGAMENTS AND TENDONS OF THE FOOT FROM ABOVE

Dorsal tarsometatarsal ligament
This is one of the many ligaments that join bones within the foot.

Tendon of extensor digitorum longus muscle
This is one of the tendons connecting this leg muscle to the toes.

Firm but flexible

Most of the body's joints have a group of ligaments and tendons around them. This can be seen with the ankle and foot joints shown in these two images, from above and below. Ligaments allow a joint to move freely, while preventing it from coming loose or falling apart.

Ligaments and tendons

Bones and muscles allow the body to move and change position. However, they could not work without ligaments and tendons—superstrong bands that make firm but flexible connections between bones, joints, and muscles.

Strong, slightly stretchy ligaments hold together the different bones around joints such as the knee, elbow, or shoulder. Tendons do a different job. They are the tough bands that attach a muscle to a bone.

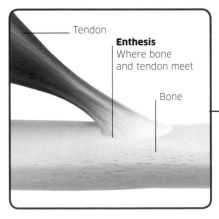

Tendon

Enthesis
Where bone and tendon meet

Bone

Making connections

At the point where tendons and ligaments join to bones, they spread out to cover a larger surface, which gives a stronger grip. Fibers, made of a protein called collagen, grow into the top layer of bone at an attachment site called an enthesis.

4,000 –the approximate number of tendons in the human body.

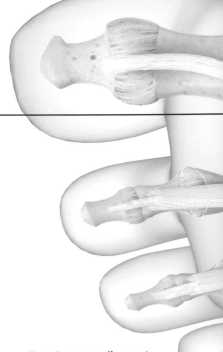

Deep transverse ligament
This narrow strip of ligament links the metacarpal bones.

People are ⅜ in (1 cm) shorter when they go to bed at night, because the joints in the spine compress as they walk around during the day.

900 –the approximate number of **ligaments** in the body.

181

Phalanges
These are the jointed bones of the toes.

Double-jointed
People with flexible bodies are often described as "double-jointed". However, these people don't have unusual joints, but extra-stretchy ligaments. Acrobats and gymnasts often have naturally loose ligaments, but still must train hard to achieve maximum flexibility.

Head held high
One of the most important ligaments in the body is the nuchal ligament, which attaches the skull to the neck bones, helping to keep the head upright and stable.

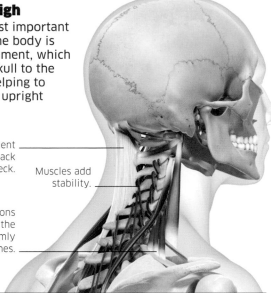

The nuchal ligament runs down the back of the neck.

Muscles add stability.

Tendons attach the muscles firmly to bones.

Stringy structure
Both ligaments and tendons are made of many bundles of collagen fibers. Collagen is a tough, stringlike protein found in many body tissues, such as bone and skin.

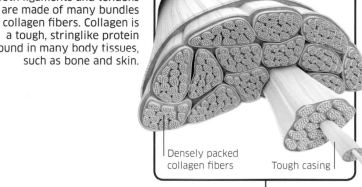

Densely packed collagen fibers

Tough casing

Tendon of flexor hallucis longus
This is the muscle at the back of the leg that bends the toe down.

Achilles tendon
This is the strongest and thickest tendon. It connects the calf muscle to the back of the heel.

Calcaneus (heel bone)

LIGAMENTS AND TENDONS OF THE FOOT FROM BELOW

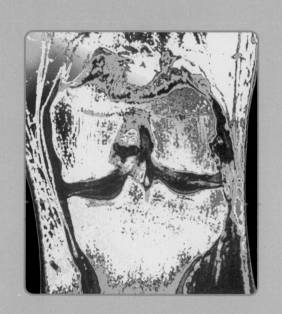
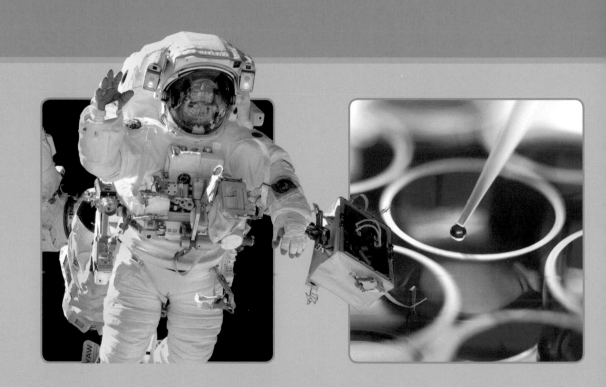

BODY SCIENCE

More is known about the human body today than ever before. Technology allows us to view the body in stunning detail, and we now understand how our lifestyle impacts health. Scientists are evolving revolutionary treatments for disease and injury, and they are even figuring out how humans could adapt to life in space!

Ancient Egyptians **preserved dead bodies** by **mummification**, which improved both their **bandaging skills** and their anatomical understanding.

1665: Hooke's discoveries
English researcher Robert Hooke publishes *Micrographia*, which contains drawings of things he has seen through his microscope. He coins the term "cell" for the smallest unit of life he finds.

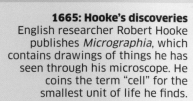

HOOKE'S DRAWING OF A FLEA

1735: Surgical success
French-born English surgeon Claudius Amyand removes the inflamed appendix of Hanvil Anderson, a young patient. To much amazement, Hanvil recovers from surgery.

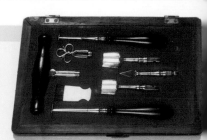

18TH-CENTURY SURGICAL INSTRUMENTS

EARLY DEPICTION OF CIRCULATION

1628: William Harvey
English doctor William Harvey explains the closed circuit of veins and arteries carrying blood around the body in the circulatory system. He understands that the heart works like a pump.

COMPOUND MICROSCOPE

1590: Compound microscope
Dutch eyeglass-maker Zacharias Janssen is said to have invented the compound microscope, a magnifying device with two or more lenses. Medical research is changed forever by this breakthrough.

Medical milestones

Humans have looked for ways to cure illnesses and heal injuries for thousands of years. The earliest people could only pray to their gods, or hope for good fortune. Gradually, as medical science progressed and knowledge of the body grew, more effective treatments were developed.

New generations of doctors and scientists build on the breakthroughs of the past. Today, we know more than ever before about how our bodies work, but there is still a lot to discover. We never stop learning about the incredibly complex machine that keeps us all alive.

c. 390 CE: Public hospital
A Roman noblewoman named Fabiola sets up the first public hospital in western Europe. She works as a nurse in her hospital and is made Saint Fabiola after her death.

SAINT FABIOLA

SURGICAL INSTRUMENTS FROM ANCIENT ROME

c. 129–200 CE: Galen
Galen is a Greek doctor who cares for several Roman emperors. He makes many discoveries by dissecting monkeys and pigs. He acts as physician to the gladiators of his hometown, Pergamon.

c. 5000 BCE: Trepanation
Early civilizations in Africa and the Americas use trepanation to try to cure a range of illnesses, from epilepsy to blindness. This involves drilling a hole in a person's skull to release evil spirits.

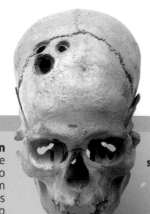

SKULL BEARING MARKS OF TREPANATION

c. 2650 BCE: Imhotep
Ancient Egyptian Imhotep is the most celebrated healer of his time, diagnosing illnesses and devising treatments for more than 200 diseases. He is worshiped as a god in Egypt, Greece, and Rome.

STATUE OF IMHOTEP

Before anaesthetics, surgery had to be speedy. Surgeon **Robert Liston** was said to be able to **amputate a leg** in just 30 seconds.

The **first blood transfusion** took place in 1818 when blood was transferred from a donor to a patient using a syringe.

185

1796: Smallpox vaccination
English doctor Edward Jenner performs the first successful vaccination against disease. He injects a boy with pus from a cowpox blister, and the boy becomes immune to smallpox.

PORTRAIT OF EDWARD JENNER

1816: First stethoscope
French doctor René Laennec invents the stethoscope. This simple wooden tube has evolved to become the twin earpieces now used by modern medics to listen to heartbeats.

LAENNEC'S STETHOSCOPE

EARLIEST SURVIVING EYEGLASSES

1306: First eyeglasses
A pair of eyeglasses is mentioned for the first time. This occurs in a sermon by Friar Giordano da Pisa.

1242: Blood revelation
Ibn an-Nafis of Damascus is the first to describe blood circulating between the heart and lungs. Galen had thought blood crossed from one heart chamber to the other, but an-Nafis was correct.

c. 1020: Cataract cure
Ammar bin Ali al-Mawsili of Iraq invents a glass tube that works like a syringe, sucking cataracts from the eyes of patients.

EARLY EYE OPERATION

c. 1025: Canon of Medicine
Persian philosopher Avicenna publishes his *Canon of Medicine*, used by doctors as a textbook for the next 500 years and translated into many languages.

PAGE FROM *CANON OF MEDICINE*

ERASISTRATUS AND HEROPHILOS

c. 250 BCE: School of anatomy
Greek doctors Erasistratus and Herophilos open a school of anatomy in Alexandria, Egypt. They make important discoveries about the heart and brain, but supposedly dissect live criminals in the process!

c. 420 BCE: Hippocrates
Ancient Greek physician Hippocrates is one of the first to realize that diseases have natural, not magical causes. The Hippocratic Oath, a vow of integrity for medical professionals, is named after him.

STATUE OF HIPPOCRATES

STATUE OF SUSHRUTA

c. 2500 BCE: Acupuncture
The healing practice of acupuncture is developed in China. Fine needles are inserted at specific points under the skin to relieve pain or cure illnesses.

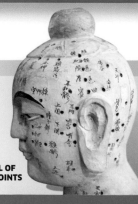

CHINESE MODEL OF ACUPUNCTURE POINTS

c. 500 BCE: Sushruta Samhita
Indian physician Sushruta publishes the *Sushruta Samhita*, a huge work on medicine and surgery. It becomes one of the founding texts of Ayurveda, the traditional Indian system of health, well-being, and healing.

1849: Pioneering doctor
British-born Elizabeth Blackwell becomes the first woman to qualify as a doctor in both the US and the UK. She goes on to practice in London and New York City.

PORTRAIT OF ELIZABETH BLACKWELL

1860: Airborne diseases
French scientist Louis Pasteur proves that infectious diseases can be spread through the air by bacteria and other microorganisms.

LOUIS PASTEUR

1953: Surgical pump
American inventor John Gibbon creates the heart-lung machine, a pump that takes over for the heart and lungs during surgery. This is used in a successful open-heart operation.

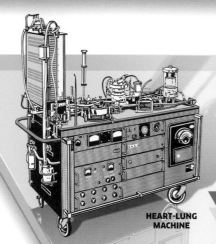

HEART-LUNG MACHINE

1933: Electron microscope
German scientists Ernst Ruska and Max Knoll produce the first electron microscope. The device revolutionizes medical imaging, by producing more powerful pictures than optical microscopes.

RUSKA WITH HIS MICROSCOPE

1953: DNA structure
James Watson, Francis Crick, and Rosalind Franklin show that DNA, the chemical molecule that sets the pattern for growth and development, has a structure like a spiral staircase. This is called a double helix.

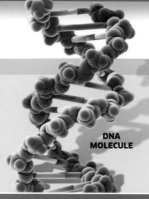

DNA MOLECULE

1954: Kidney transplant
American surgeon Joseph Murray performs the first successful human kidney transplant, in Boston. The recipient, Richard Herrick, lives another eight years.

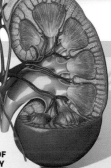

CROSS-SECTION OF A HUMAN KIDNEY

RESEARCHER IAN WILMUT WITH DOLLY

1996: Cloning sheep
Dolly the sheep is the first mammal ever to be cloned—grown in a laboratory from a single stem cell. Cloning has huge potential for treating and preventing human illness.

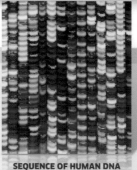

1980–83: Laser scalpels
Researchers Rangaswamy Srinivasan, Samuel Blum, and James J. Wynne use excimer lasers to cut biological tissue. This work becomes vital to the development of laser eye surgery.

LASER EYE SURGERY

2003: Human Genome Project
Scientists announce that the Human Genome Project is complete—we now have an electronic map of human DNA, which may help to treat, cure, or prevent inherited diseases.

SEQUENCE OF HUMAN DNA

2010: Robot operation
DaVinci and McSleepy, a robot surgeon and anesthetist, perform the first all-robotic operation. Human surgeons control robots' movements from a control room.

ROBOT SURGEON

3% of the world's population died from **Spanish flu** in 1918.

A **bionic eye** was successfully tested on 30 people with impaired vision in 2007–the eye is **now available** in Europe and the US.

187

1865: Antiseptic treatments
English surgeon Joseph Lister applies carbolic acid to the wound of a young boy. These antiseptic treatments kill germs and prevent infections. Lister becomes known as the "father of modern surgery."

19TH-CENTURY ANTISEPTIC SPRAYER

1895: X-ray imaging
German physicist Wilhelm Röntgen discovers X-rays, which he uses to make images of the insides of the human body for the first time. The first ever X-ray features the hand of Röntgen's wife.

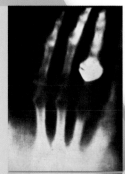

FIRST EVER HUMAN X-RAY

1928: Development of antibiotics
Scottish scientist Alexander Fleming unintentionally grows a mold that kills bacteria. He has discovered penicillin, the world's first antibiotic. By the 1940s, penicillin is mass-produced and has since saved millions of lives as treatment against bacterial infection.

FLEMING'S PENICILLIN DISH

RED BLOOD CELLS

1901: Blood breakthrough
Austrian biologist Karl Landsteiner finds and names the blood types, which are later called A, B, AB, and O. Today, doctors match a patient's blood type when giving a transfusion (injection of new blood).

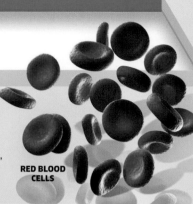

1955: Polio vaccine
American virologist Jonas Salk introduces a vaccine for polio, a disease that affects children. It is hoped polio will be wiped out by 2018.

JONAS SALK

1967: Heart transplant
South African surgeon Christiaan Barnard performs the first heart transplant operation. A 56-year-old man receives the heart of a young woman, who had been killed in a car accident.

CHRISTIAAN BARNARD

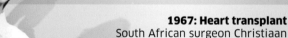

1979: Global vaccinations
The United Nation's World Health Organization declares smallpox the first disease to be officially wiped out, following a worldwide vaccination initiative.

LOGO OF THE WORLD HEALTH ORGANIZATION

DAMADIAN (ON THE LEFT) WITH HIS MRI SCANNER AND A PATIENT

1974: MRI scanner
Armenian-American Raymond Damadian gets a patent for parts of a magnetic resonance imaging (MRI) machine, a device that uses magnetic fields to make medical images.

2013: Stem cell science
In Japan, scientists grow tiny human livers from stem cells. The process could end the shortage of donor organs and save millions of lives.

STEM CELLS

2016: Genetic editing
Scientists make big advances with CRISPR, a biological system of altering DNA. It may soon be possible for doctors to replace faulty sections of our genetic sequence to prevent disease.

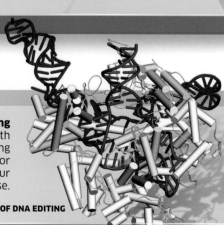

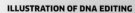

ILLUSTRATION OF DNA EDITING

THE INSIDE STORY

For most of history, knowledge of the human body has come from our own eyes—by examining the living and the dead, people have tried to understand the body and how to cure illness. In 1895, the discovery of X-rays first made it possible to see images of a living body's internal structure. Since then, many more methods of looking inside the body have been developed. Doctors now rely on imaging techniques to improve diagnosis, surgery, and treatment.

Single-photon emission computed tomography (SPECT)

This technique works with gamma rays, a type of radiation. Images can either be of 2-D sections or layered into 3-D combinations. SPECT is used for investigating the body's processes, such as blood flow.

Heart imaging

Doctors use one type of SPECT scanning to see the flow of blood in the heart. The SPECT scan can help them decide if all parts of the heart muscle are getting the blood they need. This scan shows a healthy heart.

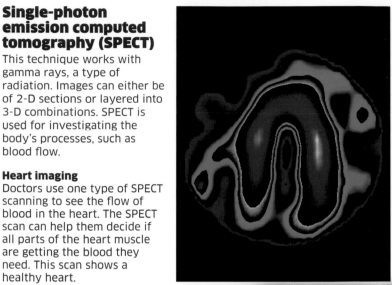

Electroencephalography (EEG)

This imaging technique uses electrodes positioned on the head to monitor electrical activity in the brain. EEGs pick up on changes in levels of brain activity to help diagnose conditions such as epilepsy.

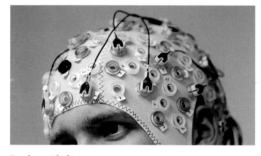

Brain activity
Electrodes attached to this man's head supply information about his brain's activity.

Positron emission tomography (PET)

Radioactive chemicals (radionuclides) are injected into the body. These show high and low levels of cell activity and can detect cancers or unusual action in the brain.

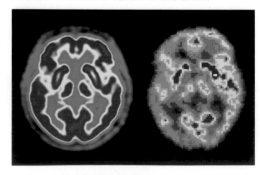

Active and sleeping brains
These two PET scans compare the brain activity of a person when they are awake (left) and asleep (right).

Magnetoencephalography (MEG)

MEG scanners record electric currents in the brain, and the magnetic forces they generate. The readings produce digital images of the brain in action, which are sometimes called "pictures of thinking."

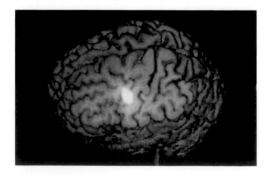

Nerve cells in action
The bright area in this MEG brain scan is where a group of nerve cells are sending commands to muscles to move a finger.

Computerized tomography (CT)

CT scanners rotate around a person and make X-ray images of 2-D "slices" of the body. These images can be layered on top of each other to produce more helpful 3-D images.

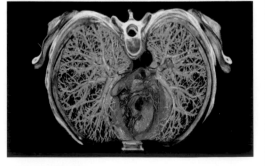

Lungs and heart
This CT scan shows a pair of lungs (green) and a heart (red). By looking at CT scans, doctors can tell whether internal organs are healthy.

Ultrasound

This scanning technique makes images from sound waves. Ultrasound is very safe and is used to check on the health of organs and of babies in the uterus. Many ultrasound scanners are small enough to use by hand.

Kidney
This ultrasound is measuring a healthy kidney inside the abdomen.

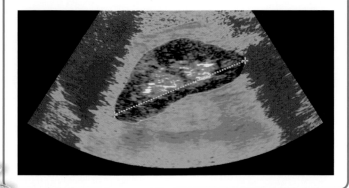

Endoscopy

An endoscope is a thin, flexible tube with a camera at the end. Doctors insert the tube through one of the body's openings, such as the mouth, then watch the images it produces on a monitor.

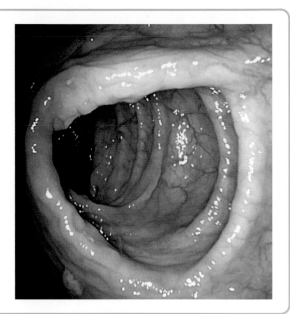

Endoscope image
This endoscope image shows a healthy large intestine. It provides a clear view of the muscular rings and many of the blood vessels in the wall of the intestine. Endoscopy is used to check for ulcers and other problems.

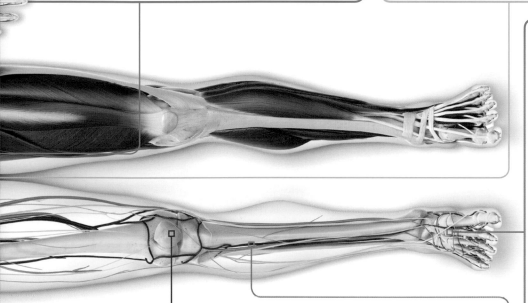

X-rays

X-rays are a type of high-energy radiation. Rays are beamed through the body and onto photographic film. Harder body parts, such as bone, absorb the rays and make a clear image on the film. Soft tissue is not as visible, because the rays pass easily through it.

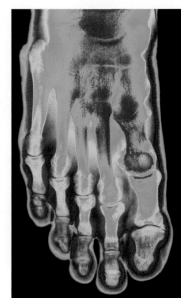

Foot bones
The bones of a right foot show up yellow, green, and blue in this colored X-ray. The red and purple areas are soft tissue.

Magnetic resonance imaging (MRI)

MRI scanners use powerful magnets to stimulate the body's tissues, which causes them to give off radio waves. The radio waves can then be used to create detailed pictures of structures inside the body.

Inside a knee
This MRI scan shows a man's knee. The yellow areas are bone, with cartilage showing in blue. This type of scan is often used to diagnose sports injuries.

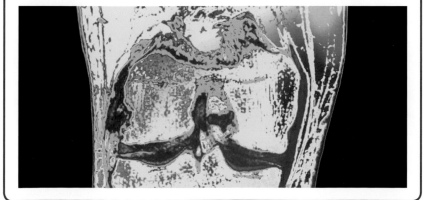

Angiogram

For this type of scan, a patient is first injected with a special dye that shows up on X-rays. The dye highlights blood vessels that are out of shape or blocked.

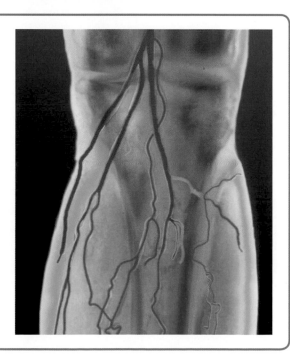

Knee and leg arteries
The arteries in the knee and lower leg are seen clearly as mauve tubes in this angiogram.

HEALTHY HUMANS

In the 21st century, people across the globe are generally healthier than ever, and live longer. Improvements in food, hygiene, and living conditions have transformed many lives. Medical breakthroughs, access to hospitals, and vaccination programs have prevented disease and provided successful treatments. But people can also play their own part in adopting a healthier lifestyle. With more known about the benefits of a good diet, regular exercise,   and plenty of sleep, many people are enjoying better health.

RECIPE FOR HEALTH

Many factors contribute to good health. Most people in developed countries can make choices about their lifestyle that will help them stay well. However, people in the developing world have fewer choices and living healthily can be a challenge for them.

A good diet

It is important to eat a balanced diet, in the right amounts—too little or too much food can harm health. The World Health Organization estimates that 39 percent of adults on Earth are overweight, whereas 14 percent are undernourished. The vast majority of hungry people live in developing countries.

Fish for health
This Japanese market sells all kinds of seafood. The average Japanese person eats 3 oz (85 g) of fish per day, which is almost as much as an American eats in a whole week. This fish-rich diet may be a factor in Japan being one of the world's healthiest nations.

Health care

Today's improved health care means many diseases can be prevented and treated, and people can also be helped in emergencies. Efficient health systems transform communities, with access to clinics, doctors and midwives, and medicines. Health education helps people spot the signs of illness so they can get medical treatment in time.

Raised standards
In Rwanda, a community health care program has helped women to give birth more safely. There has been a huge increase in the number of babies who survive childbirth.

Winding down

The human brain needs sleep to function properly. At the end of the day, the body begins to release chemicals to restrict neuron activity. This reduces brain power for a night of rest and maintenance.

Sleepyheads
In general, the younger the person, the more sleep they need. Babies sleep for up to 16 hours a day, while adults stay healthy on about seven hours' rest.

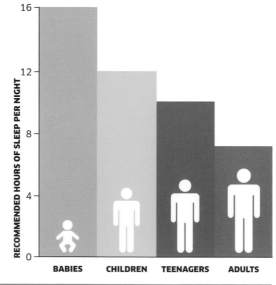

RECOMMENDED HOURS OF SLEEP PER NIGHT

| BABIES | CHILDREN | TEENAGERS | ADULTS |

Working the body

The human body is built for activity. Regular exercise strengthens the heart and helps the brain, hair, and skin stay healthy. In the developed world, most people don't get enough exercise—in the UK, recent studies show that 80 percent of adults do not even do the minimum recommended amount of exercise.

Going underground
The human body copes well with the most physically demanding jobs, such as mining. But other factors, such as dust, fumes, or accidents, can make these jobs risky to health.

MAKING PROGRESS

About 200 years ago, only half of newborn babies in the world would have lived to five years old, but now more than 90 percent of them survive. Worldwide, the average age that people can expect to reach is now 70 years old, which is twice as long as in 1913. Global health programs, such as those run by the United Nations, have played a key role in this progress.

Drinking water

Unsafe drinking water is one of the biggest threats to human health. Millions of people still die every year from diseases carried in water. In addition to germs, contamination can also come from naturally occurring chemicals such as arsenic. Providing safe water is a swift way to improve the health of entire communities.

Water pump
Public water projects can save lives in rural areas. These people in the Central African Republic are collecting water from a newly repaired pump.

ONE IN EVERY NINE PEOPLE HAS NO ACCESS TO A SAFE WATER SUPPLY.

CHALLENGES TO HEALTH

Some of the factors that affect health are beyond our control as individuals. Natural disasters, wars, and epidemics all put health at risk. The environment in which we live also has an influence on our well-being. Scientists continue to research ways to reduce the impact of the health challenges that people face.

Climate change

There is overwhelming evidence that Earth's climate is changing. This change is bringing hotter temperatures, extreme weather, rising sea levels, and periods of drought. Some of the risks to humans of climate change include hunger caused by failed crops, an increase in infectious disease, and injuries due to storms and floods.

Drop in disease

Huge advances have been made in controlling infectious diseases. In the USA in 1900, these illnesses caused 53 percent of deaths, but by 2010, this figure had dropped to 3 percent. The main factors in this drop have been: better living conditions so germs cannot spread so easily, antibiotics to kill disease-causing bacteria, and vaccinations, which give immunity to diseases.

Beating polio
This boy is receiving a vaccination against polio, a serious childhood disease. Since a vaccine was developed in the 1950s, polio cases have decreased by 99 percent.

Safer sanitation

The safe disposal of human waste stops it from contaminating land, food, and water, or attracting harmful insects. The United Nations estimates that 2.4 billion people do not have access to safe toilets.

Communal latrine
This simple toilet, or latrine, has improved life for a village in Liberia.

Air pollution

Smoke from factories and fires, exhaust fumes, and chemical pollution all pose risks to people's health. Illnesses caused by air pollution include asthma, heart disease, and some cancers. It is estimated that in 2012, 3.7 million people died worldwide as a direct result of air pollution.

Protective masks
Local people in Zhongwei, China, wear masks to help filter the polluted air.

Flood damage
This aerial view shows the impact of flooding in Germany in 2016. Flooding can cause homelessness, loss of farmland, and a rise in water-borne diseases such as typhoid or cholera.

Antibiotic resistance

One of the most important advances in medicine is the use of antibiotics to treat infection. However, some microbes are now becoming resistant to all known antibiotics. Without new treatments, lives could be lost to diseases that were once curable.

Key Normal bacteria   Resistant bacteria   Dead bacteria

Resistant bacteria
This sequence shows how a small number of mutated bacteria can quickly become dominant over unmutated bacteria.

Stage 1
A few bacteria adapt to become resistant to antibiotics.

Stage 2
An antibiotic kills most of the "normal" bacteria.

Stage 3
The resistant bacteria now have room to multiply.

Stage 4
The drug-resistant strain of bacteria takes over.

FUTURE BODIES

Scientists are constantly researching new ways to make us feel better and live longer. Some are working to prevent and cure disease by working on the body's DNA and genetic makeup. Others are developing bionic body parts to replace limbs and internal organs. These advances are transforming the lives of people around the world.

GENETIC MEDICINE

In the 1980s, discoveries about the structure of DNA—the molecule in body cells that directs growth and development—led to a new field of genetic medicine. Scientists are still learning how to use information from our genes to predict and cure health problems. In the future, it might be possible to alter our genetic makeup to avoid diseases.

Genetic testing

For people who have inherited genes for a specific illness or disorder, genetic testing is a lifesaver. Movie star Angelina Jolie was found to carry a mutated version of the gene BRCA1, giving her an 87 percent chance of developing a form of breast cancer. By choosing to have surgery in advance of any diagnosis, her cancer risk reduced to just 5 percent.

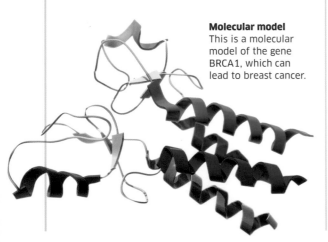

Molecular model
This is a molecular model of the gene BRCA1, which can lead to breast cancer.

Panel testing

It is not always necessary to scan the complete DNA chain. Panel testing can check for genetic mutations more quickly than ever before.

DNA panel
This revolutionary gene panel can test 60 different potentially mutated genes at once, to determine who might be at risk of disease.

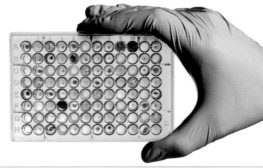

Gene editing

Scientists have found how to use enzymes called nucleases to target, remove, and replace sections of a DNA strand. The latest technologies allow researchers to remove specific areas of the DNA molecule with amazing precision. With this ability, scientists hope to be able to identify faulty genes that cause inherited diseases such as cystic fibrosis, Huntington's disease, and certain cancers.

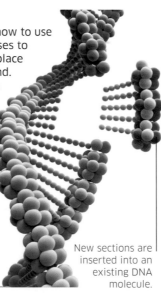

New sections are inserted into an existing DNA molecule.

NANOMEDICINE

In the future, engineers could develop tiny nanobots and inject them into the bloodstream to destroy bacteria, repair damaged cells, and deliver medicines or new strands of DNA. Miniature biotech machines are one-tenth the width of a human hair, and use proteins as motors, sensors, and arms.

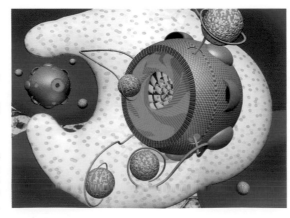

Capturing germs
Called the Pathogen Rustler, this nanobot design would involve using artificial white blood cells as minuscule robot "cowboys," ready to lasso germs and bacteria with their retractable arms.

BIONIC BODIES

Prosthetics are artificial replacements for parts of the body. Scientists are now experimenting with prosthetics that communicate more directly with the human brain. In the future, it could become common for humans to have both natural and artificial body parts, with feedback passing freely between the two.

Exoskeletons

Severe spinal cord injuries and other illnesses can make walking difficult or even impossible. American company Ekso Bionics has designed a powered exoskeletal suit to help with these problems. Originally intended to give workers superstrength when lifting heavy loads, the suit is now used to help wheelchair users regain the motor skills they need to walk independently.

Battery pack powers the exoskeleton

Motor

Computer

Bionic suit
This suit helps to rehabilitate people who have suffered strokes and spinal injuries by correcting posture and assisting them as they walk.

Braces attach the exoskeleton to the user's legs.

Bionic eyes

Many millions of people have severe problems with their eyesight. Developing bionic eyes proves an ongoing challenge for biotechnologists. Visual prosthetic solutions include Argus II, which fits to the eye, and the MVG system, which fits to the brain.

MVG system
Australia's Monash Vision Group (MVG) has designed a device to help people who have damage to the optic nerve. It works in a similar way to the Argus II (shown below), except that the electronic chipset is fitted to the brain, rather than the eye.

MVG SYSTEM

ARGUS II CAMERA

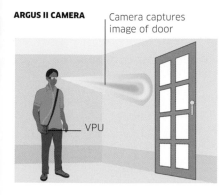

Camera captures image of door

VPU

Electronics case

Image is flipped by the eye to see the door the right way up.

Retina

Implant

Antenna

Electrodes produce visual patterns read by the user.

1 IMAGE CAPTURE
The US device Argus II is designed for people with damaged retinas. A tiny camera mounted on a pair of glasses records the view and converts it into an electrical signal, which is sent to a video processing unit (VPU).

2 ANTENNA
The processed video signal is then sent to a radio transmitter antenna on the side of the glasses. Next, the transmitted signal is picked up by a receiver attached to the eye and finally relayed to a retinal implant inside the eye.

3 ELECTRODES
The signal reaches electrodes placed inside the eye, which stimulate the retina's remaining working cells. They pass the signal along the optic nerve to the brain, and recognizable patterns of light are seen.

Synthetic skin

In the 21st century new advances in synthetic skin are making artificial limbs much more realistic and usable. Innovative technologies mean that the material has as much sensitivity to touch as human skin. Users may in future be able to feel with their prosthetic limbs, just as well as with natural ones.

Helping hand
This revolutionary, touch-sensitive hand has been designed by an American-South Korean team. It is made of silicon and gold, with a flexible plastic covering. Tiny electronic sensors can pick up on heat, cold, and moisture, just like human skin.

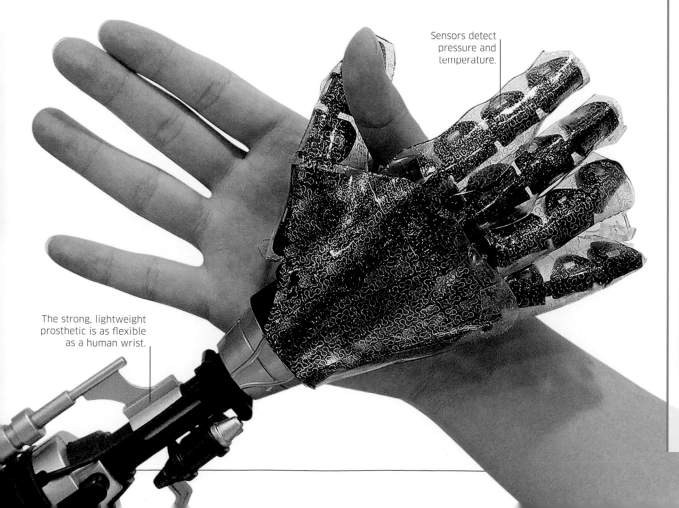

Sensors detect pressure and temperature.

The strong, lightweight prosthetic is as flexible as a human wrist.

STEM CELL THERAPY

The body contains special cells, called stem cells. Every day they divide and produce 300 billion new cells. There are about 200 cell types with different jobs to do. Scientists can now trigger certain genes in the stem cells to make them develop in set ways.

Stem solutions
Stem cells can be steered along many paths. They can be used to create insulin-producing pancreas cells, which could be implanted into diabetic people. This could lead to a cure for diabetes.

Cell cultures
These pots hold stem cells, which may one day be implanted into people to repair damaged cells.

BIOPRINTING

Human organs for transplants are always in short supply. American surgeon Anthony Atala is one of the researchers who believes the solution could lie in bioprinting—making custom-made body parts using a 3-D printer.

Printing a kidney
To make their artificial kidney, the researchers first make a CAT scan (multi-layered X-ray) of an existing kidney. This scan is then used to program the printer to build the new organ.

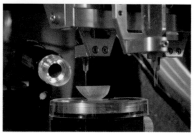

Organ print
The kidney is made up of layer after layer of bio-ink, a mixture of gel and human cells.

BODIES IN SPACE

Living in space has a dramatic impact on the human body. Scientists research ways for astronauts to stay in space, while minimizing risks to their health. Orbiting 240 miles (390 km) above Earth, the International Space Station (ISS) provides a home and workplace to astronauts for months at a time. Air comes from an onboard supply, radiation levels are high, and even everyday activities can be a huge physical challenge.

◎ DANGER ZONE

Without a space suit, a human in space would quickly die. Aside from the lack of oxygen to breathe, temperatures reach highs and lows that the body cannot cope with. Levels of radiation mean that a human stands no chance of survival. ISS astronauts experience 16 sunrises every 24 hours, which can disrupt their sleep and make them dangerously tired.

Galactic cosmic rays
These tiny particles come from outside our solar system. Without protection, they can cause cancers.

Radiation hazards

A huge magnetic field surrounds Earth, which helps to protect people against radiation from the sun and space. A space suit protects against ultraviolet (UV) rays from the sun and provides some protection against the high-energy cosmic rays coming from beyond our solar system.

Trapped radiation
Fragments of atoms whiz around Earth's magnetic field. This trapped radiation can damage body cells.

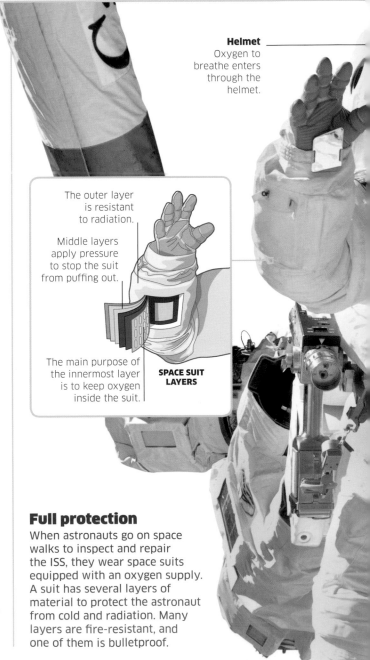

5. Space workplace
The ISS orbits 240 miles (390 km) above Earth, which creates a variety of health challenges for astronauts.

SPACE STATION

240 miles

4. Freezing cold and boiling hot
Temperatures in space can change dramatically very quickly. On the sunny side of the ISS, for example, the temperature reaches 250°F (121°C). On the shady side, it falls to –250°F (–157°C).

ROCKET-POWERED AIRCRAFT

120 miles

AURORA

3. Oxygen omission
At a height of 60 miles (100 km), there is no oxygen in the atmosphere.

60 miles

2. Altitude sickness
At the top of Mount Everest there is 33% of the oxygen there is at sea level, so people suffer from altitude sickness.

HIGHEST WEATHER BALLOON

PASSENGER AIRCRAFT

1. Oxygen assistance
Most mountain climbers have to use extra oxygen from a tank at heights over 21,000 ft (6,500 m).

ALTITUDE

0

SURVIVING SPACE

There is no air to breathe in space, so an astronaut would die very quickly from a shortage of oxygen. Technologies such as the latest space suits and breathing apparatus make it possible to stay in space safely, but the impact still takes its toll on the body. Astronauts must go through intensive testing before the mission, regular health checks while in space, and rehabilitation once they return home.

Essential oxygen

This shows how oxygen, which is essential for human life, gradually disappears from the atmosphere above Earth.

Helmet
Oxygen to breathe enters through the helmet.

The outer layer is resistant to radiation.

Middle layers apply pressure to stop the suit from puffing out.

The main purpose of the innermost layer is to keep oxygen inside the suit.

SPACE SUIT LAYERS

ASTRONAUTS IN SPACE
DO NOT SNORE
SINCE GRAVITY DOESN'T PULL THE TONGUE BACK
WHEN THEY SLEEP.

Full protection

When astronauts go on space walks to inspect and repair the ISS, they wear space suits equipped with an oxygen supply. A suit has several layers of material to protect the astronaut from cold and radiation. Many layers are fire-resistant, and one of them is bulletproof.

Space sleep

On Earth there is a sunrise about every 24 hours, but for astronauts on the ISS the sun rises over Earth every 90 minutes. Astronauts tie their sleeping bags down to stop them from floating. They also use eye masks and ear plugs to block out the light and noise of the station.

Solar flare particles
The sun fires fast-moving particles, called solar flare particles. These can damage astronauts' equipment.

Ultraviolet radiation
This strong radiation travels in sunlight. Exposure to it can cause serious harm to the eyes.

Sunrise from space
This is one of the many daily sunrises seen from the ISS looking toward Earth.

Visor
The transparent visor is coated with chemicals that filter the sun's radiation.

Gloves
Tiny heaters inside the gloves keep hands warm.

BODY BATTLES

Conditions in space mean the body is faced with very different challenges from life on Earth. Gravity in a spaceship orbiting Earth is tiny compared with the pull on Earth. This microgravity makes astronauts float in space as though they are weightless. Since their bodies are not working hard, astronauts exercise to keep their muscles and bones strong.

Muscle power

Without a specialized fitness regime, astronauts would lose up to 40 percent of their muscle mass in a few months. This is the equivalent of a 30-year-old's muscles deteriorating to resemble those of an 80-year-old.

Return to Earth
Astronauts back on Earth have weakened muscles and may struggle to walk. This Russian astronaut (cosmonaut) is being carried after a space mission.

Weaker bones

For every month in the microgravity of space, astronauts can lose up to 1 percent of their bone density—which means that the inner network of spongy bone gets more fragile and liable to break.

Outer case of compact bone | Brittle interior of weakened bone

BONE BEFORE A SPACE MISSION | **BONE AFTER A SPACE MISSION**

Space osteopenia
When astronauts' bones don't have to work against Earth's gravity when they move, they become weaker and less dense. This condition is known as space osteopenia.

Stretchy spine

The human spine expands and relaxes without the continual pressure of gravity. As a result, astronauts grow taller in space by about 3 percent. The extra height is lost within months of returning to Earth.

Tall story
American astronaut Garrett Reisman had grown almost 2 in (5 cm) taller by the end of his five months on the ISS.

Floating fluids

On Earth the body relies on gravity to help blood and other fluids circulate down through the organs and tissues. In the microgravity of space, blood is pushed up into the upper body, where it floats around without being pulled back down. The upper body swells, the face becomes puffy, and the legs shrink. Blood can also put pressure on the eye's optic nerve, blurring the vision.

Long stay
Astronaut Scott Kelly spent more than a year in space, where he experienced many of the symptoms of poor circulation that scientists expected to see.

Liquid balance
As fluid gathers in the upper body, the brain is fooled into thinking the body has too much water. This means astronauts urinate more often and must drink regularly to avoid becoming dehydrated.

SPACE WORKOUT

This picture shows British astronaut Tim Peake working out on an exercise bench on the International Space Station. The device monitors his muscles and heart as he goes through his fitness program.

Without regular exercise, astronauts would experience bone and muscle loss. This is because there is low gravity in space, so the body doesn't have to work as hard as it does on Earth. Astronauts spend two and a half hours every day on treadmills, bikes, and other fitness devices. They have to be strapped on to the equipment so they don't float away. Exercise is also important for astronauts' mental health–to keep them alert and prevent them from getting bored.

RECORD BREAKERS

The human body is the most incredible machine on Earth, but sometimes it is pushed to the limit. The body may have to contend with natural disasters, a harsh environment, or simply the challenge of competition or adventure. As people push the boundaries of human capability, new records are set. Medical advances also make their mark, helping the population grow taller and stronger, and live longer.

UNDER THE SEA

Some people can train themselves to cope with the lack of oxygen that comes when they hold their breath for a long time. This ability is useful for making long underwater dives.

Deep dive

For thousands of years people in the fishing industry have dived into the sea to catch fish and find shells. The Japanese ama and the Bajau of Malaysia and Indonesia swim to depths of 130 ft (40 m).

Japanese ama
Pearl divers (called ama) can hold their breath for several minutes underwater.

HIGH LIFE

The higher the altitude, the harder the body has to work to get enough oxygen. At first, the blood pressure and heart rate rise, and a person takes more breaths. Then the body adapts by increasing the number of red blood cells that carry oxygen, and developing more blood vessels in the muscles.

Mount Everest, Nepal/Tibet
(29,029 ft; 8,848 m)
7.7%

Oxygen levels
The air at sea level contains 20.9 percent of usable oxygen, making it easy for the blood to carry oxygen to body cells. Heading to higher ground causes oxygen levels to drop as the air gets thinner.

Aconcagua, Argentina
(22,838 ft; 6,961 m)
9%

La Rinconada
The world's highest town is La Rinconada in the Peruvian Andes. About 50,000 people live at 16,730 ft (5,100 m), with effective oxygen at 11 percent. People acclimatize so well that they mine for gold here.

Denali (Mount McKinley), US
(20,308 ft; 6,190 m)
9.5%

Kilimanjaro, Kenya
(19,341 ft; 5,895 m)
10%

Mont Blanc, France
(15,778 ft; 4,809 m)
11.5%

Mount Fuji, Japan
(12,388 ft; 3,776 m)
13%

Ben Nevis, United Kingdom
(4,413 ft; 1,345 m)
18%

Sea level
OXYGEN LEVEL: 20.9%

SPEED AND ENDURANCE

In the world of sports, athletes continually strive to be faster and stronger. And when people find themselves in the harshest environments, they have to endure huge physical challenges to survive.

Faster and faster

In 1912, the record for the 100 m sprint was 10.6 seconds. At the Mexico Olympics in 1968, American Jim Hines became the first man to officially break the 10-second barrier, aided by low air resistance at high altitude. In 2009, Jamaican Usain Bolt broke all records with 9.572 seconds. It took a whole century for the sprint time to drop by one second.

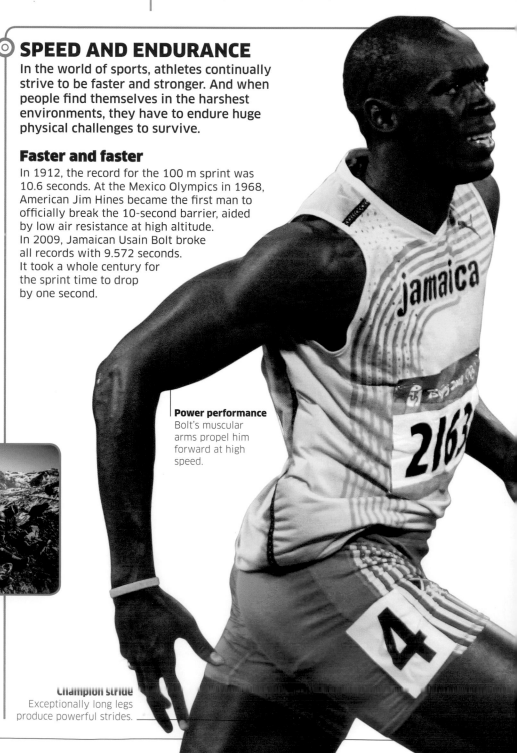

Power performance
Bolt's muscular arms propel him forward at high speed.

Champion stride
Exceptionally long legs produce powerful strides.

Free diving

Holding your breath underwater without an oxygen tank is now a popular competitive sport, called free diving. Some divers breathe pure oxygen before going underwater and also breathe hard to get rid of toxic carbon dioxide (CO_2). The human body seems to be able to respond to long dives by making changes in blood circulation so that not so much oxygen is used up.

Diving champion
In 2016, free diver Aleix Segura Vendrell held his breath underwater for a record-breaking 24 minutes.

Endurance tests

The human body is built to endure huge physical challenges or even periods without food. Accidents, such as being lost in the wilderness or trapped underground, force people into a fight for survival. Others choose to push their bodies to the limit by taking part in extreme sports and endurance events.

Underground rescue
In 2010, 33 miners were rescued from a collapsed copper pit in Chile. They were stranded 2,300 ft (700 m) below the surface for 69 days, making it the longest underground entrapment in history.

Desert challenge
The hardy participants of Morocco's Marathon des Sables (Desert Marathon) trek through sand dunes and rocky terrain for 156 miles (251 km) in scorching temperatures of 122°F (50°C).

LONG LIFE

The life expectancy of a human has risen steadily over the centuries, with women generally living longer than men. Europe is the longest-lived continent, while African countries take all three places at the bottom of the table. Poverty and lack of health care are the main health risks that many African people face.

Staying alive

Japan is usually agreed to be the longest-living nation—experts believe that its wealth, excellent health care, and healthy diet are the main factors. Japanese people can expect to live more than 30 years longer than those in Sierra Leone, the country with the shortest life expectancy.

	RANK	COUNTRY		LIFE EXPECTANCY (Years)
TOP 3	1	●	Japan	83.7
	2	🇨🇭	Switzerland	83.4
	3		Singapore	83.1
BOTTOM 3	181		Central African Republic	55.5
	182		Angola	52.4
	183		Sierra Leone	50.1

TALL STORIES

Humans are growing—people in the 21st century are taller than those from previous centuries. Currently the tallest men are from the Netherlands, while the tallest women are from Latvia.

Latvia woman: +6 in		Kenya woman: +1 in		Netherlands man: +5 in		India man: +1 in	
1914	2014	1914	2014	1914	2014	1914	2014
5 ft 1 in	5 ft 7 in	5 ft 1 in	5 ft 2 in	5 ft 7 in	6 ft	5 ft 4 in	5 ft 5 in
(155.5 cm)	(169.8 cm)	(155.9 cm)	(158.2 cm)	(169.4 cm)	(182.5 cm)	(162 cm)	(164.9 cm)

Dizzy heights

The world's tallest known person in history was American Robert Pershing Wadlow (1918–1940). He measured 8 ft 11 in (2.72 m), which is taller than an Asian elephant. His height was due to an overactive pituitary gland, which produces a hormone that makes the body grow.

Giant of Illinois
Record-breaking Robert Pershing Wadlow is seen next to a friend of normal size.

Oldest age

According to official records, the oldest person ever was Jeanne Calment of Arles, France, who reached 122 years, 164 days. She was born in 1875 and died in 1997. She credited a diet plentiful in olive oil and chocolate for her long, healthy life.

TODAY, THERE ARE 450,000 PEOPLE AGED OVER 100 YEARS IN THE WORLD. BY 2050, THERE WILL BE 2.2 MILLION.

Growing population

In 2014, a study found that men and women in every country were taller than 100 years ago, although height gains varied hugely. These increases are likely due to better nutrition, hygiene, and health care.

Glossary

ABDOMEN
The lower part of the body, between the chest and the pelvis, which contains most of the digestive organs.

ABDUCTOR MUSCLE
A muscle that pulls a limb away from the midline of the body.

ADDUCTOR MUSCLE
A muscle that pulls a limb toward the midline of the body.

ABSORPTION
The process by which nutrients from digested food pass through the wall of the small intestine and into the blood.

ADRENALINE
A hormone that prepares the body for sudden action at times of danger or excitement.

ALLERGY
An illness caused by overreaction of the body's immune system to a normally harmless substance.

ALVEOLI (singular alveolus)
Tiny air bags in the lungs through which oxygen enters, and carbon dioxide leaves, during breathing.

AMINO ACID
A simple molecule used by the body to build proteins. The digestive system breaks down proteins in food into amino acids.

ANTIBODY
A substance that sticks to germs and marks them for destruction by white blood cells.

ANTIGEN
A foreign substance, such as a bacterium, which triggers the immune system to respond.

AORTA
The largest artery of the body, arising from the left side of the heart. The aorta supplies oxygen-rich blood to all other arteries except for the pulmonary artery.

ARTERY
A blood vessel that carries blood away from the heart to the body's tissues and organs.

ATRIUM
One of two chambers in the upper part of the heart.

AXON
A long fiber that extends from a nerve cell (neuron). It carries electrical signals away from the cell at high speed.

BACTERIA (singular bacterium)
A small type of microorganism. Some types cause disease in humans, while others help to keep the body functioning properly.

BLOOD
Red liquid tissue, which contains several types of cell. Blood carries oxygen, nutrients, salts and other minerals, and hormones around the body. It also collects wastes for disposal and helps defend the body against infection.

BLOOD VESSEL
A tube that carries blood through the body. The main types of blood vessel are arteries, capillaries, and veins.

BONE
The strong, hard body part made mainly of calcium minerals. There are 206 bones in the human body.

BRAIN STEM
The lower part of the brain, which connects to the spinal cord. The brain stem controls functions such as breathing and heart rate.

BRONCHIOLE
A tiny tube through which air passes on its way in or out of the lungs.

BRONCHUS (plural bronchi)
One of the two main branches of the trachea (windpipe), a tube that leads into each lung.

CAPILLARY
A tiny blood vessel that carries blood between arteries and veins.

CARBOHYDRATE
A food group including sugars and starches that provides the body's main energy supply.

CARBON DIOXIDE
The waste gas that is expelled from the body by breathing out.

CARDIAC MUSCLE
A type of muscle found only in the heart.

CARDIOVASCULAR SYSTEM
This body system consists of the heart, blood, and a vast network of blood vessels. It is also called the circulatory system.

CARTILAGE
A tough, flexible type of connective tissue that helps support the body and covers the ends of bones and joints.

CELL
One of the trillions of tiny living units that form the human body.

CELL BODY
Part of a nerve cell (neuron) that contains its nucleus.

CENTRAL NERVOUS SYSTEM
The brain and spinal cord together make up the central nervous system.

CEREBELLUM
The area of the brain behind the brain stem. The cerebellum is concerned with balance and the control of fine movement.

CEREBRAL CORTEX
The folded outer layer of the brain. The cerebral cortex is responsible for high-level brain functions such as thinking, memory, and language.

CEREBRAL HEMISPHERE
One of the two symmetrical halves into which the main part of the brain (the cerebrum) is split.

CEREBRUM
The largest part of the brain, it contains the centers for thought, personality, the senses, and voluntary movement. It is made up of two halves, called hemispheres.

CHROMOSOME
A threadlike package of DNA found in the nucleus of every body cell. A normal cell has a total of 46 chromosomes, arranged in 23 pairs.

CILIA
Microscopic hairlike structures that project from the surface of some body cells.

CLAVICLE
Also called the collarbone, one of two slender bones that make up part of the shoulder girdle.

CONE CELLS
Receptor cells in the back of the eye, which detect different colors and send messages back to the brain for interpretation.

CONTRACTION
The shortening of a muscle to move one part of the body.

CRANIAL NERVE
One of the 12 pairs of nerves that emerge from the brain.

DENDRITE
A short branch that extends from a nerve cell, or neuron, and carries incoming electrical signals from other nerve cells.

DENTINE
The hard, bonelike material that shapes a tooth and forms its root.

DIAPHRAGM
The dome-shaped sheet of muscle that separates the thorax (chest) from the abdomen and plays a key role in breathing.

DIGESTION
The process that breaks down food into simple substances that the body can absorb and use.

DISEASE
Any problem with the body that makes someone unwell. Infectious diseases are those caused by germs.

DNA (deoxyribonucleic acid)
Long molecule found inside the nucleus of body cells. DNA contains coded instructions that control how cells work and how the body grows and develops.

EMBRYO
Term used to describe a developing baby in the first eight weeks following fertilization.

ENAMEL
The hardest material in the body. It covers the exposed part of a tooth with a thin, hard layer.

ENDOCRINE GLAND
A type of gland that makes hormones and releases them into the bloodstream.

ENZYME
A substance that speeds up a chemical reaction in the body.

EPIGLOTTIS
The flap of tissue that closes the windpipe during swallowing to stop the food from entering.

ESOPHAGUS
The muscular tube through which food passes from the throat to the stomach.

EXTENSOR
A muscle that extends or straightens a joint, such as the triceps brachii, which straightens the arm at the elbow.

FAT
A substance found in many foods that provides energy and important ingredients for cells.

FECES
Solid waste made up of undigested food, dead cells, and bacteria, which is expelled from the body via the anus.

FEMUR
The largest bone in the body, located in the leg between the pelvis and the knee.

FERTILIZATION
The joining of a female egg (ovum) and male sperm to make a new individual.

FETUS
The name given to a baby developing in the uterus from the ninth week after fertilization until it is born.

FLEXOR
A muscle that bends a joint, for example, the biceps brachii, which bends the arm at the elbow.

FORAMEN
A hole or opening in a bone through which blood vessels and nerves can pass.

FRONTAL LOBE
The foremost of the four lobes that make up each hemisphere of the cerebrum. The frontal lobes help with mental processes, such as planning and decision-making.

GASTRIC
Describes something relating to the stomach, such as gastric juice.

GENES
Part of DNA, genes contain instructions that control the way the body looks and how it works. Genes are passed on from parents to their children.

GENOME
All the DNA contained in a set of chromosomes. In humans there are 46 chromosomes.

GERM
A tiny living thing (microorganism) that can get into the body and cause illness. Bacteria and viruses are types of germ.

GLAND
A group of specialized cells that make and release a particular substance, such as an enzyme or a hormone.

GLUCOSE
A simple sugar that circulates in the bloodstream and is the main energy source for the body's cells.

HEMOGLOBIN
A substance in red blood cells that carries oxygen around the body.

HEPATIC
Describes something relating to the liver, such as the hepatic artery.

HIPPOCAMPUS
A part of the brain that helps to process long-term memories.

HORMONE
A chemical produced by glands in order to change the way a part of the body works. Hormones are carried by the blood.

HUMERUS
The long bone in the arm that extends from the shoulder to the elbow.

HYPOTHALAMUS
The small structure in the base of the brain that controls many body activities, including temperature and thirst.

IMMUNE SYSTEM
A collection of cells and tissues that protect the body from disease by searching out and destroying germs and mutated cells.

INFECTION
If germs invade your body and begin to multiply, they cause an infection. Some diseases are caused by infections.

IRIS
The colored part of the eye. The iris controls the pupil.

JOINT
A connection between two bones. Most joints allow the body to move. The hip and shoulder joints are two of the most mobile.

KERATIN
A tough, waterproof protein found in hair, nails, and skin.

LARYNX
A structure at the top of the windpipe that generates sound when a person speaks. The sound is created by folds of vibrating tissue called vocal cords.

LIGAMENT
A tough band of tissue that holds bones together where they meet at joints.

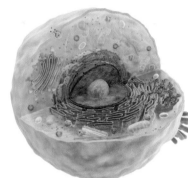
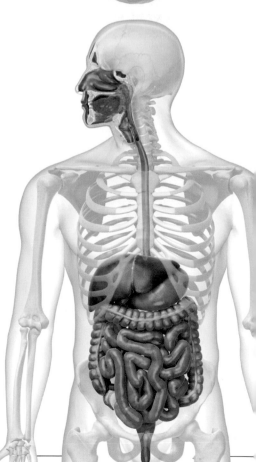

LUNG
One of two organs used for breathing. Lungs take up most of the space in the chest and are part of the body's respiratory system.

LYMPH
Liquid that is picked up from tissues, flows through the lymphatic system, and is returned to the bloodstream.

LYMPHATIC SYSTEM
A network of vessels that collect fluid from body tissues and filter it for germs, before returning the fluid to the bloodstream.

LYMPHOCYTE
A white blood cell specialized to attack a specific kind of germ. Some lymphocytes make antibodies.

MACROPHAGE
A white blood cell that swallows and destroys germs such as bacteria, mutated cells, or debris in damaged tissue.

MAGNETIC RESONANCE IMAGING (MRI)
A technique that uses magnetism and radio waves to produce images of the inside of the body.

METABOLISM
A term used to describe all the chemical reactions going on inside your body, especially within cells.

MINERAL
A naturally occurring chemical, such as salt, calcium, or iron, that you need to eat to stay healthy.

MITOCHONDRIA (singular mitochondrion)
Tiny structures found inside cells that release energy to power the cell's activity.

MITOSIS
The division of a cell into two new and identical cells.

MOTOR NEURON
A type of nerve cell that carries signals from the central nervous system to the muscles, telling them to contract or relax.

MUCUS
A thick, slippery fluid produced in the mouth, nose, throat, and intestines.

MUSCLE
A type of tissue. Most muscles contract to cause movement.

NASAL CAVITY
The hollow space behind the nose through which air flows during breathing.

NERVE
A bundle of fibers through which instructions pass to and from the central nervous system.

NERVE IMPULSE
A tiny electrical signal that is transmitted along a nerve cell at high speed.

NEURON
A term for a nerve cell. Neurons carry information around the body as electrical signals.

NEUTROPHIL
The most common type of white blood cell, which targets and defends the body from harmful bacteria.

NUCLEUS
The control center of a cell. It contains DNA-carrying chromosomes.

NUTRIENTS
The basic chemicals that make up food. The body uses nutrients for fuel, growth, and repair.

OCCIPITAL LOBE
One of the four lobes that make up each hemisphere of the cerebrum. The occipital lobe is the area that controls sight.

ORGAN
A group of tissues that form a body part designed for a specific job. The heart and lungs are organs.

ORGANELLE
A tiny structure within a cell that carries out a particular role.

OVARIES
A pair of glands that store, then release, a woman's eggs (ova).

OVUM (plural, ova)
Also called an egg, the sex cell that is released from a woman's ovaries.

OXYGEN
A gas, found in air, that is vital for life. Oxygen is breathed in, absorbed by the blood and used by cells to release energy.

PARIETAL LOBE
One of the four lobes that make up each hemisphere of the cerebrum. The parietal lobe interprets touch, pain, and temperature.

PATHOGEN
A microorganism that causes disease. Pathogens include bacteria and viruses, and they are sometimes called germs.

PELVIS
A large bony frame that the legs are connected to. It is made up of the hip bones and those at the base of the spine.

PERISTALSIS
A wave of muscle contractions in the wall of a hollow organ that, for example, pushes food down the esophagus during swallowing.

PHAGOCYTE
A general name for white blood cells, such as macrophages, which track down and kill pathogens.

PHALANGES
The bones of the fingers, thumbs, and toes.

PHARYNX
A tube that runs from the nasal cavity to the esophagus. It is also called the throat.

PHOTORECEPTOR
A type of cell found in the eye that sends signals to the brain when it detects light. The two types of photoreceptors in the eye are rods and cones.

PLASMA
A pale yellow liquid that makes up the greater part of blood, and in which the three types of blood cells float.

PLEXUS
A network of nerves or blood vessels.

PROTEIN
Vital nutrients that help the body build new cells.

PULMONARY
Describes something relating to the lungs, such as the pulmonary artery or pulmonary vein.

PULMONARY ARTERY
The artery that carries oxygen-poor blood to the lungs to pick up oxygen. Other arteries carry blood that is rich in oxygen.

PULMONARY VEIN
The vein that carries oxygen-rich blood from the lungs to the heart. All other veins carry blood that has low levels of oxygen.

RECEPTOR
A nerve cell, or the ending of a neuron, which responds to a stimulus such as light or sound.

RED BLOOD CELL
A cell that contains hemoglobin, a protein that carries oxygen and makes the blood red.

REFLEX
A rapid, automatic reaction that is out of a person's control, such as blinking when something moves toward the eyes.

RENAL
Describes something relating to the kidney, such as the renal vein.

RETINA
A layer of light-sensitive neurons lining the back of each eye. The retina captures images and relays them to the brain as electrical signals.

RIB CAGE
A flexible, protective framework of 12 pairs of bones. The rib cage surrounds soft organs in the chest, such as the heart and lungs.

ROD CELL
A light-sensitive cell in the back of the eye. Rod cells work in dim light but do not detect color.

SALIVA
The liquid in the mouth. Saliva helps a person taste, swallow, and digest food.

SCANNING
Any technique that is used to create images of organs and soft tissues inside the body.

SCAPULA
One of the two large, flat bones that form the back of the shoulder. It is also called the shoulder blade.

SEBUM
An oily substance that keeps the skin soft, flexible, and waterproof.

SEMEN
A fluid that contains sperm (male sex cells).

SENSE ORGAN
An organ, such as the eye or ear. It contains receptors that detect changes inside or outside the body, and sends nerve signals to the brain, enabling you to see, hear, balance, taste, and smell.

SENSORY NEURON
A type of nerve cell that carries signals from the sense organs to the central nervous system.

SENSORY RECEPTOR
A specialized nerve cell or the end of a sensory neuron that detects a stimulus, such as light, scent, touch, or sound.

SKELETAL MUSCLE
A type of muscle that is attached to the bones of the skeleton and which moves the body.

SMOOTH MUSCLE
A type of muscle that is found in the walls of hollow organs, such as the small intestine and bladder. Smooth muscle contracts slowly and rhythmically.

SPERM (singular and plural)
A male's sex cells, which are made in, and released from, a man's testes.

SPHINCTER
A ring of muscle around a body opening that opens and closes to allow the flow of material, such as food or urine, through it.

SPINAL CORD
The thick column of nerve cells that runs down the backbone and connects your brain to the rest of the body.

SPINAL NERVE
One of the 31 pairs of nerves that branch out from the spinal cord.

SUTURE
An immovable joint between two bones such as those that make up the pelvis and skull.

SYNAPSE
The junction where two nerve cells (neurons) meet but do not touch.

SYNOVIAL JOINT
A movable joint, such as the knee or elbow, in which the space between bones is filled with lubricating synovial fluid.

TASTE BUD
A receptor on the surface of the tongue that detects different flavors in food and drink.

TENDON
A cord of tough connective tissue that attaches muscle to bone.

THALAMUS
The mass of nerve tissue that lies deep within the brain and receives and coordinates sensory information.

THORACIC CAVITY
The area inside the thorax (chest) containing organs such as the lungs and heart.

THORAX
The upper part of the trunk (the central part of the body) between the abdomen and the neck. Also called the chest.

TISSUE
A group of cells of the same or similar type that work together to perform a particular task. Muscle is a type of tissue. Blood is tissue in liquid form.

TONGUE
The movable, muscular organ attached to the floor of the mouth. It is the main organ for taste and is also essential for speech.

TOXIN
A poisonous substance released into the body, often by disease-causing bacteria.

TRACHEA
Also known as windpipe, the tube that links the larynx to the bronchi, and carries air toward and away from the lungs.

ULTRASOUND
An imaging technique that uses high-frequency sound waves to produce images of body tissues or a developing fetus.

URETHRA
The tube that carries urine from the bladder outside the body. In males, it also transports semen.

UTERUS
The hollow, stretchy organ in which the fetus grows and is nourished until birth. The uterus is sometimes called the womb.

VEIN
A blood vessel that carries blood toward the heart.

VENTRICLE
One of two chambers (left and right) in the lower part of the heart.

VERTEBRA
One of the bones that make up the backbone.

VIRUS
A tiny, infectious, nonliving agent that causes disease by invading, and multiplying inside, body cells.

VITAMIN
One of a number of substances, required in small amounts in the diet to keep the body healthy.

VOCAL CORDS
The small folds of tissue in the larynx (voice box) that vibrate to create the sounds of speech.

WHITE BLOOD CELL
A cell found in the blood that is involved in defending the body against pathogens.

X-RAY
An imaging technique that reveals body structures, especially bones, by passing a type of radiation through the body onto photographic film.

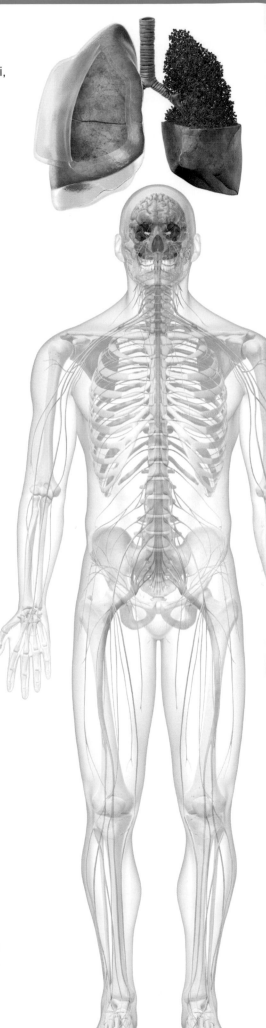

Index

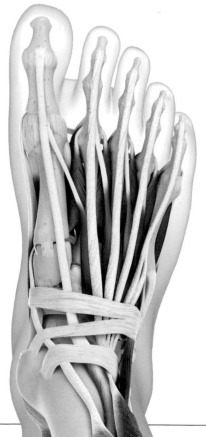

Acknowledgments

The publisher would like to thank the following people for their assistance in the preparation of this book:
Shaila Brown for editorial guidance and Helen Leech for editorial assistance; Neetika Malik Jhingan, Govind Mittal, and George Mihic for design assistance; Steve Crozier for retouching; Katie John for proofreading; Hilary Bird for the index.

Smithsonian Enterprises:
Kealy E. Gordon, Product Development Manager
Ellen Nanney, Licensing Manager
Brigid Ferraro, Vice President, Education and Consumer Products
Carol LeBlanc, Senior Vice President, Education and Consumer Products
Chris Liedel, President

Reviewers for the Smithsonian:
Dr. Don E. Wilson, Curator Emeritus, Department of Vertebrate Zoology, National Museum of Natural History

The publisher would like to thank the following for their kind permission to reproduce photographs:
(Key: a-above; b-below/bottom; c-center; f-far; l-left; r-right; t-top)

6 Science Photo Library: Keith R. Porter (cl). **8 Dorling Kindersley:** Colin Keates / Natural History Museum, London (br). **Science Photo Library:** Keith R. Porter (cr). **8-9 SuperStock:** Science Photo Library (tc). **9 Science Photo Library:** Alvin Telser (fcl, cl, c). **12-13 Science Photo Library**. **15 123RF.com:** luchschen (br). **17 Getty Images:** Indranil Mukherjee / AFP (cra). **23 123RF.com:** Wavebreak Media Ltd (ca). **24 Alamy Stock Photo:** Panther Media GmbH / micut (cl). **iStockphoto.com:** Artem_Furman (bl); Mikolette (tr). **25 Alamy Stock Photo:** Cultura Creative (RF) / Ben Pipe Photography (br); Gallo Images / David Malan (bl). **iStockphoto.com:** antorti (bc). **31 Science Photo Library:** Biosphoto Associates (fbr); R. Bick, B Pointdexer / UT Medical School (bc, br). **40-41 Science Photo Library:** Thomas Deernick / NCMIR. **44 Dreamstime.com:** Syda Productions (r). **Science Photo Library:** Steve Gschmeissner (bl). **45 123RF.com:** stockyimages (cl). **Alamy Stock Photo:** Jim West (bl). **Dreamstime. com:** Saaaaa (tc). **Paul Thompson, UCLA**

School of Medicine: Time-Lapse Map of Brain Development. Paul Thompson (USC) and Judith Rapoport (NIMH) (cb). **50 Science Photo Library:** James Cavallini (cl, cr); Dennis Kunkel Microscopy (tc, cla, ca, bc); Steve Gschmeissner (bl, br). **51 Science Photo Library:** Juergen Berger (ca); Steve Gschmeissner (cra, fcra); Dr. John Brackenbury (bc). **52-53 Science Photo Library. 64 Science Photo Library:** K H Fung (clb). **66 Science Photo Library:** Science Picture co (cl). **71 Science Photo Library:** Ted Kinsman (clb). **72-73 Science Photo Library:** Tom Barrick, Chris Clark / SGHMS. **74 Alamy Stock Photo:** Sport Picture Library (cra). **75 Alamy Stock Photo:** SIBSA Digital Pvt. Ltd. (cr). **77 Science Photo Library:** Steve Gschmeissner (cra). **79 Science Photo Library:** Eye of Science (cra). **80 Dreamstime.com:** Katarzyna Bialasiewicz (bl). **81 Science Photo Library:** Steve Gschmeissner (cr). **82-83 Science Photo Library:** Prof. P. Motta / Dept. Of Anatomy / University "La Sapienza", Rome. **85 Science Photo Library:** Omikron (bl). **86 123RF.com:** Baloncici (cl). **87 Depositphotos Inc:** Tristan3D (tr). **Dreamstime.com:** Eveleen007 (br). **Getty Images:** Fuse / Corbis (clb); Edgar Mueller (ca). **91 Science Photo Library:** Steve Gschmeissner (tl, cr); Veisland (crb). **93 123RF.com:** Volodymyr Melnyk (cr). **98 123RF.com:** anatols (bl); Patryk Kośmider (clb); sam74100 (fclb). **99 Science Photo Library:** Bo Veisland (cb). **102-103 Getty Images:** Steve Gschmeissner / Science Photo Library. **104 Science Photo Library:** (clb); GCA (cl). **105 Science Photo Library:** Steve Gschmeissner (bl). **107 Science Photo Library:** Philippe Plailly (bc). **108 Science Photo Library:** Overseas (cb). **114-115 Science Photo Library:** Thomas Deernick / NCMIR. **117 123RF.com:** Wavebreak Media Ltd (tl). **127 123RF.com:** Todd Arena (br); Vladislav Zhukov (bl). **Dreamstime.com:** Berc (clb). **Science Photo Library:** Joseph Giacomin / Cultura (cr); Kent Wood (cra). **128-129 Science Photo Library:** Steve Gschmeissner. **133 123RF. com:** Phanuwat Nandee (cr); Sayam Sompanya (cra); wckiw (br). **Dreamstime. com:** Flynt (fcra); Typhoonski (tc); Konstantin Zykov (fcr). **137 Robert Steiner MRI Unit, Imperial College London:** Dr Declan O'Regan, MRC London Institute of Medical Sciences (bc). **138 Science**

Photo Library: Dr. K. F. R. Schiller (cr). **139 Science Photo Library:** Steve Gschmeissner (br). **142 Science Photo Library:** Gastrolab (bl); Steve Gschmeissner (tl). **143 Dreamstime.com:** Clickandphoto (br). **148-149 Science Photo Library:** Steve Gschmeissner. **150 Science Photo Library:** Scimat (cr). **151 Science Photo Library:** (tr). **155 Alamy Stock Photo:** ZUMA Press, Inc. (br). **156-157 Science Photo Library:** Susumu Nishinaga. **158 Science Photo Library:** Dennis Kunkel Microscopy (clb, cb); Steve Gschmeissner (bl); Ted Kinsman (bc). **159 Dreamstime.com:** Alexander Raths (tr); Wxin (bl). **Getty Images:** Digital Art / Corbis (cr). **164-165 Science Photo Library:** Thierry Berrod, Mona Lisa Productions. **171 Alamy Stock Photo:** A Room With Views (cra). **173 Science Photo Library:** Steve Gschmeissner (cl). **174-175 Science Photo Library:** Steve Gschmeissner. **179 Getty Images:** Dan Mullan (cr). **181 Getty Images:** Tristan Fewings (ca). **182 NASA:** (c). **Science Photo Library:** Simon Fraser (cl); Tek Image (cr). **184 Alamy Stock Photo:** ART Collection (cr). **The Trustees of the British Museum:** Peter Hayman (br). **National Museum of Health and Medicine:** Alan Hawk (c). **Science Photo Library:** (tc, tr); Photo Researchers (cla); Science Source (crb). **Science Museum, London:** Adrian Whicher (bc). **185 Alamy Stock Photo:** Art Directors & TRIP / Harish Luther / ArkReligion.com (br). **Getty Images:** De Agostini / A. Dagli Orti (cla); DEA / A. Dagli Orti (cb). **Science Photo Library:** (tr); Paul D. Stewart (tl); Sheila Terry (ca); New York Public Library Picture Collection (cl); National Library of Medicine (cr); John Greim (bl). **Wellcome Images http://creativecommons.org/ licenses/by/4.0/:** (clb). **186 Getty Images:** Colin McPherson / Corbis (clb). **Science Photo Library:** (cla); National Library of Medicine (tc); Humanities and Social Sciences Library / New York Public Library (tr); Thomas Hollyman (cra); Evan Otto (c); Alexander Tsiaras (cb); J. C. Revy, ISM (bc); Dr P. Marazzi (br). **187 Getty Images:** Bettmann (cb); PhotoQuest (cl); Mondadori Portfolio (cr). **Science Photo Library:** (tr); St. Mary's Hospital Medical School (cla); Sebastian Kaulitzki (ca); Steve Gschmeissner (bl); Molekuul (br); Dorling Kindersley (tl). **World Health Organisation:** (clb). **188 Alamy Stock Photo:** Roger Bacon / Reuters (cl). **Science Photo Library:**

Centre Jean Perrin / ISM (fbl); Sovereign, ISM (br); Hank Morgan (bl, bc); ISM (tr). **189 Science Photo Library:** (tl); Gastrolab (tr); Simon Fraser (bl); Mehau Kulyk (cr); BSIP VEM (br). **190 123RF.com:** myroom (clb). **Alamy Stock Photo:** Paul Felix Photography (bc). **Getty Images:** William Campbell / Corbis (cra). **191 Alamy Stock Photo:** Olivier Asselin (cr); My Planet (tr); Peter Treanor (crb); dpa picture alliance (bl). **Getty Images:** Jean Chung (tl). **192 123RF.com:** angellodeco (c). **Courtesy of Ekso Bionics:** (br). **Copyright 1999 by Tim Fonseca:** (bc). **Science Photo Library:** Evan Oto (clb); Alfred Pasieka (cb). **193 Getty Images:** New York Daily News Archive (tc). **Science Photo Library:** Tek Image (cr). **Seoul National University:** Dae-Hyeong Kim / Nature Communications 5, 5747, 2014 (b). **Wake Forest Institute for Regenerative Medicine:** (br). **194-195 NASA:** (bc). **195 NASA:** (cra, crb); Reid Wiseman (cla); Bill Ingalls (c); ESA (br). **196-197 NASA:** ESA. **198 123RF.com:** yokokenchan (tr). **Getty Images:** Al Bello (br); Sebastian Castaneda / Anadolu Agency (cb). **199 Alamy Stock Photo:** Sergey Orlov (cla). **Getty Images:** Bettmann (br); Pascal Parrot / Sygma (cra); Government of Chile / Handout / Corbis (cl); Pierre Verdy / AFP (bl)

Cover images: *Front:* **Dorling Kindersley:** Arran Lewis b

All other images © Dorling Kindersley
For further information see: www. dkimages.com